Supporting Inclusive Practice and Ensuring Opportunity is Equal for A

This third edition of *Supporting Inclusive Practice* builds on the successful format of the previous two editions, both in content and structure. It explores many aspects of inclusive practice relevant to those who work with children in schools and other educational settings, aiming to provide the most up-to-date theoretical knowledge and understanding in the field, and illustrating the theory with examples of good practice in the areas explored.

Many of the topics that have appeared in the previous editions, including supporting children for whom English is a second language, children on the autistic spectrum and children with neurodiversity conditions, also appear in this edition. The revised content of this third edition also covers recent and relevant changes in national policy and legislation, particularly, for example, around changes in equality and disability, same-sex parenting and transgender children and parenting policy and legislation. It explores the impact on aspects of inclusive practice legislation such as the Equality Act 2010, Marriage (Same Sex Couples) Act 2013 and the Children and Families Act 2014. It also explores in detail the revised 2014 SEN Code of Practice and the introduction of the pupil premium in 2011, which provides support for the education of children from low income families or who may be children who are fostered or in care.

Throughout, the book is informed by the solution-focused social model of special educational needs and disability, and reflects current national policy that sees inclusive practice as fundamental to ensure equality of educational opportunity is achieved for all children.

Gianna Knowles is an Associate Professor in Educational Studies at London South Bank University. She has also worked with teacher trainee students from across Europe at the University of Jönköping in Sweden. Gianna has over 12 years' experience of teaching in primary schools in England, in London and the Midlands, and working in Local Authority Advisory services. Gianna has experience of being an Ofsted inspector and reviewer for the Quality Assurance Agency. Her research interest is in the area of social justice, inclusion and diversity, and critical disability studies.

Supporting Inclusive Practice and Ensuring Opportunity is Equal for All

Third Edition

Edited by Gianna Knowles

Routledge
Taylor & Francis Group

LONDON AND NEW YORK

Third edition published 2018
by Routledge
2 Park Square, Milton Park, Abingdon, Oxon, OX14 4RN

and by Routledge
711 Third Avenue, New York, NY 10017

Routledge is an imprint of the Taylor & Francis Group, an informa business

First edition published by David Fulton 2006
Second edition published by Routledge 2010

British Library Cataloguing-in-Publication Data
A catalogue record for this book is available from the British Library

Library of Congress Cataloging-in-Publication Data
Names: Knowles, Gianna, editor.
Title: Supporting inclusive practice and ensuring opportunity is equal for all / [edited by] Gianna Knowles.
Description: Third edition. | New York : Routledge, 2017. | "First edition published by David Fulton 2006"—T.p. verso. | "Second edition published by Routledge 2010"—T.p. verso.
Identifiers: LCCN 2016058697| ISBN 9781138674387 (Paperback) | ISBN 9781138674370 (Hardback) | ISBN 9781315561325 (eBook)
Subjects: LCSH: Inclusive education.
Classification: LCC LC4015 .S87 2017 | DDC 371.9/046—dc23
LC record available at https://lccn.loc.gov/2016058697

ISBN: 978-1-138-67437-0 (hbk)
ISBN: 978-1-138-67438-7 (pbk)
ISBN: 978-1-315-56132-5 (ebk)

Typeset in Times New Roman
by Keystroke, Neville Lodge, Tettenhall, Wolverhampton

Printed and bound in Great Britain by
TJ International Ltd, Padstow, Cornwall

Contents

Notes on contributors

Fabienne Benoist is a Senior Lecturer in the Division of Education at London South Bank University, teaching and lecturing in psychology and sociology of education. She has extensive experience of teaching in urban inner London mainstream primary schools as well as Special Educational Needs teaching experience with children on the autism spectrum.

Jenny Fogarty is an Assistant Professor in Learning and Teaching at the London School of Hygiene and Tropical Medicine, part of the University of London. Jenny has considerable experience working with trainee teachers and before moving into academia she was a deputy head in primary schools in Hertfordshire and Essex. Her research interests include creative pedagogies and effective university partnerships.

Anna Jones is a Lecturer in Education at London South Bank University. Anna has twelve years' experience as a classroom teacher and senior leader in primary schools in Yorkshire and inner London. She has experience of working in early years settings and after-school clubs as a play leader. Anna is particularly interested in how schools can effectively support children's mental health and well-being and her research is currently around teachers' experiences of implementing a social and emotional skills curriculum.

Gianna Knowles is an Associate Professor in Educational Studies at London South Bank University. She has also worked with teacher trainee students from across Europe at the University of Jönköping in Sweden. Gianna has over twelve years' experience of teaching in primary schools in England, in London and the Midlands, and working in Local Authority Advisory services. Gianna has experience of being an Ofsted inspector and reviewer for the Quality Assurance Agency. Her research interest is in the area of social justice, inclusion and diversity and critical disability studies.

Zoë Leadley-Meade is a Senior Lecturer in the Division of Education at London South Bank University, with interests in Media Studies education and creative pedagogies, as well as the experience of LGBT students and same-sex parents in educational contexts. Prior to joining LSBU in 2015, Zoë had accumulated seven years of experience as both an English and Media Studies teacher and curriculum leader in a range of education contexts, in inner London. Zoë's area of research is currently around the experiences of same-sex parents.

Nicola Martin is a Professor at London South Bank University and has lead responsibility for the Education Research Centre, with its focus on equality, diversity and sustainability and she has recently become a National Teaching Fellow. She joined LSBU from the London School of Economics and Political Science (LSE), where she took a lead on disability equality. Nicola has expertise in inclusive practice in education and Critical Disability Studies and she is currently Principal Investigator in a collaborative project with Cambridge and Research Autism, which explores good practice in mentoring young adults with autism.

Damian Milton is a member of the programme board for the Autism Education Trust, and a member of the scientific and advisory committee for Research Autism. Damian works for the National Autistic Society as Head of Autism Knowledge and Expertise (Adults and Community) and is a researcher for London South Bank University. Damian's interest in autism began in 2005, when his son was diagnosed as autistic at the age of 2. Damian was also diagnosed with Asperger's in 2009 at the age of 36.

Vicki Ryf is a Senior Lecturer in Education at London South Bank University. She is currently module leader for primary English across PGCE and UG programmes. She has had wide experience of teaching in urban inner London schools and was deputy head teacher of a multi-lingual infant school in Lambeth.

Edlene Whitman is a Senior Lecturer in the Division of Education at London South Bank University. She is a former South London primary school head teacher with almost twenty years' experience. Throughout her teaching career Edlene has worked in schools with many challenges serving diverse communities. Edlene has been an Ofsted inspector, and has particular interest in school leadership and management and school improvement and support for vulnerable pupils. Edlene is also a hub leader for the Spinnaker Trust, a charity which provides RE teaching and collective worship in primary schools as well as being a member of the Bromley Standing Advisory Council for Religious Education (SACRE).

Introduction

Gianna Knowles

... every child has unique characteristics, interests, abilities and learning needs.

(UNESCO 1994, p.viii)

The first edition of *Supporting Inclusive Practice* was published in 2006 and although the Salamanca Agreement and subsequent *Framework for Action* (UNESCO 1994) had already been in place for over ten years, many schools and educational settings at that time were still working on achieving fully embedded inclusive practice. However, by the publication of the second edition in 2010, only four years later, the strides were evident that schools and educational settings had made in their understanding and practice around inclusive education. One of the fundamental principles established by the 1994 Salamanca Agreement was not only the right that all children have to gain an education, but that it also acknowledged the diversity of need that children bring to the learning environment. As a result, governments who signed the agreement, including the British government, agreed that they would ensure the education systems of their country would: 'accommodate' these factors 'within a child entered pedagogy capable of meeting these needs' (UNESCO 1994, p.viii). In this way, building on the work of the previous editions, this edition of *Supporting Inclusive Practice* has sought to bring to the reader the most current aspects of good practice in both understanding how a range of needs might impact on a child's capacity to achieve in their learning, and in exploring what is regarded as good pedagogical practice in meeting those learning needs.

A third edition is timely for a number of other reasons. Since 2011, there has been further considerable progress made in educational settings in the area of inclusive practice and a range of significant developments in research and thinking around the terms 'special educational need' (SEN) and 'disability'. There has also been an increasing understanding of the range of diverse needs children bring to the classroom unrelated to SEN or disability. Alongside a growing understanding of children's diverse needs, there has been a considerable number of changes to the laws and legislation affecting this area of education and, since 2010, a restructuring of government policy in this area.

An example of some of these changes can be seen in how understanding has moved on regarding what it means to say that some children are *different*, or special, because they have a particular educational need, or mental or physical condition that deems them to be disabled. Many argue that all children are special, all are unique and individual and all, at some point, need particular consideration when it comes to enabling them to engage with learning activities. While some children have physical, social, or cognitive characteristics that are individual to them, other children experience life events or have factors in their families' lives, over which they have no control and that will impact on how they approach their learning. For some children, learning and achieving at school and in educational settings is very straightforward, but because, for example, English is an additional language for them, or because they come from a low income background where there are not the resources at home to support their learning, they may be unable to achieve all they are capable of. Similarly, there may be children who use a wheelchair to aid their mobility, but this will have no bearing on their capacity to learn and achieve.

As well as development in educational approaches to what is regarded as good practice in inclusive education there have been changes in the law around equality, same-sex marriage and the revision of the national curriculum and Special Educational Needs Code of Practice, all of which have impacted on understanding of what constitutes inclusive practice. The Equality Act passed in 2010 now compels schools and educational settings to make reasonable adjustments to ensure a child who has a disability has their needs met, whereas previously schools were not obliged, if they could make a reasonable case, to admit children with disabilities. Indeed, critical disability studies, social models of disability and greater understanding of neurodiversity conditions have had a huge impact on attitudes to and support for children with SEN and/or disability. Chapter 6 explores these concepts in more detail and Chapters 7 and 8 discuss how to best support children with neurodiversity conditions such as dyslexia, dyspraxia, ADHD and autism.

Similarly, legislation and changes in society's attitudes have seen a marked improvement in the inclusion of children who may be experiencing gender dysphoria, which is discussed, alongside other aspect of gender, in Chapter 2. The Marriage (Same Sex Couples) Act, passed in 2013, has meant schools and educational settings need to be more aware of and proactively inclusive of LGB children and families. Discussion of these aspects of inclusive practice which did not feature in previous editions of *Supporting Inclusive Practice*, can be found in Chapter 3 of this edition. More recently, the Children and Family Act 2014 has effected many changes to the care of vulnerable children, extending support to them and their families from birth to age 21 or 25, depending on need; this is covered in more detail in Chapters 6, 7 and 8. The Children and Family Act 2014 has also impacted on the regulations around adoption and fostering regulations and requires settings and schools to support children at school with medical conditions (Gov.uk 2014); this is explored in Chapter 10.

One of the significant changes in the field of inclusion has been the introduction of the new SEN Code of Practice and the move from Statements of Special Need to the Health and Care Plan (the EHC plan), which includes ensuring that the child's 'voice' – their aspirations and wants – is included in any support provided for the child, much of which is discussed in detail in Chapter 6.

In 2012, Sylva and colleagues published the outcomes of research into the impact of early educational experiences on later educational achievement. The research had been commissioned before the change of government in 2010 and while the current government does not necessarily endorse all its findings, key points which the report makes include the positive impact that early, pre-school learning experiences and home background have on children's immediate and long-term educational attainment. That is to say children 'who had a more favourable early years Home Learning Environment (HLE) had better academic and socialbehavioural outcomes' by the end of their secondary education (Sylva et al. 2012, p.ii). They also concluded that children who experience 'socio-economic disadvantage predicted poorer outcomes in KS3 in line with results in pre-school and primary school'. The research also noted the ongoing trend of higher attainment for girls, although girls 'were more likely to report themselves as having anxious behaviours, lower "popularity", lower "maths academic self concept"' (Sylva et al. 2012, p.ii). While Chapter 2 discusses the impact of gender on attainment, Chapter 11 explores how poverty and coming from low income homes can affect children's education. Chapter 11 also discusses how the government measure called the 'pupil premium' can support children in disadvantaged economic circumstances. The pupil premium is significant in that the government recognises that children from low income families (and, in this instance, also children who are being fostered or in care), can be adversely affected by the economic aspect of their backgrounds in terms of their capacity to achieve in their learning. In this way, the introduction of the pupil premium has meant that educational settings have had to act positively to ensure that they are including and supporting the specific needs of these children.

This edition also acknowledges that throughout their childhoods children will experience many events that will impact on their capacity to learn; some of these events will have a temporary effect, while others will be more long-lasting; for example, when children experience the loss of a loved one when a family member or person significant in their lives dies. Children will also experience loss when families break up or when they move to new places. Chapter 9 explores how loss and bereavement can impact on children and how schools and educational settings can support them through these difficult times.

One final point to be noted about changes in inclusive practice that have impacted on the writing of this edition of *Supporting Inclusive Practice* is how the wider government policy agenda with regard to inclusion has changed since 2011. Current government policy in this area of education now rarely uses the term 'inclusion'; instead policy has built on previous successful inclusive practice and broadened the term to focus more on equality of opportunity. The Department for Education states on its website that 'we work to achieve a highly educated society in which opportunity is equal for all, no matter what their background or family circumstances' (Department for Education 2016).

The notion of achieving equal opportunities for all has embedded within it the need for good, if not better, inclusive practice, since only by ensuring that all children are included in learning environments and can access learning, can we ensure they will be able to achieve the opportunities available to them. Ofsted is the review body that inspects educational settings and makes judgements about how effective these settings are in terms of enabling children to achieve, and it looks for evidence that practice is in line with government policy. Its current handbook for inspecting schools does not include the term 'inclusion' (Ofsted 2016). However, in relation to ensuring children are included and that all are enabled to have equal access to educational opportunities, it rigorously evaluates practice that supports: 'individuals and groups, such as pupils for whom referrals have been made to the local authority . . . pupils who have special educational needs and/or disabilities, [and] children looked after' (Ofsted 2016, p.51).

With regards specifically to children with SEN and/or disabilities, Ofsted looks for evidence that schools and educational settings are enabling children to make 'improvement in progress' (Ofsted 2016, p.56). It will also inspect how the pupil premium is used and make a judgement 'about the promotion of equality of opportunity' (Ofsted 2016, p.12) for all children, whatever their needs or background. Inspectors will also evaluate 'evidence relating to the achievement of specific groups of pupils and individuals, including disadvantaged pupils [and] the most able pupils' (Ofsted 2016, p.21). It is also concerned with evidence that supports how schools and educational settings are promoting 'all forms of equality and foster greater understanding of and respect for people of all . . . genders, ages, disability and sexual orientations . . . through their words, actions and influence within the school and more widely in the community' (Ofsted 2016, p.35). In this way, we can see that while the shift in focus broadens out the term inclusion to embrace the notion of ensuring that equality of opportunity is achieved, we can also see how, given the diverse range of needs and abilities children bring to the learning environment, a good understanding of how to include all children in the learning environment is now needed as much as it ever was.

What follows is a more detailed summary of content of each chapter in this edition, beginning with Chapter 1, which starts the book by exploring what is meant by 'inclusive practice' and examines the whole concept of what it means to be a child and what is meant by 'childhood', as our understanding of these concepts has a bearing on how we understand inclusion. Similarly, the chapter also explores theories of child development and what enables children to thrive, particularly as expressed through Maslow's hierarchy of needs and Bronfenbrenner's ecological systems theory of child development. These are important concepts to consider as how we understand what it is to be a child and what we want for children has an impact on how we view what it means to have an SEN or disability, and how we ensure equality of opportunity is available to all children and barriers to their learning are removed.

Having discussed the main themes running through this book, particularly those of equality of opportunity, Chapter 2 looks in more detail at how gender can still operate as a barrier to learning. In discussing gender, the chapter examines in detail what is meant by gender and the impact of culture and society on defining gender and gender roles. The chapter also considers what it means to be transgender and the experience of being a girl or boy in contemporary Britain, particularly in relation to how gender continues to impact on educational achievement.

In light of the Marriage (Same Sex Couples) Act 2013, Chapter 3 explores inclusion in respect of working with lesbian, gay and bisexual (LGB) children and families in schools. The chapter discusses what it means to identify as lesbian, gay, or bisexual and provides some background on the political, legal and social contexts which impact on LGB children and families. It examines the concept of 'heteronormativity' and why it is important to challenge it within the classroom in order to provide a truly inclusive environment; the chapter also discusses roles and relationships in families with same-sex parents and the need to include family diversity within the curriculum. It also raises awareness around the role of schools and individuals in enabling LGB children and young people to fulfil their potential and maintain mental health and well-being alongside their peers.

In beginning to look at specific needs some children bring to the learning environment, Chapter 4 explores good practice in including bilingual learners and children with English as an additional language (EAL). It discusses what is meant by the terms 'bilingualism' and 'EAL' and the links between language and identity. It explores how children acquire additional languages and provides practical guidance on inclusive practice when supporting bilingual learners.

Chapter 5 considers how schools and educational settings support and include children who are highly able. It discusses what is meant by the term 'highly able' and how we might know a child is more able than their peers. It explores the barriers which exist for highly able children in terms of their learning and provides guidance on what are effective inclusive practices for highly able children.

Chapter 6 is the first of three chapters that look specifically at the inclusion of children deemed to have a special educational need or disability and, in particular, looks critically at our understanding of what being disabled might mean. It discusses in detail the 2014 Special Educational Needs Code of Practice and explores medical and social models of disability and SEN. It also provides guidance on what good practice, in terms of support for disabled children in educational settings, might look like.

Continuing the theme of SEN, Chapter 7 deals more specifically with inclusion and neurodivergency. It explores what is meant by the term 'neurodiversity' and what it means to be neurodivergent, and discusses aspects of neurodivergency often recognised as dyslexia, dyspraxia and ADHD. The chapter also provides ideas for removing barriers to learning for children with neurodivergent approaches to learning.

Chapter 8 explores how to support the inclusion of autistic children. It explains what is meant by the term 'autism spectrum' and how autism is about a different way of thinking. The chapter discusses autism and sensory processing, and stress, and anxiety and autism in relation to social interaction and Theory of Mind. It examines autism, communication and language, and the importance of managing transitions for autistic children. The chapter also provides a range of strategies to support the inclusion of autistic children.

Chapter 9 discusses the impact of loss, grief and bereavement on children and how schools and educational settings need to be aware of the impact these factors can have on children's learning. Having explored the range of loss, grief and bereavement children can experience, the chapter examines the emotional processes children go through in such situations and the conceptual understanding they have of these events. It looks at how schools can support children through loss and bereavement and provides guidance for schools and educational settings in supporting children who are bereaved, particularly by the death of a parent.

Chapter 10 discusses the inclusion of looked after children, and fostered or adopted children. The chapter explores what is meant by the term 'looked after child' and the reasons why children may be being looked after. It examines the barriers to learning typically faced by looked after children and the importance of practitioner awareness of such barriers. It discusses the ways in which practitioners working with looked after children may reduce barriers to learning to further inclusion and improve educational outcomes, and explores the importance of empathy, relationships and understanding to enable all children to thrive.

The final chapter, Chapter 11, discusses how to include and support children from low income families. It explores what is meant by low income and poverty, and how poverty is defined. It discusses who are the families on low income in the UK today and addresses some of the myths attached to those living in poverty. The chapter examines the impact on children's well-being, development and learning when living on low income or in poverty, and what the research suggests about supporting children from low income families. It explores the attainment gap between children from poor backgrounds and their peers, how the pupil premium works and how schools have used the extra funding to raise attainment. It also provides examples of good practice in this area of inclusion, and outlines what schools can do to enable all children to achieve, regardless of income.

References

Department for Education (2016) www.gov.uk/government/organisations/department-for-education [accessed 28 October 2016]

Gov.uk (2014) Landmark Children and Families Act 2014 gains royal assent. www.gov.uk/government/news/landmark-children-and-families-act-2014-gains-royal-assent [accessed 10 May 2015]

Ofsted (2016) School inspection handbook for inspecting schools in England under section 5 of the Education Act 2005. Ofsted

Sylva, K., Melhuish, M., Sammons, P., Siraj-Blatchford, I. and Taggart, B. (2012) Pre-school, Primary and Secondary Education 3–14 Project (EPPSE 3–14) Final Report from the Key Stage 3 Phase: Influences on students' development from age 11–14. Institute of Education

United Nations Ministry of Educational, Scientific and Education and Science Cultural Organization (UNESCO) (1994) The Salamanca Statement and Framework for Action on Special Educational Needs. UNESCO. www.unesco.org/education/pdf/SALAMA_E.PDF [accessed 3 March 2015]

Chapter 1

What do we mean by inclusive practice?

Gianna Knowles

This chapter explores:

- What it means to be a child and the concept of childhood
- Theories of child development
- Maslow's hierarchy of needs and Bronfenbrenner's ecological systems theory of child development
- What is meant by inclusion
- Special educational needs and disability
- The SEN Code of Practice
- Equality of opportunity and barriers to learning
- Factors that children experience that may act as barriers to their learning.

Children and childhood

What does childhood mean?

- What does the term childhood mean to you?
- How is being a child different from being an adult?
- The next time you see a child in an advert, a magazine, or through some other medium, notice how they are portrayed: what are they wearing, what activity are they engaged in, how do they behave, are they happy, sad, noisy, curious?
- Think about the similarities between what is shown and your own experience of childhood.

Many adults can reflect on their own childhood as a time which was free from work, financial worries and concerns about a range of other responsibilities; for many, their childhood can seem to have been a time when things were more straightforward and the future was always a promise of exciting new possibilities. However, in reality, there are few adults who had a truly charmed childhood, where they were not at some point having to deal with situations and circumstances that worried or frightened them. Many adults can cite times when things happened at school that caused anxiety, or when changing family and wider social situations brought challenges; some adults, including many of you reading this book, will have had very challenging childhood situations to deal with.

Often the media can ignore the struggles some children face and represent childhood as a time filled with joy, wonder and excitement. While this is the experience of many children, for others in reality they are facing many of the challenges and problems that adults face. Most children have strong, loving and caring homes, but others experience upheavals in family life, or live in poverty, or are subjected to abuse and neglect. Some children are looked after children or are marginalised and vulnerable because they have a special educational need or disability. However, these issues aside, there does seem to be a general belief that childhood is a 'special' time, distinct and different from adulthood. Childhood is a point in a developing human being's life when it is acknowledged, by both individual families and wider society, that particular things are unique to this time in life – freedom from responsibility, for example, and possibly a greater tolerance of personal whims and indulgence of wants. However, from the child's point of view, it is also a time of intense learning both through the structured compulsory education system and through the day-to-day learning involved in growing up and learning to live in society.

Historically, in Europe and the West, the notion of childhood as a special time, different from adulthood, began to develop from the fifteenth century. Prior to this, children were treated in a similar way to the treatment of adults. Children were expected to undertake chores and work alongside adults, although the tasks they were given to do would be in keeping with their physical and cognitive development. It is not until the nineteenth century that the notion of childhood begins to develop, in a way we would understand now, where the notion of childhood brings with it distinct expectations of how families and society should provide for and treat children, which will be different to the ways adults might expect to be treated.

The end of children in the workplace and the development of compulsory schooling

In the late eighteenth and early nineteenth century, Britain moved from being a largely agricultural nation to a highly industrialised one. Thousands of families who had lived and worked on the land moved to cities for jobs in the new factories. Just as children had worked on the farms alongside the adults, when families moved to the cities, children continued to work with adults in the factories and mines. However, in the early nineteenth century, there was a growing belief that it was inappropriate for children to be working in such conditions. It began to be recognised that children were being exposed to considerable physical and emotional harm and were vulnerable to exploitation.

Below is a list of key dates and legislation that eventually made it illegal for children to work and legally require children to attend school:

* *1833 Factory Act* – This law stopped children under age 9 from working in textile factories. Children from age 9–13 were allowed to work, but only for forty-eight hours a week.
* *1836 Registration of Births, Deaths and Marriages* – This law meant that because a child's birth date was recorded, it was possible for factory inspectors to check the ages of children and ensure that the children working in the factory were old enough to do so.

- *1842 Mines Act* – This stopped all women and girls being allowed to work underground and boys under the age of 10. It also prevented everyone under 15 from being in charge of machinery.
- *1844 Factory Act* – Girls under the age of 18 had their working hours limited to twelve hours on week days (including Saturdays) and nine hours on Sundays. In 1847, the Ten Hour Act reduced working hours for girls under 18 to ten hours a day and fifty-eight hours a week.
- *1870 Education Act* – This was one of the first pieces of legislation relating to education. Significantly it allowed money to be raised from local rates to provide schools in all areas for children, although schools were not free and could charge fees for attending.
- *1880 Education Act* – This piece of legislation made attendance at school compulsory for children between the ages of 5 and 10. However, fees were still payable until 1891. In 1893, the school-leaving age was raised to 11, and in 1899 it was further raised to 12.
- *1893 Elementary Education (Blind and Deaf Children) Act* – This law extended compulsory education to blind and deaf children, which led to the development of special schools.
- *1899 Elementary Education (Defective and Epileptic Children) Act* – This law made educational provision for disabled children.

Throughout the nineteenth century, there was significant resistance to these laws being passed. Factory owners resisted the laws as children were cheaper to employ and their physical size meant they could work in smaller spaces and, with their smaller hands, do more specialised jobs than adults were able to undertake. Parents too were resistant to the laws as it meant a reduction in family income; not only were children not bringing in an income, but if they were going to school, school fees also had to be found. This was a time before welfare support, so there were no benefits available to a family if someone was too ill to work, or was unemployed; without housing benefit, there was an ever-present fear of eviction and homelessness. In reality, despite the changes in legislation, many children continued to work, either lying about their age and not attending school, or working after school.

Sources: Victorian Children 2016; Parliament UK 2016

The social changes brought by the Industrial Revolution and the legislative changes relating to children that followed as a result, have had a significant impact on the development of the idea of 'childhood'. In making it illegal for children to work, it was recognised that children, by comparison with most adults, are more physically, cognitively and emotionally vulnerable and therefore should not be exposed to situations that are potentially dangerous or might lead to exploitation. Further to this, by compelling children to go to school, it was acknowledged that education serves to inform and develop skills, knowledge and understanding that in the longer term provide choice and wider long-term work and lifestyle possibilities for the individual, and also ensure an educated workforce for society.

In this way, making child labour illegal and instituting compulsory and, later, free education has contributed to our understanding of childhood as being a time where specific things do and do not happen for children. They do go to school, but do not go to work. However, this is to somewhat over-simplify the situation. Many see a significant purpose of education as being to prepare children for adulthood and there is, arguably, increasing pressure on children to achieve particular levels of academic success at school, to ensure that they are able to take full advantage of the opportunities employment might provide for them, and to ensure that they contribute to wider society by doing so. However, not only is education for some children a far from happy time, but also, as noted above, many children still face challenges throughout their childhood years. For example some children continue to work, while others may be carers for parents or siblings.

Child exploitation in the UK

In Britain there are a number of laws that prevent children under the age of 18 being employed in paid work. However, from the age of 16, young people can work in jobs such as babysitting and delivering newspapers, and they may also do odd jobs for a parent, relative or neighbour; with special licences which restrict the number of working hours, a child can take part in television and other entertainment work and, with permission from parents or carers, young people aged 16 can join the armed forces (Citizen's Advice 2016).

However, despite these laws, there is a darker side to the lives of working children in Britain. In 2015 it was reported that up to 3,000 children may have been trafficked and forced to work 'running cannabis factories, nail bars, garment factories, brothels and private homes' (*The Guardian* 2015). And it is not only 'trafficked' children who end up working and being exploited in the ways described above. The NSPCC reports that between 2010 and 2011 nationally 'Over 2,400 children were victims of sexual exploitation', including prostitution (NSPCC 2016). Other children worked long hours after school in parents' or a relative's shops, or alongside adults working in the home.

As discussed above, there are very good reasons it is illegal for children to work: children are still developing physically, cognitively and emotionally, and long working hours, the work environment and the work itself will have a negative impact on the child's health and wellbeing and may interfere with some children being able to attend school.

Child carers

The 2011 census identified 178,000 young carers in England and Wales alone; an 83 per cent increase in the number of young carers aged 5–7 years and a 55 per cent increase in the number of children caring who are aged 8–9 years. When figures from the Northern Ireland and Scottish census are taken into account, the total number of young carers in the UK is at least 195,000 (Barnardo's 2016).

Just as in Britain we have seen how the development of our current understanding has come about for social change and through historic reasons, so too the second half of the twentieth century saw the beginning of a more global move to recognising and protecting childhood in a similar manner.

The United Nations Convention on the Rights of the Child

The United Nations Convention of the Rights of the Child (UNCRC) was established in 1989. Many governments across the world have signed the convention, agreeing that they will observe the rights for children set out in the convention. This is a significant agreement, since it seeks to provide for all 'children civil, political, economic, social and cultural rights that all children everywhere are entitled to' (Unicef.org 2016), thereby recognising that children are entitled to particular treatment, specifically because they are children.

The Convention has fifty-four articles that set out the rights of the child. The articles define a child as being someone under the age of 18 and as having the right to a national identity, to stay with their family and parents, to have their views acknowledged, to have education and health care, and to have leisure and play.

While many countries have signed to abide by the UNCRC, the UNCRC itself is a convention or agreement, not a law. The UK Government has signed the UNCRC, but that does not make the articles law in the UK. Only Acts passed by the UK Government are laws, therefore no one in the UK can be punished for not upholding the UNCRC. However, many of the UNCRC's articles are covered by other laws in the UK, which, if broken, can lead to punishment.

Although we have explored how children and childhood is protected by laws, particularly those that prevent children from working, there is still concern that the very concept of childhood, as conceived in the way we have discussed, can leave children open to exploitation. Foley, Roche and Tucker (2001) discuss how childhood has become an 'industry', that is, toy makers and the children's fashion industry, the children's media industry and, to a certain extent, the education industry, all owe their existence and, for some their vast profits, to the current concept of children and childhood. If childhood were not a special time, it would not need these special services. Wyness writes that children are 'providing employment for adults', which possibly 'strengthens the economic power of adults at the cost of children's own interests' (Wyness 1999, p.24). That is to say, the development of the idea of childhood has, in some ways, disempowered children. It is usually adults who make decisions for and about children, and the extent to which children's concerns and wishes are taken into account is questionable, when decisions that directly affect their welfare are made.

Some would argue that, while we have sought to protect children from the worst aspects of the adult world and provide them with a time to grow up, learn and mature before taking on adult responsibilities, we have also infantilised them for longer than we should. That is, by keeping young people in education or training until the age of 18, we have prevented them from growing into young adults, under the guidance of older work colleagues, as would have happened for previous generations; the knock-on effect can be that it comes as a shock to move suddenly from childhood to adulthood, rather than it being a gradual transition, or that some young people who are ready for more responsibility at an earlier age rebel against being kept in education when they want to be doing other things. However, more recent UK legislation – and the UNCRC – does require that children have a voice in deciding for themselves what is in their best interests in certain aspects of their lives and we will come back to this in later chapters in this book.

Theories of child development

So far we have discussed the notion of childhood and what it means to be a child in terms of society's views about children and what a child should and should not be able to do. This next section looks at what is meant by the term 'child' from a human developmental point of view. In Europe and North America, the beginning of the twentieth century saw a rise in interest, led by psychologists and doctors, particularly paediatricians, around the idea of 'child development'. Starting in the 1930s, the Swiss-born developmental psychologist Jean Piaget led the way in codifying the stages of cognitive development children passed through from birth to adulthood. For example, he detailed at what age a child might be expected to be able to move from concrete thinking to abstract thinking. That is, from the pre-operational stage from age 2–7, of seeing things from an egocentric or self-focused point of view, to the concrete operations stage at age 7–11 where children begin to de-centre and understand the nature of others and be able to empathise with others' feelings and needs.

In physical development terms, just as Piaget established that children pass through given stages of cognitive development, the American psychologist and paediatrician Arnold Gesell developed a similar set of stages relating to children's physical development – as well as their social and emotional development. Over the course of the twentieth century, others working in the area of child development established influential and significant theories around many aspects of child development, with a number of theorists fiercely arguing against the work of others. So, for example, Margaret Donaldson, who also researched children's cognitive development, contested aspects of Piaget's theory. Lev Vygotsky established ideas about children's language development and John Bowlby theorised about how children form attachments to caregivers from birth and how these attachments, depending on their nature, will impact on how children form later attachments to others in wider society – that is, friends and potential partners.

While all these theories are important, in terms of helping us understand what might be happening for children as they develop, one of the unforeseen consequences of these ideas has been the medicalisation of childhood and the increasingly dominant idea that there is a *normal* pattern for how a child should grow and develop, cognitively, physically and emotionally, and that any child who does not develop in these possibly quite prescriptive ways is *not normal*.

Maslow and wellbeing

While the theorists above are concerned to set out developmental trajectories for children growing into adults – to indicate a typical line of development in the areas of physical and cognitive development – all these theories explain development in terms of what should normally happen for a person or child. These theories also overlook other factors that can impact on development. Maslow, for example, explores how what is happening around a child will impact on that child's growth and development, particularly in terms of achieving what Maslow defines as 'self-actualisation' (Knowles and Holmstrom 2012). For Maslow, the goal of human growth and development is self-actualisation or 'full-humanness' (Maslow 2014, p.3).

For Maslow, too, this gets away from notions of 'illness' and 'health' (Maslow 2014), which are fundamental to the 'normal' trajectories just discussed and the binary notion of ability/ disability; though he does acknowledge that the word 'self' is not necessarily helpful as it implies selfishness.

Self-actualisation

Being self-actualised includes the following characteristics:

- Accepting the self and others for what they are, understanding that others will have different views and not feeling threatened by or needing to change those views
- Having strong relationships with a few people and enjoying privacy
- Being able to see challenges as problems 'outside the self' and be objective about them
- Being able to deal with uncertainty
- Creativity, be that scientific as well as artistic
- Being able to accept and reject fashions and ideas on their own terms, not because they are forced on them, or are what 'everyone' is doing/thinks
- Concern for others and seeking to help and support others
- Having a strong moral sense, but not being a bigot

Source: www.simplypsychology.org/maslow.html#self2

However, for a human being to achieve this state, it requires a foundation of other aspects of support and care to already be in place, which self-actualisation can build upon. For this reason, Maslow represented this process as a hierarchy, most often shown as a pyramid and referred to as Maslow's 'hierarchy of needs'.

At the bottom of the pyramid are the basic psychological needs we all have and that ensure survival and growth: shelter, water and food. These are the most basic needs that must be met and the ones that will ensure physical health, without which the journey to self-actualisation cannot begin. The next level of needs contains affection and relationships and the following level moves on to feelings of self-esteem and confidence and feeling respected by others. Education is placed in level three of this hierarchy and, importantly, we can see that for level three to be achieved, the needs in level one and two must be being met.

Understanding Maslow's hierarchy of needs

- Work your way through Maslow's hierarchy of needs, beginning at the bottom, and think about how your own needs are being met.
- Consider who is around you and helps you meet some of the needs listed – and who you support to help meet the needs of others.
- Think about your experience of working with children in an educational setting. How do such settings actively encourage children to develop self-esteem, confidence and respect for others?
- How does this happen for all children in the setting, depending on their gender, ethnicity, or if they have SEN or a disability?

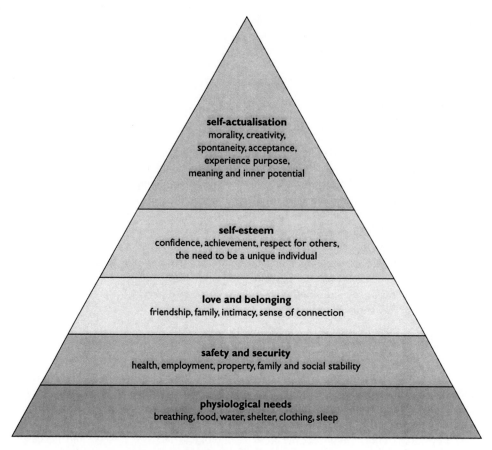

Figure 1.1 Maslow's hierarchy of needs (Dirt 2012, p.19)

Maslow states that we do not necessarily start at the bottom of the pyramid and work our way up in a smooth trajectory. Life for most people is much messier than that. Many people struggle with ensuring they have their basic needs met and this can significantly impact on their capacity to achieve self-respect and self-esteem. For children, achieving wellbeing can be even more challenging as having their needs met is much more dependent on who is around them to support and provide for them.

The Scottish Government's *Getting it right for every child approach (GIRFEC)*

The Scottish Government has recently passed The Children and Young People (Scotland) Act 2014. This Act recognises that 'each child is unique and there is no set level of wellbeing that children should achieve' and that all children 'should be helped to reach their full potential as an individual'.

inclusion'. From the 1994 Salamanca Statement and the *Framework for Action* onward, classroom educational practice in all UK mainstream schools began to adopt an approach to teaching and learning that was to be inclusive of all children's learning needs and is now a fundamental principle of UK educational practice. Those working with children in educational settings understand that learning activities must take into consideration those needs pertaining to particular aspects of children's backgrounds; for example, coming from a low-income family, or having a particular learning need or disability. Inclusion meant, and continues to mean, that all children must be able to enter their classroom, be that with or without assistive technologies, and be able to access the learning activities being presented by the adults in the classroom. Having a particular learning need, such as dyslexia, needing to use a wheelchair, having English as an additional language, an autistic spectrum condition, being a gifted mathematician, or having parents of the same sex should not be a barrier to learning, or mean that a child faces discrimination.

Since Salamanca, the principle of inclusion has shaped both social and educational policy in the UK. From 1997 and even earlier, educational settings had been developing their inclusive practice and there is now a great deal of good and outstanding practice happening in Early Years settings and schools. The first two editions of this book, published in 2006 and 2010, sought to bring to the reader key aspects of relevant government and educational policy and present aspects of good practice to help put that policy and practice in place.

Over the past fifteen years, educational settings and schools have understood that as they have developed their approach to learning activities to ensure the activities are accessible to children with a range of needs, the result is that the learning of all children has improved. For example, the use of visual timetables in classrooms, which were often initially introduced to better support the learning of children on the autistic spectrum, is now generally regarded as good practice for all children, since they offer all children the opportunity to see how their day will be structured and to understand the learning they will be engaged in. In this way, settings and schools have moved to an approach to learning that focuses on a social model of learning and meeting children's needs. That is, the learning environment is inclusive because all children can access the learning – irrespective of their needs or ability. Nothing 'special' needs to be done or provided for them.

What is an inclusive learning environment?

Below is a list of features that identify an inclusive learning environment – next time you are in an education setting look for examples of these indicators of good practice:

- Learning activities are designed to enable all children to join in and learn in a way that meets their needs and abilities.
- There is evidence of collaboration between pupils, either through talk partners clarifying ideas for each other, or team players working together to solve problems.
- The educational setting or learning environment has an ethos where children are encouraged to understand and empathise with the needs of others.
- Aspects of the educational setting's provision are informed by the children's voice – that is, children have an input into how the learning environment is designed and, where appropriate, how aspects of the curriculum are approached.

- 'Barriers to learning are overcome including for those pupils with disabilities and complex needs. These experiences include a wide range of well-planned visits, visitors to the school, dance and drama activities and a varied menu of extra-curricular options which ensure all, regardless of ability are fully included' (Ofsted 2013).
- Good inclusive practice not only improves the learning experience and wellbeing for individual children, but also encourages all children to expect diversity in their lives.

The development of educational approaches to what is regarded as good inclusive practice is also supported by a range of recent changes to legislation and educational policy.

Recent legislation relating to inclusion

- *The Equality Act 2010* – this piece of legislation replaced and brought together a wide range of laws relating to many forms of discrimination: race, disability and gender, to name a few. In particular, it introduced a list of specific *protected characteristics* a child or adult may have, that make it unlawful to discriminate against people on grounds of having that characteristic. Protected characteristics are: age, disability, gender reassignment, pregnancy and maternity, marriage and civil partnership, race, sex and sexual orientation.

  This piece of legislation recognises that we all, at some point in our lives, may experience being discriminated against, unless we live in a truly inclusive society. Some aspects of this legislation have an obvious and direct bearing on schools and children, while other aspects have a more complex impact. For example, an educational setting is now compelled to make reasonable adjustments to ensure a child who has a disability has their needs met; similarly, trans children – that is, children who may be experiencing gender dysphoria – must be supported in their educational setting. An example of a more complex impact of this legislation is ensuring there is no discrimination with regards to same sex marriages, where there may be indirect discrimination experienced by children whose parents may be lesbian, gay, bisexual, or transgender (LGBT). Indeed the Act itself states there must 'be protection for people discriminated against because they are perceived to have, or are associated with someone who has, a protected characteristic' (Gov.uk 2015). These issues are discussed in more detail in Chapters 2 and 3.
- *The Marriage (Same Sex Couples) Act* was passed in 2013. The possible impact of this legislation, with regard to children and inclusive practice, has been briefly outlined above in relation to discussing protected characteristics around gender and sexuality. However, there are also wider aspects around this discussion to consider – how, for example, settings must ensure they are being inclusive of all families and children when, for example, they are exploring through curriculum topics such as 'My Family'.

> • *The Children and Families Act 2014* introduced many changes to the care of vulnerable children, extending support to them and their families from birth to age 21 or 25, depending on need. In particular, it made changes to adoption and fostering regulations and requires settings and schools to support children at school with medical conditions (Gov.uk 2014).

Special educational needs and disability

The SEN Code of Practice

In 2014 the new – and long-awaited – *SEN Code of Practice* was introduced. This built on the successes of the previous Code of Practice (2001), while introducing significant changes, in that it now covers children and young people from birth to age 25. It has also made the following changes: the views of children and young people must be sought and taken into account; there must be joint planning and commissioning of services to ensure close co-operation between education, health services and social care; the statement of SEN is replaced by the Health and Care Plan (the EHC plan), and it includes new guidance on the support pupils and students should receive in education and training settings.

What is meant by 'equality of opportunity' and 'barriers to learning'?

In 2013, the latest version of the *National Curriculum* was published. Section 4 of the National Curriculum reiterates what inclusion means for the current generation of primary school children. It states educational settings must ensure they are 'responding to pupils' needs and overcoming potential barriers for individuals and groups of pupils'. It makes explicit reference to the Equality Act 2010, stating that 'Teachers should take account of their duties under equal opportunities legislation that covers race, disability, sex, religion or belief, sexual orientation, pregnancy and maternity, and gender reassignment.' It also reinforces the continuation of the excellent inclusive practice already in operation in educational settings by reiterating that 'a wide range of pupils have special educational needs, many of whom also have disabilities. Lessons should be planned to ensure that there are no barriers to pupil achieving' (DfE 2013, p.8).

Factors that children experience that may act as barriers to their learning

In 2011, the government introduced the *pupil premium*. This was the first time it had been officially recognised that children from low-income families (and, in this instance also children who are being fostered or in care) could be adversely affected by their backgrounds in terms of their capacity to achieve in their learning. The introduction of the pupil premium has meant that educational settings have had to act positively to ensure that they are including and supporting these children's specific needs. This support is directly funded by the government, which gives schools 'extra funding to raise the attainment of disadvantaged pupils from reception to year 11' (Gov.uk 2014). With regard to this book, the chapters on looked after children, fostering and adoption and children from low-income families explore not only the particular challenges faced by these children, but also how educational settings can ensure they are including and supporting these children in terms of their educational success – and using the pupil premium to do so.

Conclusion

This chapter, as the first chapter in this book, has sought to raise and discuss key points that will be discussed in more detail in subsequent chapters. At the heart of inclusive practice is the notion that truly inclusive learning environments will allow any child, whatever their needs, to access the learning activities provided and thrive in that learning environment. In beginning to explore how this might happen for children, we have firstly explored what it means to be a child – our view of what children are, and what childhood is about, will impact on how we work with children and seek to ensure they are included. We have also looked at theories around how children can be supported to thrive and achieve self-actualisation and we have discussed theories of child development. It has been noted that depending on how these theories are approached, they can either aid or impair our understanding of how children thrive and learn.

In exploring these ideas, many general points about children have been raised; however, what must be remembered is that every child is unique and will bring to any learning situation a specific range of individual needs, abilities and expectations. A child's needs may arise because of their home background, their gender, their ethnicity and/or whether they have an SEN or disability. Indeed, all children's learning needs are a combination of all or some of these factors. Having now raised these points, the following chapters of this book will examine in more detail some of these factors, and provide more insight and understanding into how to consider these factors when thinking about developing an inclusive environment.

References

Barnardo's (2016) Young Carers www.barnardos.org.uk/what_we_do/our_work/young_carers.htm [accessed 12 September 2016]

Citizen's Advice (2016) Young people and employment https://www.citizensadvice.org.uk/work/young-people/young-people-and-employment/ [accessed 12 September 2016]

DfE (Department for Education) (2013) The national curriculum in England Key stages 1 and 2 framework document. DfE

Dirt, N. (2012) *Recent Posts* www.researchhistory.org/2012/06/16/maslows-hierarchy-of-needs/ [accessed 10 September 2016]

Foley, P., Roche, J. and Tucker, S. (2001) *Children in Society*. London: Palgrave

Gov.scot (2016) Key facts about wellbeing www.gov.scot/Topics/People/Young-People/gettingitright/wellbeing/keyfacts [accessed 21 August 2016]

Gov.uk (2014) Landmark Children and Families Act 2014 gains royal assent www.gov.uk/government/news/landmark-children-and-families-act-2014-gains-royal-assent [accessed 10 May 2015]

Gov.uk (2015) Equality Act 2010: guidance www.gov.uk/equality-act-2010-guidance [accessed 10 May 2015]

Knowles, G. and Holmstrom, R. (2012) *Understanding Family Diversity*. Routledge

Maslow, A. (2014) *Toward a Psychology of Being*. Lushena Books

NSPCC (2016) Child sexual exploitation https://www.nspcc.org.uk/preventing-abuse/child-abuse-and-neglect/child-sexual-exploitation/ [accessed 12 September 2016]

Ofsted (2013) Effective integration of pupils with disabilities and complex needs into mainstream school: St John Bosco Roman Catholic Voluntary Aided Primary School. Ofsted

Parliament UK (2016) Going to School www.parliament.uk/about/living-heritage/transformingsociety/livinglearning/school/overview/1870educationact/ [accessed 6 June 2016]

The Guardian (2015) 3,000 children enslaved in Britain after being trafficked from Vietnam https://www.theguardian.com/global-development/2015/may/23/vietnam-children-trafficking-nail-bar-cannabis [accessed 12 September 2016]

UNESCO (United Nations Ministry of Educational, Scientific and Education and Science Cultural Organization) (1994) The Salamanca Statement and Framework for Action on Special Educational Needs. UNESCO www.unesco.org/education/pdf/SALAMA_E.PDF [accessed 3 May 2015]

Unicef.org (2016) United Nations Convention on the Rights of the Child (UNCRC) www.unicef.org.uk/unicefs-work/un-convention/ [accessed 6 September 2016]

Victorian Children (2016) Victorian Child Labor and the Conditions They Worked In www.victorianchildren.org/victorian-child-labor/ [accessed 6 September 2016]

Wyness, M. (1999) *Contesting Childhood*. London: Falmer Press

Chapter 2

Gender and inclusion

Gianna Knowles

This chapter explores:

- Gender roles – employment and educational achievement by gender
- The impact of culture and society on defining gender roles
- What do we mean by gender?
- Transgender, and children and transgender
- Gender and identity
- What it's like being a girl or boy in contemporary Britain
- Gender and education.

> Gender affects every aspect of our personal lives. Whether we identify as a man or woman determines how we look, how we talk, what we eat and drink, what we wear, our leisure activities, what jobs we do, how our time is deployed, how other people relate to us.
>
> (Bradley 2013, p.6)

Gender roles: employment by gender

Recent statistics exploring employment by gender in the UK (Stone 2015; ONS 2013) show that while more women are part of the workforce than at any other time over the past forty years, 'men have consistently higher employment rates aged 22 and above' (ONS 2013). Not only this, but 'men tend to work in the professional occupations associated with higher levels of pay . . . women dominate employment within caring and leisure occupations' (ONS 2013). Stone (2015) discusses how, apart from Finland, Sweden and France, the world's governments are composed of mainly men, with the UK coming behind many European nations, having only 22.70 per cent (less than a quarter) of its government composed of women. Further to this, both in the UK and internationally, the majority of those who dominate the financial and business world are men.

Gender expectations

There is little, if any, convincing evidence that human brains are neurologically either 'boy' brains or 'girl' brains. However, wider society and the media project very strong ideas about what it is to be a 'girl' or a 'boy'. Images and examples exist everywhere that reinforce the idea that girls behave in a particular way and that boys behave in another – that there are girls' clothes and boys' clothes, girls' toys and boys' toys, etc. And, eventually, as girls become women and boys men, there are women's jobs and men's work and, possibly, different roles for women and men in the family.

- Write a list of ten words that describe popular beliefs about how girls look and behave. Try the same activity for boys.
- As adults, are there particular jobs women and men do and particular roles they should take in long-term partnerships and in bringing up families?

In thinking through the activity above, it is likely you came up with some of the usual gender stereotypes – that girls like pink, frilly clothes and looking good, while boys like adventurous games and football. However, very quickly it is also likely that you began to question these stereotypes, particularly if you began to think about the experiences of yourself and your friends, and to argue that, in reality, both boys and girls like a range of activities and clothes and both want very similar things for their adulthood. Indeed, with the increasing diversity in the ways families now configure themselves – be they blended families, single-parent, same-sex parents, or mixed heritage families – fewer adults now fulfil traditional gender stereotypical roles within families. In terms of jobs, women can now serve as soldiers in the front line of battle and men can be midwives, both roles seen up until recently as definitely gender specific; that is, men are soldiers, women are midwives. Yet the media still projects stereotypes about gender and there is still a gender imbalance in the employment and elected government members' statistics.

The ideas of the dominant culture

Why does this continue to happen, despite legislation moving towards equality? The dominant discourse suggests that some behaviours belong to one gender rather than the other, that girls and women are genetically more nurturing and caring than boys and men and therefore more suited to bringing up children and working in occupations that involve caring for others. In the dominant discourse, boys and men are the 'hunters' in society and should be working away from the home, being the breadwinners – their jobs are regarded as the socially more important roles.

These behaviours we have learnt as children, but cultures change, as the next generation generates new expressions of culture, and not necessarily because one culture has swamped another. Adhering to traditional cultural values provides a sense of certainty and continuity – if we take on the cultural norms of the society around us, it gives us a sense of belonging. Being part of a group supports our sense of self, or identity. However, we are not necessarily born with these ideas; they are 'something we learn about as we grow-up and therefore what we describe as being "our culture" will depend on what we have been taught it should be' (Knowles and Holmstrom 2012, p.26).

What do we mean by gender?

The terms 'gender' and 'sex' are often used interchangeably (Bradley 2013), and to make the distinction between male and female, boy and girl, man and woman. However, these terms are increasingly coming to have two distinct meanings. The term 'sex'

> . . . is usually understood to represent the physical differentiation as male or female, indicated by the external appearance of the genitalia and the presence of gonads (testes in a boy/ovaries in a girl) which will determine reproductive function, and differences in brain structure and function.
>
> (GIRES 2008)

'Gender', on the other hand, is about how we wish to and present ourselves as meeting the social categories of male or female. For many people, their sex – that is, whether they are biologically male or female, having testes or ovaries – will also be the gender they assign to themselves. We have discussed above how aligning ourselves with one gender or another may carry with it certain behaviours which society expects from that gender.

In this way, gender is now generally recognised as a social construct (Bradley 2013; Giordano 2013). That is, it is a 'way of categorizing social relations' (Bradley 2013, p.4). It is about what is culturally expected in the way those who gender themselves male/female should behave, what they should wear and the social roles they should perform. Unlike the term 'sex', which is ascribed to particular given biological features, gender is not so fixed and what is expected of the different genders will vary from culture to culture and in different historical periods. It can also be argued that there is a power dynamic inherent in the notion of gender.

Gender is also a lived experience (Bradley 2013). While sex is about biological characteristics and the physical factors that result from this, for example, whether one can have a baby or not, gender is about how we are positioned in society and the relationships we have that result from our acquired or chosen gender. These are not only the relationships we choose to have, but also how others will view us and treat us because of the gender we portray; in many instances there persist 'disparities of power between women and men . . . in every aspect of our lives, whether we realize it or not' (Bradley 2013, p.6).

Impact of culture

Activity

Culture is that complex whole which includes knowledge, belief, art, morals, law, custom and other capabilities and habits . . . culture includes all aspects of human activity from the fine arts to popular entertainment.

(Rai and Panna 2010, p.8)

- Spend some time reflecting on the media you engage with – what are the images and behaviours of men and women it projects?
- How do women dress, how do men dress?
- How do men and women behave?

- Do you see reflected traditional views of the roles and behaviours of men and women represented, or are both seen as being more in line with each other?
- Thinking about more complex cultural beliefs, do your views on marriage, bringing up children, rules about right and wrong and the role of men and women in society reflect a particular cultural view?

Scenario 1: Coombe Hage Primary School

Justyn is the assistant head teacher of Coombe Hage Primary School. She says she has always been concerned about how notions of gender impact on children's engagement with education and developing identities. She comments:

'We live in quite a diverse community and all cultures, white and black, have their own views of how girls and boys should be. In our reception class, we use an Early Years model of teaching and learning, so in many ways we're always thinking about how to create an environment that allows all children to experience and engage with the learning activities available.

'We have an outside area with sand and water play, scooters and trikes. When I first started here there was a culture of only the boys going outside, they would race out and grab the scooters and monopolise them and this was accepted by the adults, so the boys and girls accepted it was how things should be. We had to work quite hard to get a shift in this way of doing things – and I met with resistance from the children, and staff and the children's families! The girls had to be encouraged to go out – many wanted to, but even at five said the scooters were "boys toys". Then some were worried about getting dirty, so we invested in "school" wellies and outdoor protective clothing a bit like plastic onesies. We insisted both the boys and girls wear them too, to show that everyone's clothing has to stay clean. We also asked the key workers to go out and encourage all the children to play with the different things outside and the learning activities we set-up out there.

'We worked to ensure all our inside learning activities were gender neutral, or had a gender balance and we created an ethos that celebrates everyone having a go at all the activities. We're working on developing times when families and members of the community can come in and read with the children. At the moment it still tends to be mainly women coming in and we're very glad to see them, but I'd like a few more men in, to be role models for the boys; we're working on finding some retired grandads we can share around! Older brothers, who are further up the school, come – which gives the older boys a great sense of responsibility too. The Children's Centre attached to the school has Saturday morning sessions for "dads", where they bring the children along, have breakfast with them and engage with whatever activities have been set up. It works really well, but we don't have the facilities here for that kind of activity.'

Transgender

For some, while they may be born with testes and initially defined as being male, or ovaries and therefore defined as being female, they may experience gender variance or dysphoria. There is a notion that once a baby is at birth assigned a sex, that they will follow the typical gender development associated with the sex they have presented as. By contrast, 'gender variance is an atypical development in the relationship between the gender identity and the visible sex of an individual' (GIRES 2008). That is, a child may be identified at birth as being female, but may themselves identify as male (Giordano 2013).

Sometimes, the doctors get it wrong at birth, for medical reasons, for example, in cases where a person may have complete Androgen Insensitivity Syndrome (cAIS), which can cause 'a mixture of female and male characteristics' (GIRES 2008). However, gender variance also occurs though 'gender dysphoria (dysphoria means "unhappiness")' (GIRES 2008). This is thought to happen where a child may be born with matching chromosomal and visible physical sex characteristics, for example, typical female XX chromosomes and genitalia, but 'may have some male brain characteristics and therefore, identify as a man' (GIRES 2008). Therefore, GIRES argues, although others will contest this argument, that 'gender identification . . . is rooted in the brain, and is regarded by the individuals concerned, and is demonstrated by research, to be largely determined pre-birth and more or less stable thereafter' (GIRES 2008).

Gender dysphoria

On its website, the NHS offers the following information and guidance about gender dysphoria. It discusses how 'gender development is complex' and outlines that there can be 'a mismatch between a person's biological sex and their gender identity' (NHS 2016). While the official view of the NHS is that 'the exact cause of gender dysphoria is unclear' (NHS Choices 2017), it is acknowledged it can be due to hormones, or may also be the result of other conditions, such as 'congenital adrenal hyperplasia (CAH) – where a high level of male hormones are produced in a female foetus' (NHS 2016), or 'intersex conditions – which cause babies to be born with the genitalia of both sexes (or ambiguous genitalia)' (NHS 2016). In instances of intersex conditions, 'parents are recommended to wait until the child can choose their own gender identity before any surgery is carried out' (NHS Choices 2017).

The Gender Recognition Act 2004

The Gender Recognition Act (GRA) provides for those who have had medical treatment to enable them to be formally recognised as their chosen gender. Those who wish to have their gender recognition reassigned may apply to the Gender Recognition Panel (GRP) for a Gender Recognition Certificate (GRC). The GRC then entitles a person to be recognised 'as the gender stated on that certificate "for all purposes"' (GIRES 2008). To obtain a GRC, the applicant must 'provide the GRP with evidence of a diagnosis of persistent gender dysphoria, and must convince it of their intention to live in the new role for the rest of their lives' (GIRES 2008). However, the GRA 2004 does not require that sex change surgery has taken place for the GRC to be issued and in this way 'disconnects genital anatomy from gender identity' (Giordano 2013, p.7).

Children and transgender

Children and transgender

In her *Guardian* article, 'Transgender children: "This is who he is – I have to respect that"', Kleeman (2015) tells the story of Tom, age 5, who used to be called Melanie, and Julia, age 8, who used to be Callum. The article explores with Tom's and Julia's parents their experience of realising their children wanted to be recognised as being a different gender to the one they had been assigned and how they, the children and wider society have responded to the situation.

In talking about Tom, Tom's mother says she 'can pinpoint the moment her daughter Melanie became her son, Tom. They were in the supermarket and Melanie, then 2½, said: "I don't want to be a girl any more – I'm going to be a boy, and I'm going to be called Tom"' (Kleeman 2015). Similarly, Julia's mother says that Julia was given the name Callum at birth, 'but as soon as she could talk, she said she was a girl . . . "She used to draw herself as a girl as soon as she could hold a pencil," Daniel [father] says. "I've never seen her draw herself as a boy, ever." And both Julia's parents describe how Callum, from a very young age, was relentless in presenting himself as Julia.'

The article goes on to outline the challenges faced by Tom, Julia and their families in terms of having the children's chosen gender acknowledged. It explains the support they received from other parents and help groups and the mixed reactions experienced from their own, wider families and from society at large, including the children's schools. While schools must acknowledge gender dysphoria and accept children as the gender presented by the child, there are individual teachers and support staff in schools who can still be unsupportive of children with gender dysphoria.

Kleeman (2015) also discusses how, if unsupported, children with gender dysphoria may become increasingly unhappy as they grow up, particularly through puberty and beyond, as their bodies begin to develop into their adult form and reinforce how their physical gender is completely at odds with the gender they feel they are. Lack of support at this time can lead to self-harm and, in some cases, suicide. Recent research 'has found that 48% of trans people under 26 said they had attempted suicide, and 30% said they had done so in the past year, while 59% said they had at least considered doing so' (Strudwick 2014).

For further information about children and transgender, gender dysphoria and support available for transgender children, visit the Mermaids website: www.mermaidsuk.org.uk. Mermaids was formed by parents of children experiencing challenges with their assigned gender. It aims 'to raise awareness about gender issues amongst professionals and the general public' (Mermaids 2016), and is a good source of resources to use in schools, both to raise awareness about gender challenges and to help children needing support.

Gender and identity

The notion of identity is a contested term – that is, there is no one agreed idea about what it means and it can mean different things in different cultures. To further confuse things, the terms 'identity' and 'personality' are often used interchangeably, but actually have subtle differences. Identity is usually seen as being more fluid; that is, it can change, while personality has traits that are more fixed. That is to say, we may have particular characteristics and behaviours which are fundamental to who we are, which is our personality; but how we present ourselves to others, what we choose to believe, the choices we make about our appearance, what we do in our social lives are what form our identity. Adelson (1980) discusses how, in constructing our identity, we are constantly adding to and discarding things from our identity, as we change with age and experience. Thus, in this way, our identity will include how we choose to gender ourselves, the values and ideals we hold, and what we want to do and 'be' in life.

For Adelson (1980) and Klimstra and colleagues (2010), the development of identity 'begins with the self-object differentiation at infancy and reaches its final phase with the self-mankind integration at old age' (Adelson 1980, p.160). That is, the beginning of developing an identity is as a small child beginning to understand that 'I' am a separate being to those around me and, as such can have control over what I might want to do, what I want to eat or wear and the things I like doing. Young children are particularly very dependent on those around them and this will impact on their developing identities. However, as children grow up, they become more independent and Adelson writes, that when children reach adolescence: 'this is the first time that physical development, cognitive skills, and social expectations coincide to enable young persons to sort through and synthesize their childhood identifications in order to construct a viable pathway toward their adulthood' (Adelson 1980, p.160). Which is part of the reason, Adelson argues, that teenagers can seem to change from the children they were into rebellious creatures forever pushing boundaries, wearing different clothes and seeking new experiences.

In Europe and North America, there is a strong notion that part of achieving well-being includes having 'a sense of self' and that it is important to know 'who we are'. In Chapter 1, we looked at Maslow's notion of flourishing and self-actualisation, which explores what the individual needs to survive and thrive. Surviving is dependent on having very basic needs met, such as the need for food and shelter. The idea of thriving, however, is about having more than basic needs met: it is about what makes us 'feel good' as people and allows us to take advantage of the opportunities around us, to move on in life and develop in ways that bring us satisfaction and enable us to live positively alongside others. For Maslow (2014), someone who is thriving is a person who has confidence, self-esteem and supportive relationships around them. While it is usually a child's family that provide for children's basic needs of food and shelter, the family also impacts on a child's developing confidence and self-esteem and teaches a child about how to build relationships with others. If we now consider Bronfenbrenner's ecological systems theory (Knowles and Holmstrom 2012), we know that the family provides a child's first experiences of being around others and the child will learn, through the mesosystem, how to behave and interact with others, particularly as they move from the family into wider social environments, such as educational settings and school.

Theories about how children begin to develop their identities also debate to what extent a child's genetic heritage is the major influence on how a child's identity and personality develops, as compared to the impact of the social environment they have grown up in. That is to say, are we a product of our genes, or the environment we have grown up in? This dichotomy is often referred to as 'nature or nurture'.

Erik Erickson

Marcia's ideas build on those of Erikson, who in turn was building on Freud's work (McLeod 2013). The importance of Erikson's work is that it introduces the notion that social interactions play a significant part in how we develop and grow as human beings, particularly in relation to our developing identities.

Erik Erikson's stages of psychosocial development

- *Trust vs. Mistrust* – As a baby and young child, trust is placed in the primary caregiver. This may be a parent, older sibling, other family member, or foster or adoptive family. This is the person who initially provides for the basic needs described by Maslow. The sense of trust, or lack of trust, present in this relationship we will carry into relationships in the wider social arena.
- *Autonomy vs. Shame and Doubt* – From age 2–3, the child starts to realise they are independent of the carers around them and can make their own choices about what toys to play with and what to eat. They also begin to discover and test out other skills they have, such as being able to dress themselves. It is important children are provided with positive support in exploring these skills as criticism that they are 'too slow', or failing to do things correctly can have a lasting effect on confidence and self-esteem at this crucial development age.
- *Initiative vs. Guilt* – Between the ages of 3 and 5, children begin to develop a more definite sense of themselves and, in the UK, this will coincide with children starting compulsory schooling. In this way, children begin to develop and refine their interpersonal skills: they learn to be around others, making friends and inventing games with other children. This helps them 'develop a sense of initiative, and feel secure in their ability to lead others and make decisions' (McLeod 2013). Again, if this is a positive experience for children, their confidence and self-esteem will continue to flourish. However, if their ideas and initiatives are squashed or ignored, they may begin to doubt themselves and develop feelings of guilt, in that their wants and desires are somehow 'wrong'.
- *Industry (competence) vs. Inferiority* – This stage usually lasts from around age 5 to age 12. Not only is this a very intense time for learning at school, but the child's social life outside the family will gradually become more important to them than family life. This is in preparation for becoming an independent adult. In this way, 'the child now feels the need to win approval by demonstrating specific competencies that are valued by society, and begin to develop a sense of pride in their accomplishments' (McLeod 2013). Being able to demonstrate the skills and abilities valued by society will reinforce the child's belief in themselves, while failing to do so may lead to the child developing a sense of inferiority.
- *Identity vs. Role Confusion* – This stage of development, from approximately age 12 to 18, marks the transition from childhood to becoming a young adult. It is during this time the child begins to experience and explore the adult world and develop some sense of what and how they want to be as an adult. Uncertainty about the self and how to meet the seeming demands of the adult world can lead to feelings of identity uncertainty and unhappiness or rebellion.

Erikson's remaining stages apply to identity development throughout adulthood to old age. They include: Stage 6 Intimacy vs. Isolation, Stage 7 Generativity vs. Stagnation, and Stage 8 Ego Integrity vs. Despair. In these stages, Erikson discusses the positive impact adults can feel where they establish themselves in society, through having long-term relationships, possibly their own families and/or contributing to society through their work, finally leading to feeling a sense of achievement in old age. However, the reverse side of this experience happens when the individual feels they have not achieved these expectations of adulthood and they can become lonely, isolated and develop a sense that they have 'wasted' their life (McLeod 2013; Erickson 1995; Scheck 2014).

Identity, family and school

What is useful about the work of Erickson and Marcia is the notion of how the environment around the child impacts on their developing sense of self and identity. Since children spend a large part of their childhood in educational settings and schools, their educational experience will have huge impact on their developing identity. Not only will the abiding culture and ethos of the school or educational setting have an impact on the child, but also identities are shaped by our sense of a need to belong. As Weedon states: 'Identity is about belonging, about what you have in common with some people and what differentiates you from others' (Weedon 2004, p.1). In terms of academic success at school, children are more likely to succeed if they feel they can identify with and belong to the culture and cultures promoted by the school and will therefore 'try and fit in', which may mean adapting their behaviour, sometimes giving up doing things they like, because their wants do not 'fit' with the predominant ways of doing things. In this way, it is also understood that if a child comes into a school which has a culture and practices it cannot identify with, it may be that the child will fail to thrive and achieve in its learning. As Knowles and Lander state: 'where individuals or organisations transmit messages that suggest only particular aspects of certain cultures are acknowledged and others are ignored or marginalised . . . it can marginalise children and erode their sense of self, or who they identify themselves as being' (2011, p.8).

Being female in contemporary Britain

In 2016, the charity Plan International UK, in conjunction with the University of Hull (Lyons 2016), published 'The State of Girls' Rights in the UK' (Russell et al. 2016). The report states:

> Our analysis poses the question, 'What is the current state of girls' rights in the UK?' Sadly, the answer is clear. We may be the fifth-richest country in the world, but we are failing our girls, and failing to meet international standards set out in human rights frameworks and the United Nation's new Sustainable Development Goals (SDGs).
>
> (Russell et al. 2016, p.2)

The report goes on to outline how issues such as poverty, sexual harassment – including bullying and harassment through cyber technologies – violence against girls – including sexual violence – gender stereotyping and rising incidents of self-harm blight the lives of many girls in the UK. The report also discusses how the quality of life experienced by girls varies in different parts of the UK; it shows, for example, that 'Middlesbrough is the worst area to be a girl in England and Wales and Waverley in Surrey is the best' (Lyons 2016), with inner-city areas being the areas where girls are the most marginalised and vulnerable.

In undertaking the study the researchers investigated 'childhood poverty levels, life expectancy, teenage conception rates, GCSE results and percentage of girls aged under 18 not in employment, education or training' (Lyons 2016) across all UK local authorities.

One hundred and three girls took part in the research and their comments show that despite legislation to ensure that, by law, there is no preferential treatment for boys over girls, or men over women, inequalities in terms of life experiences between males and females still exist in our society.

While there has been much reported over recent years about girls outperforming boys in schools, the headline data tells only part of the story:

> Although results seem to show that girls are 'doing well' the researchers also found that: the school environment tends to reinforce stereotypes about girls' capabilities, whether that's through the sports they play or the subjects they choose. School can also be a location for abuse and harassment for girls.
>
> (Russell et al. 2016, p.4)

The girls also reported that there are few female role models, particularly in the media, who offer an alternative example to the stereotyped, often sexualised image presented by celebrity women. Further to this, the current representation of women in the media is leading to many girls having a poor body image and feelings that 'their choices are constrained by expectations about their bodies that are reproduced and reinforced across society – and strongly amplified in the digital world' (Russell et al. 2016, p.5). This research is supported by the Girlguiding (2016) Attitudes Survey. The report of the survey, conducted with 1,600 girls and women, states that girls' 'overall happiness is dropping' (Girlguiding 2016, p.1), and that a significant contributing factor to this finding is that 'Young women face more pressures affecting their body confidence . . . Too many of us are made to feel that our looks are the most important thing . . . girls don't feel free to use their voice online because they're afraid of abuse' (Girlguiding 2016, p.1).

Being male in contemporary Britain

Since the early 1990s, it has been regularly reported in the media that girls are outperforming boys in terms of educational attainment (Younger et al. 2005; Lloyd 2009; McCartney 2016). However, when we hear or read these comments, it must be remembered that this is not *all* boys; some boys *are* doing well, but just as we need to be concerned for the girls being marginalised we need also to understand why it is that some boys do not make the educational achievements they are capable of. Exploring the 'attainment gap' between girls and boys, McCartney (2016) writes that some boys are already beginning to underachieve – that is, achieve less than they are capable of – by the end of primary school, where on average as a group, girls outperform boys by six percentage points. By GCSE level, 'the gap for five A*-C grades, including English and Maths, is nine percentage points in England and more than seven in the other three home nations' (McCartney 2016). The knock-on effect of this is that fewer boys are becoming apprentices or going to university and more are falling into the NEET category (Not in Education, Employment, or Training) after leaving school. This in turn poses a problem, both for the skills needed for the UK job market and the economy and for the boys themselves, since underachievement can have a long-term effect on well-being and the opportunity to thrive and flourish.

Why the situation is as it is seems more difficult to discern. As we have discussed already in this chapter, in a society that ascribes gendered behaviour to young children in a binary way – that is, boys should engage in noisy, rough play and are expected to be uninterested in reading and 'quiet' activities; while girls should play indoors, dress-up, play with dolls, tell stories and engage in quiet activities – very quickly children are 'trained' in certain behaviours, some of which are more congruent with how learning takes place in schools than others. If a child has learnt that it wins praise and the admiration of those around if it sits down and gets on with quiet activities, then that child has already learnt one of the most important lessons about how to succeed with learning activities. In contrast, if their sense of self has been developed around being daring and noisy and wanting to 'play outside', they may feel challenged and confused by being expected to sit down and 'get on' quietly. This is not to say that young children think these things out consciously, but in a society that expects different genders to behave in different ways, very clear messages are signalled to young children about what is expected of them, messages which we have seen above in the case of girls and body image, which can be very damaging to how children grow up to view and understand themselves.

Some schools have tried to address the gender attainment gap by introducing same-sex teaching groups. However, it is possible this is 'missing the point', as all children are individuals and need to be taught in relation to their needs. Others have argued the move towards more male/female equality has served girls and women well – in some instances – but has left 'masculinity in crisis' as the old certainties of 'men needing to be the breadwinners' are lost.

Masculinity in crisis

Blayac and colleagues write that 'the crisis of masculinity has been a recurrent feature – although with different names – of political and scholarly discourses for decades' (Blayac et al. 2011, p.6). Indeed, they go on to suggest that the notion of 'masculinity in crisis' is not new to the twenty-first century, and that at times of 'social and political changes' (ibid.), throughout history there has been a notion that men experience a crisis in terms of understanding what it is to be a man. Indeed what Blayac and colleagues suggest is that boys and men, just as we have seen is the case for girls and women, feel confined and sometimes alienated by how masculinity is portrayed by the media and dominant discourses. While society seems to offer a view of what being a boy or man should be, individual boys and men find this view is a stereotype that does not represent who they are. The crisis then arises as boys and men feel they are failing to be a 'true' man, just as girls are feeling in crisis that they are failing to live up to female stereotyped body images.

In order to readjust this situation, the South Bank Centre in London has for the past few years run a festival that 'addresses the pressures of masculine identity in the 21st century' (South Bank Centre 2016). The discussion, exhibitions and workshops aim to raise ideas and awareness around the issues that impact directly on boys and men; these include 'shared paternity leave to shyness, from video games to transgender identity' (South Bank Centre 2016). The festival also provides the opportunity for boys and men to explore emotion and their emotional lives and how this impacts on their mental health and family relationships. This is just one example of an arena where boys and men can have the opportunity to explore what it is to be male.

Gender and achievement at school

In 2009, the then Department for Children Schools and Families, now the Department for Education, wrote:

> Myth: All boys underachieve, and all girls now achieve well at school.
> Reality: Many boys achieve highly, and conversely many girls underperform.
>
> (DCSF 2009, p.3)

Nearly ten years on, as we have discussed, there still persists the idea that, collectively, girls achieve better at school and in other educational settings, than do boys. We have acknowledged that the reality of the situation is much more complex than this. Ethnicity and family income have a greater bearing on educational attainment than does gender and what has the greatest impact on achievement is having high expectations for all children. In their 2013 evidence report 'Unseen children: Access and achievement 20 years on' (Ofsted 2013), Ofsted make it quite clear that a significant factor that contributes to children's achievement in school and other educational settings, is where there are high expectations that all children can succeed. The report discusses the particular challenges faced by children from low-income families. Educational success is often measured by 'the outcomes for pupils at the end of secondary school' (Ofsted 2013, p.7). While the report acknowledges that 'if we could get the earlier years right for everyone, that would make much more of a difference' (ibid.), the outcomes at the end of secondary school mark the end of the compulsory education process and, therefore, how successful it has been for children, in terms of their educational achievement. The qualifications with which children leave secondary school 'also account to a large extent for success in courses and qualifications thereafter' (ibid.). What has changed for girls, however, is a greater expectation by families and the girls themselves that they will go on to further and higher education after school, and use achievement at school as a stepping stone to a career.

It is also suggested that the 'male' and 'female' brain are different and that in young children, this somehow makes girls more likely to engage with their education. However, again, 'there is little evidence to suggest that neurological ('brainsex') differences result in boys having different abilities/ways of learning to girls' (DCSF 2009, p.4). While there may be marginal evidence of differences, 'even proponents of neurological gender difference caution that there is more within sex difference in abilities than between sex difference' (DCSF 2009, p.7). Therefore, little is likely to be gained by separating children into groups of 'boys' and/or 'girls' and teaching them in split gender groups, as this runs the risk of overlooking what is actually needed for learning – which is attending to the individual needs of each child, irrespective of their gender.

What makes a difference to children's achievement?

One of the themes we keep coming back to in this book, whether we are thinking about socio-economic factors, gender, or ability and disability, is the notion of values, attitudes and belief. Children's achievement in school and their confidence, self-esteem and sense of self are most largely impacted on by the behaviours of those around them.

Scenario 2: Coombe Hage Primary School

'I think some people around here think I'm the gender police,' says Justyn, assistant head teacher of Coombe Hage Primary School. 'However, I know that if people aren't challenged about what they say to the children, the children will begin to limit their aspirations for themselves. I've managed to stop people saying things like "Well, that's boys for you!" Or "These are girls' books and these ones are boys' books", or, "You won't get the boys to do that." They might still think these things – or say them, but not when I'm around!

'We do ensure that displays in the school reflect both the achievements of both men and women and we continue, at KS2, to encourage all children to have a go at everything. We have a girls football team, who play against other girls teams and we have a great street dance club which is very popular with both boys and girls.

'We've also worked on how we structure our learning activities and give feedback to the children; there has been research that shows boys respond better to structured tasks with a clear focus and clear time limit to complete the task in, that they work better if there's speaking and listening built in to tasks and the chance to use the computer. What we've actually found is that we need to use a range of these approaches as different things work for different children, irrespective of gender. But what it has made us do is increase our range of teaching and learning strategies and everyone has benefited because of that.

'We can do all sorts of things in school to let all children develop their identity and interests, including their sense of who they are in terms of their gender, and we can have great success, but what we're really battling with is the wider world. Certainly by years five and six we can see that the children are beginning to take more notice of what's in the media and what wider society is saying about how girls and boys should be. That's where the real work needs to be done.'

References

Adelson, J. (1980) *Handbook of Adolescent Psychology*. New York: Wiley

Blayac, A., Conilleau, C., Delahayes, C. and Quanquin, H. (2011) Critical masculinities, *Culture, Society & Masculinities*, 3(1):3–12

Bradley, H. (2013) *Gender*, 2nd edition. Bodmin: Polity Press

DCSF (Department for Children Schools and Families) (2009) *Gender and Education – Mythbusters Addressing Gender and Achievement: Myths and Realities*. DCSF

Erikson, E. (1995) *Childhood and Society*. Vintage

GIRES (Gender Identity Research and Education Society) (2008) Gender variance (dysphoria) www.gires.org.uk/assets/gdev/gender-dysphoria.pdf [accessed 29 August 2016]

Giordano, S. (2013) *Children with Gender Identity Disorder: A Clinical, Ethical, and Legal Analysis*. Taylor and Francis

Girlguiding (2016) Girls' Attitude Survey https://www.girlguiding.org.uk/globalassets/docs-and-resources/research-and-campaigns/girls-attitudes-survey-2016.pdf [accessed 25 October 2016]

Kleeman, J. (2015) Transgender children: 'This is who he is – I have to respect that' https://www.theguardian.com/society/2015/sep/12/transgender-children-have-to-respect-who-he-is [accessed 1 November 2016]

Klimstra, T. A., Hale III, W. W., Raaijmakers, Q. A. W., Branje, S. J. T. and Meeus, W. H. J. (2010) Identity formation in adolescence: Change or stability? *J Youth Adolescence*, 39:150–162

Knowles, G. and Holmstrom, R. (2012) *Understanding Family Diversity and Home School Relations*. Routledge

Knowles, G. and Lander, V. (2011) *Diversity, Equality and Achievement in Education*. Chippenham: Sage

Lloyd, T. (2009) Boys' underachievement: What schools think and do. A University of Ulster Research Project

Lyons, K. (2016) Girls' quality of life shows huge variation in England and Wales www.theguardian.com/society/2016/sep/12/girls-quality-of-life-shows-huge-variation-around-the-country-report?CMP=Share_iOSApp_Other [accessed 25 October 2016]

Maslow, A. (2014) *Towards a Psychology and Being*. Bensenville, IL: Lushena Books

McCartney, K. (2016) Our schools are failing boys, which is bad news for Britain https://www.theguardian.com/commentisfree/2016/sep/06/schools-colleges-failing-boys-masculinity [accessed 25 October 2016]

McLeod, S. A. (2013). Erik Erikson. Retrieved from www.simplypsychology.org/Erik-Erikson.html [accessed 30 September 2016]

Mermaids (2016) www.mermaidsuk.org.uk/about-mermaids.html [accessed 1 October 2016]

NHS (2016) What causes gender dysphoria? www.nhs.uk/Conditions/Gender-dysphoria/Pages/Introduction.aspx [accessed 1 October 2016]

NHS Choices (2017) Gender dysphoria www.nhs.uk/conditions/Gender-dysphoria/Pages/Introduction.aspx [accessed 2017]

Ofsted (2013) Unseen children: access and achievement 20 years on: Evidence report. Ofsted

ONS (Office for National Statistics) (2013) Women in the labour market 2013 www.ons.gov.uk/employmentandlabourmarket/peopleinwork/employmentandemployeetypes/articles/womeninthelabourmarket/2013-09-25 [accessed 29 August 2016]

Rai, R. and Panna, K. (2010) *Introduction to Culture Studies*. Mumbai, India: Global Media

Russell, L., Alsop, R., Bradshaw, L., Clisby, S., King, C. and Smith, K. (2016) The state of girls' rights in the UK: Executive summary Plan International and the University of Hull file:///C:/Users/knowl/Downloads/Plan-International-UK_The-state-of-girls-rights-in-the-UK-2016_Executive-Summary.pdf [accessed 25 October 2016]

Scheck, S. (2014) *The Stages of Psychosocial Development According to Erik H. Erikson*. GRIN Verlag GmbH

South Bank Centre (2016) Being a man www.southbankcentre.co.uk/whatson/festivals-series/being-a-man [accessed 25 October 2016]

Stone, J. (2015) This is what gender inequality in Britain looks like in charts www.independent.co.uk/news/uk/politics/this-is-what-gender-inequality-in-britain-looks-like-in-charts-10386937.html [accessed 29 August 2016]

Strudwick, P. (2014) Nearly half of young transgender people have attempted suicide – UK survey https://www.theguardian.com/society/2014/nov/19/young-transgender-suicide-attempts-survey [accessed 1 October 2016]

Weedon, C. (2004) *Identity and Culture: Narratives of difference and belonging.* Maidenhead: Open University Press

Younger, M., Warrington, M., Gray, J., Rudduck, J., McLellan, R., Bearne, E., Kershner, R. and Bricheno P. (2005) *Raising Boys' Achievement.* University of Cambridge Faculty of Education

Chapter 3

Working with lesbian, gay and bisexual children and families in schools

Zoë Leadley-Meade

This chapter explores:

- What it means to identify as lesbian, gay or bisexual and provides some background on the political, legal and social contexts which impact on LGB children and families
- The concept of 'heteronormativity' and why it is important to challenge it within the classroom in order to provide a truly inclusive environment
- Roles and relationships in families with same-sex parents and the need to include family diversity within the curriculum
- The role of schools and individuals in enabling LGB children and young people to fulfil their potential and maintain mental health and well-being alongside their peers.

What it means to identify as lesbian, gay or bisexual

Where Chapter 2 explored the concept of gender, transgender and gender identity, this chapter looks at what it means to identify as lesbian, gay or bisexual (LGB). The chapter covers what this might mean, both in terms of sexual orientation and identity, and how living in a heteronormative society impacts on identifying as LGB.

Sexual identity or sexual orientation is a way of describing the feelings that we have for someone that we are attracted to, are dating, or want to be in a relationship with. For some people, this is someone of the opposite gender to themselves and for others this is someone of the same gender as themselves. Put simply, to identify as lesbian means a woman who has relationships with women; to identify as gay means a man who has relationships with men (although this can be a gender-neutral term and women may call themselves gay also). To identify as bisexual is to be someone who has relationships with both men and women.

Stonewall and sexual orientation

Stonewall is a lesbian, gay, bisexual and transgender (LGBT) rights charity, founded in 1989. Its role is to work for 'the social and legal advancement for LGB people living in Britain'. In 2015, Stonewall extended its remit 'to campaign for trans equality'.

In discussing sexual orientation Stonewall states:

- 'We don't know what causes someone's sexual orientation, but we know that it isn't a choice – no one can change who they fancy. Sexual orientation is a part of who we are.

- You can't tell what someone's sexual orientation is by looking at them – the only real way to know this is if they tell you.
- Someone else can't tell you what your sexual orientation is – only you know how you feel and you should never feel pressured to label yourself. Some people know their sexual orientation from a young age and some people take a while to work out what makes them feel comfortable. This is completely fine – everyone is unique.'

Source: Stonewall 2016

Often people reduce the label 'LGBT' to one that defines sexual activity alone and although sexual orientation is in part about who you are attracted to or have a sexual relationship with, it is also about who you love. The relationships that we have with others play a central role in reinforcing our identity and, after our family, romantic relationships are some of the most important relationships that we form over our lifetime. Romantic relationships are complex and cannot be reduced to a matter of sexual activity alone; instead, they are about who we share our life with and are often about being a supportive and committed partner.

From a psychological perspective, Abraham Maslow argues that as humans we all have needs that must be met if we are to reach self-actualisation. Maslow identifies a hierarchy including physiological needs, safety and security, love and belonging and self-esteem as categories of need, which are central to our development as human beings. He argues that without these categories of need being met, individuals are unlikely to fulfil their potential and reach a state of self-actualisation and maintain mental health and well-being (Maslow 1998).

As we have seen in previous chapters, Maslow's hierarchy of needs highlights the importance of gaining a sense of love and belonging from relationships in order to develop self-esteem. At a young age, we form loving relationships with family and friends, and as we mature, we begin to form more intimate romantic and sexual relationships. The relationships that we form throughout our lifetime become a core part of our identity. It is important for individuals to be able to express the various aspects of their identity freely, including being free to express their love openly, without fear of discrimination, if they are to reach a state of self-actualisation and maintain mental health and well-being.

In the UK, in the past, many LGB people have been denied the opportunity to be open about their relationships or to feel the sense of pride that comes with introducing your girlfriend, boyfriend, partner, husband, or wife to family, friends and colleagues.

The changes in law over recent decades and the continued challenge of homophobia means that more and more lesbian, gay and bisexual people feel able to be open about their relationships with people of the same sex. A recent YouGov poll (Dahlgreen and Shakespeare 2015) found that younger generations are more likely to view sexuality as fluid, meaning that it is not necessarily fixed as either heterosexual or homosexual, and 43 per cent of 18–24-year-olds identify as other than exclusively heterosexual. This can mean anything from being attracted to someone of the same sex, having a sexual experience, or being in a relationship with someone of the same sex. Although many people still prefer to use the labels of 'lesbian', 'gay', 'bisexual', or 'heterosexual' to identify themselves, there are now more diverse labels

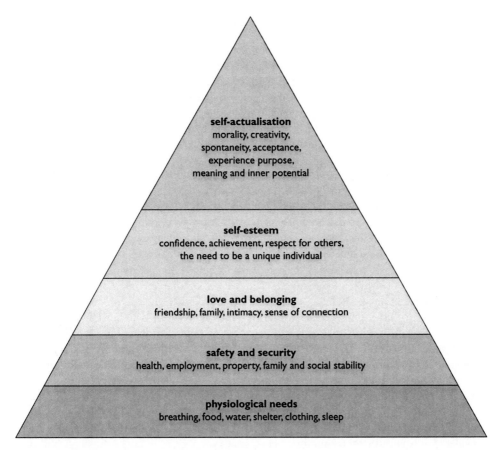

Figure 3.1 Maslow's hierarchy of needs (Dirt 2012)

such as 'pansexual' (not limited in sexual choice with regard to biological sex, gender, or gender identity), 'asexual' (without sexual feelings or association), 'homoromantic' (romantically attracted to a member of the same sex or gender but not necessarily sexually attracted), and many more to choose from. To older generations that have grown up being told that sexuality exists as binary opposites of straight (heterosexual) and gay (homosexual), this can seem confusing and complicated. What is important to remember is that people are free to identify as they wish and that their identity may change, therefore you should try to avoid making assumptions about someone's sexual identity or relationship status. Instead of trying to put people into narrow categories, we should see them as individuals and listen to the way in which they describe themselves and respect the way in which they identify themselves.

There are now laws in the UK to protect people against discrimination according to their sexual orientation; however, there are still many countries where this is not the case. There are also people in the UK who feel the need to hide their sexual orientation because of fear of discrimination. So while we can celebrate the progress of equal rights for LGB people, it is important to remember that not everyone is able to live without fear of discrimination and therefore it is not surprising that rates of mental illness, self-harm and suicide are much higher within the LGB community:

> **Three in five** people still say there is public prejudice against lesbian, gay and bisexual people in Britain today. People think negative attitudes at school, work, of parents and in the media are the main sources of public prejudice against gay people today.
>
> However, **four in five** people (81 per cent) believe it is right to tackle prejudice against lesbian, gay and bisexual people where they say it exists. People think parents, the media and schools have the greatest role to play in tackling prejudice against gay people.
>
> (Guasp and Dick 2012, original emphasis)

While there has been much progress in recent decades, the quality of life and the rights available to LGB people still varies greatly across the globe, with those countries that fully recognise LGB people as equal from a political and legislative perspective being in the minority.

At the end of 2015, consensual adult same-sex relations were criminalised in seventy-five countries, and in up to ten countries, could be punished by death, with same-sex marriage legal nationwide in only nineteen countries worldwide (Human Rights Campaign 2016b). Same-sex parent adoption is legal in only fourteen countries, and many countries prohibit it. As the debate on the rights of lesbian, gay and bisexual people has been at the forefront of political and social debate in many countries, it has led to some backlash and a resurgence in discriminatory laws introduced in countries such as Russia, where a law banning the promotion of 'non-traditional' sexuality to under-18s was introduced in 2013, leading to violent attacks on the LGBT community. Also in 2013, India reinstated a 153-year-old colonial era law criminalising gay sex, and Uganda recently outlawed same-sex marriages, gay groups and shows of same-sex public affection (BBC 2014). Most recently in 2016, forty-nine men and women were killed in a lesbian and gay nightclub in Orlando, Florida; it was the largest attack on the LGBT community since the Holocaust when some 10–15,000 people were deported to concentration camps for being gay. When the global picture is considered, it is clear that the fight for equality is not yet over, as many LGB people still face barriers when attempting to access the same rights as their heterosexual counterparts.

LGB legislation in the United Kingdom

In many ways the UK is one of the most progressive countries in regards to LGB rights; however, much of this change has occurred in recent years and as a result of persistent protest and campaigning:

- 1982 – Homosexuality is decriminalised in 1982.
- 2001 – The age of consent for gay men and lesbians is brought in line, at age 16, with the age of consent for heterosexual men and women.
- 2002 – The Adoption and Children's Act (which came into effect in December 2005) changed so that a single person or couple outside of marriage could adopt, allowing a same-sex couple to apply.
- 2003 – The Criminal Justice Act (which came into effect 2005) empowered courts to impose tougher sentences for offences motivated or aggravated by the victim's sexual orientation.

Updated August 2016

CRIMINALISATION OCCURS IN 72 COUNTRIES:

Africa (Algeria, Angola, Botswana, Burundi, Cameroon, Central African Republic, Comoros, Egypt, Eritrea, Ethiopia, Gambia, Ghana, Guinea, Kenya, Liberia, Libya, Malawi, Mauritania, Mauritius, Morocco, Namibia, Nigeria, Senegal, Sierra Leone, Somalia, South Sudan, Sudan, Swaziland, Tanzania, Togo, Tunisia, Uganda, Zambia and Zimbabwe)

Asia (Afghanistan, Bangladesh, Bhutan, Brunei, India, Iran, Kuwait, Lebanon, Malaysia, Maldives, Myanmar, Oman, Pakistan, Qatar, Saudi Arabia, Singapore, Sri Lanka, Syria, Turkmenistan, United Arab Emirates, Uzbekistan and Yemen)

Caribbean (Antigua and Barbuda, Barbados, Dominica, Grenada, Guyana, Jamaica, St. Kitts and Nevis, St. Lucia, St. Vincent and the Grenadines and Trinidad and Tobago)

South Pacific (Kiribati, Papua New Guinea, Samoa, Solomon Islands, Tonga and Tuvalu)

Entities (Cook Islands, Gaza, South Sumatra and Aceh Provinces of Indonesia)

PUNISHABLE WITH DEATH PENALTY IN 10 COUNTRIES:

Africa (Mauritania, Sudan, as well as parts of Nigeria and Somalia)

Asia (Brunei (enacted May 2014, to be enforced in 2015), Iran, Qatar, Saudi Arabia, United Arab Emirates and Yemen)

SO-CALLED ANTI-PROPAGANDA LAWS INHIBIT LGBT ADVOCACY IN 3 COUNTRIES:

Africa (Nigeria*)

Europe (Lithuania, Russia)

* Nigeria is in all 3 categories.

Research based on news reports, discussions with local advocates, the U.S. State Department's Country Reports on Human Rights Practices for 2013 and the 2014 State-Sponsored Homophobia Report of ILGA (the International Lesbian, Gay, Bisexual, Trans and Intersex Association).

HUMAN
RIGHTS
CAMPAIGN
FOUNDATION

CRIMINALISATION AROUND THE WORLD

Figure 3.2 Criminalisation around the world (Human Rights Campaign, 2016a)

- 2004 – The Civil Partnership Act was passed, giving same-sex couples access to some, but not all, of the same rights and responsibilities as married heterosexual couples.
- 2008 – The Human Fertilisation and Embryology Act 2008 (which came into effect in 2009) gave legal recognition to lesbian parents who conceive a child through fertility treatment, so that both parents can be on the birth certificate.
- 2010 – The Equality Act included extension of the single public Equality Duty to cover lesbian, gay and bisexual people.
- 2013 – The Marriage (Same Sex Couples) Act was passed and came into effect from March 2014.

This timeline demonstrates just a fraction of the progress that has been made to ensure political, legal and social equality for LGB people in the UK. Although these changes in law have had a significant positive impact on the lives of LGB people, it does not necessarily mean that social values and attitudes have progressed at the same rate and many LGB people still experience the detrimental impact of social stigma and discrimination. In the UK, one in six lesbian, gay and bi people have experienced a homophobic or biphobic hate crime or incident, and a quarter (26 per cent) of lesbian, gay and bi people alter their behaviour to hide their sexual orientation to avoid being the victim of a hate crime (Guasp et al. 2013). It is important to be aware of the political and social context which impacts on the lived experiences of LGB children and parents in order to be able to challenge homophobia and prejudice.

Why do schools, educational settings and practitioners need to be aware of this information?

Historically, in the UK there has been an intentional erasure of the recognition or discussion of homosexuality in educational settings due to Section 28 of the Local Government Act 1988, which was repealed as recently as 2003. Section 28 had a direct impact on schools, as it stated that schools should not 'intentionally promote homosexuality or publish material with the intention of promoting homosexuality' nor 'promote the teaching in any maintained school of the acceptability of homosexuality as a pretended family relationship' (Greenland and Nunney 2008, p.243).

The LGBT charity Stonewall UK was formed in 1989 in response to Section 28, and since the Section's repeal, Stonewall has conducted research in schools which has driven a recognition of the need to tackle homophobia in schools and in wider society as a whole. Stonewall have produced large-scale research on the experience of LGB children and children with same-sex parents in schools across the UK, which highlights the level of homophobia present in our schools and the impact of this on the well-being and achievement of learners. This research has helped to prompt a focus on reducing homophobia in schools, as well as the need to include different families within schools so that all children and families feel safe and included in their school, regardless of their sexual orientation.

The original *School Report* (Guasp 2012) in 2007 highlighted for the first time the full extent of homophobia in UK schools; two-thirds of lesbian, gay and bisexual young people reported experiencing homophobic bullying at school and only a quarter of schools were saying that such bullying was wrong (Guasp 2012). The 2012 report showed a 10 per cent decrease in homophobic bullying levels; however, more than half of lesbian, gay and bisexual students still reported experiencing homophobic bullying and over two in five gay pupils who experience homophobic bullying attempt to take, or think about taking, their own life as a direct consequence. Such statistics emphasise the important role of schools and all educational settings in reducing homophobia, which has now been recognised by the Department for Education and Ofsted. All schools (including faith schools) are expected to take action to prevent and tackle homophobic and transphobic bullying, as schools have a statutory duty to prevent all forms of discrimination and bullying. Ofsted now identify lesbian, gay and bisexual children as a key group of learners which schools must support to fulfil their potential, and this support must be demonstrated during Ofsted inspections (HM Government 2015).

Stonewall's slogan is 'acceptance without exception' which is a central theme to this chapter, as for too long the rights of lesbian, gay and bisexual children and parents have been ignored within schools, as sexual orientation can be viewed as problematic or too controversial to discuss in an educational setting. However, an educational setting cannot claim to be inclusive if it does not also consider the needs of LGB children and parents. It is no longer possible to use fear or ignorance as an excuse; instead schools and professionals working with children and young people must support LGB children and families.

Heteronormativity in the classroom

If educators are going to support LGB children and families, then we must challenge discrimination and homophobia within our classrooms and to do this we must first understand the role that the classroom plays in reinforcing heteronormative attitudes.

From a young age, we are taught the values, attitudes and norms of our society through a process which sociologists call 'socialisation'. The aim of the socialisation process is to enable children to become participating members of society and therefore, as children, we are taught what is considered to be socially acceptable and unacceptable behaviour. The socialisation process continues throughout our lives and this regulation of behaviour extends to sexuality, as we are also taught what are considered to be socially acceptable and unacceptable expressions of sexual identity. To identify as lesbian, gay, or bisexual can still be viewed as a challenge to social norms and expectations. It can be argued that we live in a heteronormative society, meaning that society views heterosexuality as most valued and most 'normal' and therefore alternative sexualities are devalued, as they are viewed as deviating from this norm (Warner 1991, in Dellinger Page and Peacock 2013).

Those who identify as heterosexual may find it difficult to understand this point of view as they are in the majority, so are unlikely to face many challenges to the expression of their sexual identity. One way to understand the impact of heteronormativity is to consider the types of relationships which are represented in advertisements; it is difficult to think of an advertisement that includes any non-heterosexual couples, from the housewives in cleaning product adverts to the men who attract women by the smell of their aftershave. When adverts neglect to include representations of relationships that are non-heterosexual, the underlying message is that these types of relationships have no value in society and are not acceptable. If you identify as heterosexual, then when you see these adverts they reinforce your sexual identity and enable you to openly express your sexual identity without fear of prejudice. However, if you identify as lesbian, gay, or bisexual, then you are not provided with such easy access to images that reinforce your sexual identity; instead, when you see these adverts they reinforce the idea that your sexual identity is not accepted and can lead to feelings of marginalisation, isolation and fear of prejudice if you openly express your sexual identity.

It can be argued that this message underlies all aspects of society from the media to religion, the work place and education. If we view the classroom as a central site of social-isation, then our role as educators is not only to develop academic knowledge and skills in our pupils, but also to provide a space where pupils can develop their sense of self and their role within wider society. Therefore we must first address heteronormativity within the class-room if we aim to provide an inclusive space where pupils and their families feel free to express all aspects of their identity, including their sexual identity, without fear of prejudice.

Books, other media and relationships

- Think of the books and the films from your childhood. What types of relationships were represented in these texts?
- Were there any characters that were not in heterosexual relationships and if so how were they represented; for example, were you expected to approve or disapprove of these characters?
- Now consider the books and films that are available to the children or young people that you work with. What types of relationships are represented in these texts and are there any alternatives to heterosexual relationships?
- What are the benefits to providing texts with a range of relationship types?
- What are some of the arguments against including texts with non-heterosexual relationships in a school context?
- Explore some of the books available with LGBT characters at www.letterbox library.com. How could these books be used in the classroom?

Roles and relationships in families with same-sex parents (surrogacy, artificial insemination, adoption, co-parents)

The most important things children need to thrive and flourish are capable, loving and caring people around them with whom they can form mutually supportive attachments (Mayseless 2002, in Knowles and Lander 2011; Prior 2006, in Knowles and Lander 2011). It is now recognised that the quality of the care provided for children outweighs the importance of who the care giver is, thus the gender of the care givers, the marital status, or the relation of the care givers to the child is of much less importance.

It may appear that same-sex parent families are a relatively modern phenomena, and while the changes in law and social attitudes have made it somewhat 'easier' for same-sex parents to form families, in fact such families have been in existence prior to the changes in law but were often less visible in society for fear of facing discrimination. What has changed is that many lesbian, gay and bisexual people feel more able to be open about their sexual orientation and this is the same for many lesbian, gay and bisexual parents who feel it is important to bring up their children with a sense of pride in their family in the same way that heterosexual parents do.

It is important to remember that all families can take many different shapes and be formed in many different ways, from single parents to a mum and a dad who live together or are married, or step-families or extended families with grandparents and other relatives living in the same home. When we consider all of the different types of families that there are, same-sex parent families are just another type of family which add to this variety and, just like other families, same-sex parent families come to be formed in different ways. There are some same-sex couples who are in a civil partnership or are married and then have a baby either through artificial insemination for women or surrogacy for men; this means that there will be a parent who is biologically related to the child, but both parents can be named on the birth certificate as legal parents.

Other same-sex parents may have decided to adopt a child as it has been legal for same-sex couples (alongside single people) to adopt children since 2004. In some same-sex families, children may have been conceived in previous relationships meaning that there is a step-parent, in the same way as heterosexual step-families. Some same-sex couples decide to co-parent children with another gay or lesbian person or couple and share parental responsibility. Although schools need to be aware of who a child's legal parents are or who has parental responsibility, it is as important to be aware of who cares for a child and who plays an important role in their upbringing. When working with any family, we should not make assumptions about who does and doesn't play an important role in a child's upbringing; instead, we should get to know the child and the members of their family so that we develop a better understanding of how to work with them to support their child's educational development.

Activity

Read through this scenario from a parents evening and consider the questions below.

Janelle and Lisa have been in a relationship for five years and live together with their 10-year-old son Jordan, who was conceived by Janelle in a previous heterosexual relationship. They are a loving and supportive family and parental roles are shared equally between Janelle and Lisa. When Jordan started at a new primary school, there was no space on the application form to explain Lisa's relationship to Jordan as it only had space for the details of 'Mother' and 'Father'. However, Lisa has been present at all school meetings and plays an active role, alongside Janelle, in supporting Jordan's education. When Jordan had parents evening, Lisa booked time off work to make sure that she could attend with Janelle and Jordan. Janelle was pleased to have Lisa there to support her, as she had been a single parent previously and Jordan was looking forward to showing his books to Janelle and Lisa. However, Lisa was nervous as this would be her first parents evening and she wasn't sure if she would be recognised as Jordan's parent, as she had no biological or legal connection to him. In the meeting, Janelle greeted the teacher and introduced Lisa as her partner, the teacher said 'oh' and looked a little surprised.

Both Janelle and Lisa discussed Jordan's progress and asked questions about how best to support him at home; however, when the teacher responded she tended to direct her response at Janelle only and at one point said to Jordan 'Why don't you show your Mum all of your good work in your books?' and put the books in front of Janelle.

- How might Lisa feel in this situation?
- What message does this give to Jordan?
- What could the teacher have done differently to make sure that she included both parents?

Why it's important to include family diversity in the curriculum

Some people may argue that sexual identity has no place in schools and the discussion of sexual identity is not age appropriate. However, this is a somewhat naïve perspective, as sexual identity is ever present in school. For example, teachers will often speak about their family and may bring their partner/husband/wife or children to school events. Children will read books with characters in relationships and even children in nursery and primary school will role play relationships as they begin to explore their own identity. Therefore it is important to be open and honest with children about the different types of relationships that exist and to discuss them with sensitivity in an age-appropriate manner. In 2000, the DFEE published guidance on Sex and Relationship Education (SRE) to be followed in all schools and stated:

> The objective of sex and relationship education is to help and support young people through their physical, emotional and moral development. A successful programme, firmly embedded in PSHE, will help young people learn to respect themselves and others and move with confidence from childhood through adolescence into adulthood.
>
> (HM Government 2000, p.3)

More recently, the Department for Education highlights the need for schools to actively promote 'an understanding of the importance of identifying and combatting discrimination' (HM Government 2014, p.6) in the guidance for promoting fundamental British values as part of SMSC in schools.

As the number of same-sex parent families rises (alongside a rise in other 'non-traditional' family types), it is increasingly important to recognise and to discuss family diversity within the curriculum. Stonewall's report, 'Different Families', asked children with same-sex parents about their experiences and found that 'children with gay parents want their schools to talk about different families and stop homophobic bullying. This would make them feel more able to be themselves in school' (Guasp 2013, p.3).

Celebrating LGB families in schools and educational settings

Read this scenario from a primary school lesson and consider the questions below:

Charlotte is 6 years old and lives at home with her two Dads who she calls Daddy and Pappa; Charlotte also has a surrogate mum who carried her in her tummy called Sally who lives at the seaside with her family. Every summer Charlotte, Daddy and Pappa visit Sally and her family and have picnics on the beach. Charlotte has just started Year 2 and has a new teacher called Mr Sangha. As Mr Sangha is new to the school, he wants to get to know his class and asks them to draw a family tree and bring in pictures of their family. Charlotte spent all weekend with Daddy and Pappa creating their family tree, sticking in her favourite pictures and using her special glitter pens to decorate it. In class on Monday, Mr Sangha asks for a volunteer to show their family tree to the whole class. Because Charlotte is so proud of her special family she stands up and tells the class about everyone in her family, including her pet tortoise Max. When Charlotte talks about her two Dads that she lives with, one of the boys in the class puts up his hand and says 'How can you have two Daddies? That sounds silly!'

- Think of the different ways that Mr Sangha could respond to this.
- How can Mr Sangha make sure that Charlotte isn't made to feel embarrassed or ashamed about her family?
- How can Mr Sangha use this as an opportunity to celebrate the diversity of families in the classroom?
- How can Mr Sangha make sure that the boy who said this, and the other students, understand why it isn't acceptable to talk about different families or gay people in a negative way?

Indeed, there are now many examples of primary and secondary schools acting upon the government's guidance to include family diversity within the curriculum. If this isn't the case in your school, then you could look at the many resources available to support schools and begin by introducing the discussion of different families in your own classroom.

Why it's important to provide a safe environment for LGB children

People discover their sexual orientation at different ages and for many lesbian, gay, or bisexual children it can be an isolating time if they are only exposed to negative attitudes towards homosexuality. LGB children may feel worried about disclosing their sexual orientation to their families as they feel their family members may be disappointed or even angry. Although this is the case in some families, most families are accepting of their child as LGB, even if the news is a shock and takes some time to sink in. You might be familiar with the term 'coming out' to describe when someone is open about being lesbian, gay, or bisexual. Some people 'come out' as soon as they realise their own sexual orientation, while others may only 'come out' to their closest family members and friends. It is important to remember that 'coming out' is a personal choice and no one should be forced to be open about their sexual orientation if they are not comfortable. No one has the right to 'out' someone and tell others about their sexual orientation; if you are asked if someone is lesbian, gay, or bisexual, it is better to say 'why don't you ask them?' instead of answering for them, unless you are sure that they would be happy for you to answer.

As stated earlier, a person's sexual orientation is about more than just sexual activity; it is about relationships and love, which are an important part of any individual's life, and when people are unable to be open about who they love, it can have serious consequences for their ability to be happy and to self-actualise.

Supporting LGB children in schools

Read this scenario from a secondary school and consider the role a school can play in supporting a student like Tayo.

Tayo is 14 years old and in Year 9 at secondary school. Ever since Tayo can remember, he has been called names like 'wimp', 'weirdo', 'mummy's boy' and 'soft boy', and told 'you're such a girl'; since Year 6, these names have turned into 'gay boy' and 'batty boy' (slang for gay boy, similar to the term 'faggot'). Sometimes Tayo's teachers hear the other children calling him names, and sometimes tell the boys to stop 'winding him up' or tell Tayo to ignore them, but none of the teachers have ever said that it is wrong to call him these names or that it is OK to be gay. When Tayo was younger, he knew that he wasn't the same as the other boys, but he didn't really know why. At home, his parents noticed that Tayo wasn't as boisterous as his older brother and cousins and that he preferred to spend time on his own or with girls. Tayo's Dad didn't like this and sent him to boxing club with his brother to 'toughen him up' and 'turn him into a real man'. Tayo hated boxing club and the other boys there would pick on him like the boys at school did. He really enjoyed singing and writing his own lyrics, but he had to hide this from his parents. The only time Tayo could sing was at his family church services which he went to on Thursday evenings from 7 until 10 pm and on Sundays from 10 am until 6 pm. Tayo liked the services, except when his pastor started to talk about the devil and how some people had the devil inside them which made them do things they shouldn't, like being gay and that they would all burn in hell. Tayo used to be friends with a girl in the church, but he didn't see her anymore because her parents had sent her back to Nigeria to get married when they found out she had a secret girlfriend. Tayo's parents agree with the pastor and they think the law in the UK should be the same as it is in Nigeria, where you can go to prison if you are gay or lesbian. As Tayo grew older, he couldn't ignore the feelings he had about boys and he knew he didn't have the same feelings for girls that he should. Tayo loved his

*family and he knew they would never accept him if he said that he was gay, so he
started to think that it would be easier not to be alive.*

- What actions can a school take to ensure that all teachers challenge
  homophobic bullying?
- What support can the school give to students like Tayo to prevent self harm or
  suicide?
- Explore what services are available in your local community to support LGB
  young people.

Luckily, cases like Tayo's are becoming rarer within British society; however, for some
LGB youth, this is their reality. The increased need to support the mental and physical well-
being of LGB youth is recognised by the National College of Nursing (NCN) and Public
Health England (PHE) in their toolkit to prevent suicide amongst LGB young people:

> We know that LGB people are at higher risk of suicidal behaviour, mental disorder and
> substance misuse and dependence than heterosexual people. This gap is even greater
> for ethnic minority LGB people and those with disabilities. The most reliable indicators
> of suicide risk are self-harm, suicidal thoughts and prior suicide attempts. Self-harm
> remains one of the leading causes of acute medical admissions in the UK, with some of
> the highest in Europe. Among LGBT youth in the UK, one in two reported self-harming
> at some point in their life and 44% reported having thought about suicide. These are all
> young people at risk.
>
> (Varney et al. 2015)

Research like this highlights the significance of supporting young people during the
adolescent years; however, as Tayo's story demonstrates, homophobic bullying often begins
at primary school and thus primary schools are not exempt from the need to provide a
safe environment for LGB children. Although younger children are unlikely to describe
themselves as lesbian, gay, or bisexual as they have yet to fully form their sexual identity,
they may recognise that they feel 'different' in some way from other children. This may be
more directly related to gender identity as gender stereotypes also reflect heteronormative
expectations. For example, in dressing up, girls are expected to be princesses and boys
are expected to be superheroes; these narrow gender roles also reflect the expectations of
traditional heterosexual relationships where men are dominant and women are passive. As
younger children explore their identity at a young age, it can have a lasting impact on their
self-esteem if they are prevented from expressing themselves in the way that they choose.
Primary school and secondary school teachers alike play a part in ensuring the mental health
and well-being of all students and should be aware of the increased need of protecting LGB
children and young people.

Conclusion

When faced with the task of supporting LGB children and families in schools, it can feel
overwhelming, particularly for those who feel that they have little experience in this area.

The aim of this chapter has been to highlight the need for this support and to develop an understanding of the challenges that LGB children and families may face. To support LGB children and families, it is not enough to respond to homophobia and bullying; instead, schools, teachers and all members of staff should be proactive in creating an environment which is welcoming to all children and families and actively promotes diversity in all its forms, including sexual orientation. When working with children and young people, we each play a role in promoting the mental health and well-being of our students and cannot underestimate the significance of the role we play in reducing the self-harm and suicide rate in LGB young people. This is not only necessary for the well-being of those who identify as lesbian, gay, or bisexual, but for the well-being of all children and young people, as inclusive practice fails if we make exceptions. While increasingly schools are recognising the need to develop school-wide strategies to combat homophobia as well as celebrating family diversity, it is the responsibility of individuals to reflect on their own practice and consider if it is truly inclusive of LGB children, young people and same-sex families.

Additional advice to support schools and educational settings can be found at:

* www.stonewall.org.uk/our-work/education-resources
* www.educateandcelebrate.org
* www.each.education/resources/
* www.letterboxlibrary.com

References

BBC (2014) *Where is it Illegal to be Gay?* Available at: www.bbc.co.uk/news/world-25927595 (Accessed: 10 September 2016).

Dahlgreen, W. and Shakespeare, A.-E. (2015) *1 in 2 Young People Say They Are Not 100% Heterosexual.* Available at: https://yougov.co.uk/news/2015/08/16/half-young-not-heterosexual/ (Accessed: 10 September 2016).

Dellinger Page, A. and Peacock, J. (2013) 'Negotiating Identities in a Heteronormative Context', *Journal of Homosexuality*, 60, pp. 639–654.

Dirt, N. (2012) *Recent posts.* Available at: www.researchhistory.org/2012/06/16/maslows-hierarchy-of-needs/ (Accessed: 10 September 2016).

Greenland, K. and Nunney, R. (2008). The Repeal of Section 28: It ain't over 'til it's over, *Journal of Pastoral Care in Education*, December (Vol. 26, No. 4), pp. 243–251 [Online].

Guasp, A. (2012) *The School Report: The experiences of gay young people in Britain's schools in 2012.* Available at: www.stonewall.org.uk/sites/default/files/The_School_Report__2012_.pdf (Accessed: 11 September 2016).

Guasp, A. (2013) *Different Families: The experiences of children with lesbian and gay parents.* Available at: www.stonewall.org.uk/sites/default/files/Different_Families__2010_.pdf (Accessed: 11 September 2016).

Guasp, A. and Dick, S. (2012) *Living Together: British attitudes towards lesbian, gay and bisexual people.* Available at: https://www.stonewall.org.uk/resources/living-together-2012 (Accessed: 10 September 2016).

Guasp, A., Gammon, A. and Ellison, G. (2013) *Homophobic Hate Crime: The Gay British Crime Survey 2013.* Available at: www.stonewall.org.uk/sites/default/files/Homophobic_Hate_Crime__2013_.pdf (Accessed: 10 September 2016).

HM Government (2000) *Sex and Relationship Education Guidance.* Available at: webarchive.nationalarchives.gov.uk/20130401151715/https://www.education.gov.uk/publications/eordering download/dfes-0116-2000%20sre.pdf (Accessed: 11 September 2016).

HM Government (2014) *Promoting Fundamental British Values as Part of SMSC in Schools Departmental Advice for Maintained Schools*. Available at: https://www.gov.uk/government/uploads/system/uploads/attachment_data/file/380595/SMSC_Guidance_Maintained_Schools.pdf (Accessed: 11 September 2016).

HM Government (2015) *The Common Inspection Framework: Education, skills and early years*. Available at: https://www.gov.uk/government/uploads/system/uploads/attachment_data/file/461767/The_common_inspection_framework_education_skills_and_early_years.pdf (Accessed: 11 September 2016).

Human Rights Campaign (2016a) *Criminalization Around the World*. Available at: http://hrc-assets.s3-website-us-east-1.amazonaws.com//files/assets/resources/Criminalization-Map-042315.pdf (Accessed: 10 September 2016).

Human Rights Campaign (2016b) *Equality Rising: 2015 global equality report*. Available at: http://issuu.com/humanrightscampaign/docs/equalityrising-2015-052016/8?e=1357809/35693864 (Accessed: 10 September 2016).

Knowles, G. and Lander, V. (2011) *Diversity, Equality and Achievement in Education*. Thousand Oaks, CA: Sage Publications.

Maslow, A.H. (1998) *Toward a Psychology of Being*, 3rd edn. New York: Wiley, John & Sons.

Stonewall (2016) *Sexual Orientation*. Available at: www.youngstonewall.org.uk/lgbtq-info/sexual-orientation (Accessed: 10 September 2016).

Varney, J., Walsh, D., Watson, S., Dockerty, C., Hulatt, I., Bosanquet, J., Appleby, L., Aaltonen, G., Nodin, N., Carney, D. and Garnham, H. (2015) *Preventing Suicide Among Lesbian, Gay and Bisexual Young People: A toolkit for nurses preventing suicide among lesbian, gay and bisexual young people*. Available at: https://www.gov.uk/government/uploads/system/uploads/attachment_data/file/412427/LGB_Suicide_Prevention_Toolkit_FINAL.pdf (Accessed: 11 September 2016).

Chapter 4

Including bilingual learners and children with English as an additional language

Vicki Ryf

This chapter explores:

- What is meant by the terms 'bilingualism' and 'EAL'
- The links between language and identity
- How children acquire additional languages
- Practical guidance on inclusive practice when supporting bilingual learners.

In this chapter, we will explore what it means to be a bilingual learner in an English school – that is, a learner with English as an additional language to their first language or languages. We will consider how language and personal identity are inextricably linked and explore ways that classroom practitioners can provide inclusive and enabling environments for all children to flourish in.

According to the 2015 government census of schools, nearly 19 per cent of all primary school children in the UK, that is almost one in five children, 'is known or believed to have a first language other than English' (DfE 2015). In 2016, The British Council (n.d.) put this number at over 1 million children in maintained British schools (https://eal.britishcouncil.org/teachers/eal-learners-in-uk), with over 300 different languages spoken by UK schoolchildren.

The key thread running through this chapter is that what is good practice for including bilingual learners in the classroom is good practice for all children:

- Know your children and plan carefully to build on individual children's prior knowledge, experience and interests
- Review, revisit and reinforce learning regularly to secure progress
- Have clear language-based teaching supported with concrete and visual resources
- Make learning fun, interactive and memorable.

Terminology

The language we use to describe these learners in British schools has changed several times during the past few decades in an attempt to identify the status of children's English-language learning development. Schools previously commonly used the terms 'English as a second language' or 'E2L' or 'English Language Learners' (ELL). These terms have increasingly been replaced in the UK as they offer a rather pejorative and hierarchical view with English being seen as the most important language. Other terms sometimes used in educational settings refer to the government's previously ring-fenced money devolved to schools to support learners speaking languages other than English; for example, the Ethnic Minority Achievement Grant (EMAG). Although this grant is no longer available to schools, the language remains in use, with some schools using the terminology 'EMAG teacher', for example.

Government documentation currently refers to these children as English as an Additional Language (EAL) learners. This term is now most commonly used in schools and recognises the importance of the other language(s) the children have proficiency in. Other educationalists prefer to use the term 'bilingual learners' in order to promote a more positive awareness of the skills these learners have in their emerging linguistic ability, even where children are at the very earliest stages of English language development. Bilingualism in this context refers to children exposed to, or inhabiting, more than one language at the same time. So, a child may speak one language at home with their family but be surrounded by English on the TV, and in the high street, playground and school.

In this chapter, we use both the terms 'EAL learners' and 'bilingual learners' interchangeably and to mean the same thing: children who are living with more than one language in their lives. They may not yet be fluent in both (or more) of the languages they are experiencing.

Who are EAL learners?

EAL learners should not, however, be considered as one homogenous group with similar experiences or needs. On the contrary, they are individual children operating in a diverse group with many different backgrounds and requirements. They could be children newly arrived in the UK or they could be children who were born in the UK. They could be refugees from conflicts or economic hardships, or they could be children of foreign diplomats. They could reside in the UK permanently or they could be in transition. They may already have a confident grasp of spoken and written English, or they may be at the earliest stage of English language acquisition. They could have a special educational need or disability, or they could be very experienced and confident learners. It is important to note here that children who are bilingual should not to be considered as having a special educational need because they speak another language:

> A child is not taken as having a learning difficulty solely because the language (or form of language) in which he is, or will be taught is different from a language (or form of language) which has at any time been spoken in his home.
>
> (1981 Education Reform Act)

Within British society, there is sometimes a perception of a language hierarchy – that is, to be bilingual in French may be viewed as an asset, while to be bilingual in Urdu may be viewed as a difficulty. These discriminatory perceptions are sometimes referred to as language 'value' or 'attractiveness' by sociolinguists (Chand, in Jenkin 2014) and seem to be linked to the socio-economic advantages that language may be perceived to have and to the familiarity we as individuals have of a particular language or culture. It is crucial therefore that, as practitioners, we are very well informed about the culture and experiences that the children in our settings may have so that we can confidently support each learner.

Knowing your children and their linguistic backgrounds

In order to plan and support all of the children that you are working with, it is essential to understand something about each child's background and prior experiences. No two children are the same – all have their own history and language biography. This is true for all learners and particularly so for the children with EAL. The more knowledge we have, the more we are able to build in the child's prior experience and knowledge and interests.

The 2014 National Curriculum is clear on this need to understand our learners in order to ensure our teaching and provision is clearly targeted:

> Teachers must also take account of the needs of pupils whose first language is not English. Monitoring of progress should take account of the pupil's age, length of time in this country, previous educational experience and ability in other languages.
>
> (DfE 2013: NC)

A key recommendation in Arnot and colleagues' *School Approaches to the Education of EAL Students* reinforces the importance of gathering detailed information:

> . . . our research signals that there is a need to encourage more transfers of knowledge about the EAL families, their motivations and aspirations, levels of support and their concerns for their children's education to improve communication with EAL families and to avoid (potential) stereotyping which restrict the schools' view of such families.
>
> (Arnot et al. 2014: 108)

Scenario 1: My language story

My parents were both immigrants to the UK in the 1950s. My brother, my sister and I were born in England. Our parents believed that we should only speak English at home. 'Mixing up our languages would only confuse us' and 'if you live in England, you must speak English'. My parents used a mixture of German and French to keep secrets from us – there was much hidden talk before Christmas, 'Geschenke', and in hushed tones when there was a minor disagreement between them. I picked up words and phrases when we visited our relatives in summer holidays and I did well in school in my German and French classes but I never did become bilingual. I never had a truly in-depth discussion with my grandmother, as we didn't share the same first language.

Schools and early years settings have many different ways to gather this information and it is important not to 'single out' bilingual pupils in this process. It is essential to know about all of our children and of their prior experiences. Showing an interest in, and a respect for, our children's lives beyond our classroom should be at the root of effective and inclusive practice. Examples of common school practices to strengthen the relationships between home and school include:

- *Home visits in the EY* – Many early years settings organise home visits where teachers and key workers will visit each new child before commencing nursery or YR in their own homes. Where it is known that a child and their family speak another language, it may be beneficial for all to take an interpreter if at all possible or to invite the family to have a friend with them who can converse in both languages.

- *'All About Me' booklets* – Some schools encourage all the children themselves to record in pictures or writing their own mini biography at the beginning of a school year. There are many free downloadable examples of these, which can be adjusted to suit the age/needs of the learners. It is a good idea to then collate these into a class book for all of the children to share and review at the end of the year. When working with children at the earliest stages of English, it is important to give out the leaflet with a dual language text. Most local authorities have the facility to translate key school documents into languages other than English. Alternatively, try using internet translation sites.
- *Parent/carer conversations* – Many schools and early years' settings invite parents and carers of new children into the school for the child's first day to help them settle. This is a wonderful opportunity to talk informally to the parents and child – again utilising any bilingual support where possible – this could include an older child in the school who may share the new child's first language. It is important to make these discussions as informal and conversational as possible to make everyone feel at ease and to be non-judgemental. It is useful to plan some very specific questions to guide the conversation, questions that will help you to get to know each child in order to better provide for them in school.

Talking to families and children new to your school or educational setting – getting started

You should try to find out:

- How to pronounce the name correctly of each child
- What the child likes to do at home and what they are interested in
- If the child/family has ever lived abroad and if they have ever had any formal education (remember not all countries begin school at the same time)
- If the child/family can speak any other languages
- If the child can read or write in English and/or any other languages
- If the child/family has any religious or cultural requirements the school should be aware of
- If the family have any concerns about the child.

You should also ensure time for the child and family to ask questions about you and the school. The most effective conversations are reciprocal and should not appear like a formal job interview!

It is important to consider that finding out about the child's language history is not always straightforward, however. There is still a legacy amongst some families to be fearful that the school may not see bilingualism as an asset and therefore they might not share the information in order to protect their child. Schools have to make determined efforts to show how much they appreciate the skills of bilingualism:

> Operating in more than one language is normal. It is not in itself a problem and it certainly does not constitute a learning difficulty. Yet those of us who live in England live in a country in which monolingualism is still regarded as the norm.
>
> (Savva 1991)

Language and identity

> Identity, whether on an individual, social, or institutional level, is something that we are constantly building and negotiating throughout our lives through our interaction with others.
>
> (Thornborrow 2004)

What we say and how we say it forms a crucial aspect of our identity. We all use different 'voices' depending on who we are talking to and where we are. We speak very differently to our friends, our teachers, our employers. We use different registers with a range of formalities depending on the environment, irrespective of what language we are speaking in. This is what we call 'linguistic diversity'. Bilingual learners have an additional dimension to this diversity. They are learning how to communicate in all of these registers in another language simultaneously.

Our identity changes all the time. Who we are and how we define ourselves is complex and multi-layered. I am a university lecturer. I am a mother. I am a woman. I am white. I am European. I am a dog owner. I am the child of immigrants. I am an *Eastenders* fan . . . . We choose which of these to present to others and which to conceal. The language we speak is very much a part of this identity – it is the medium through which we can present ourselves – the way we can tell others about ourselves: 'Identity and language are intrinsic, identity is negotiated through dialogue' (Val and Vinogradova 2010).

Children at the earliest stages of becoming bilingual may find it hard to tell us who they are in words we understand: 'Languages are formed in the cultural settings in which they are situated, their meanings shaped through everyday use' (Conteh 2015: 34). Teachers have a responsibility to enable all children to show their interests, their skills and their attributes – they need opportunities to show us who they are. It can be helpful here to consider ways of communicating that do not rely on the formal model of the teacher questioning and the child responding. There are many alternative ways to invite contribution that can enable all learners to participate. For example:

- Show me what you have found out about floating and sinking in the water trough
- Draw everything you already know about the human body
- Make a film of the day in the life of a snail
- Make a PowerPoint presentation to show me all about you.

Modelling instructions through clear examples and partnered work with a more fluent English speaker can clarify your meaning, and regular, supportive reinforcement can enable the child to know they are on the right track.

Reflection: Your language biography

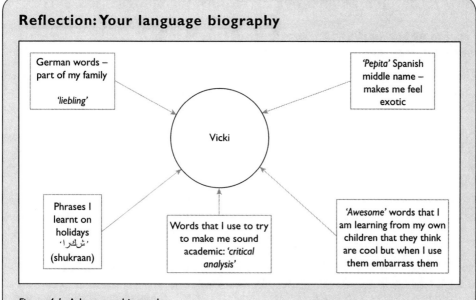

Figure 4.1 A language biography

It is useful at this point to consider your own language history to review how closely aligned language and identity is in all of our lives. Write your name or place a picture of yourself as a child in the centre and draw lines coming from your picture identifying any influences on your own language development. Consider languages or dialects spoken in your family; words or phrases you collected from holidays or friends or from school. Consider how the way we speak defines aspects of who we are.

Celebrating bilingualism in the school environment

Planning and preparing the environment in which you work to ensure all children feel welcome and included is a crucial aspect of creating a positive and accepting classroom culture. This is particularly true for bilingual learners whether they have recently arrived in the country or if they have lived all of their life in the UK. The previous section showed how closely language and identity are interlinked. The culture of our classrooms needs to show how we welcome and celebrate the different languages and cultural experiences our children have, to ensure that all children feel safe and prepared to take the necessary risks in order to progress. The examples below can help you signal to all the children in the class that you see bilingualism as aspirational and celebratory: 'Ignoring children's cultural capital can lead to conscious and unconscious discrimination, which leads to low expectations and can result in low attainment' (Gravelle 2005).

How to develop an inclusive classroom for bilingual learners

Provide opportunities to share languages spoken or understood by members of the class

These ideas can help to normalise and celebrate bilingualism and encourage monolingual children to develop their knowledge and experience of language diversity. Examples of practice might include:

*   *Signage* – Develop opportunities in the classroom to use a range of languages in notices and displays. These could include a commercially produced welcome poster in a range of languages, dual language instructions on how to feed the class hamster, and numbers in a range of alphabetic scripts.
*   *Children could be encouraged to respond to the register in different languages* – In one classroom I visited the children would vote each month on the language of the greetings to be used each day: 'Guten Morgen, Ms Jones', 'صبح بخير (subha bākhair), Mr Chilvers'. On Friday, the children would choose a language of their choice to respond in. The children loved to share their own knowledge and expertise in languages they already knew and all were excited to learn new greetings.
*   *Bilingual learners as teachers* – It is powerful for all children to be seen as the expert teaching the adults in settings. A Russian heritage girl in my reception class would laugh riotously and correct me every day when I tried to say 'hello' – 'Здравствуйте' (*Zdravstvuyte*).

Figure 4.2 'Welcome' poster (freely downloadable from: www.earlylearninghq.org.uk/popular-resources/multilingual-%E2%80%98welcome%E2%80%99-poster/)

Ensure resources and artefacts that are familiar to members of the class

These will enable the children to feel that their culture and identity are acknowledged and accepted and will broaden the experience of all the children in the class. Examples of classroom practice might include:

* *Dual language books and books in prevalent languages* – These should be freely available in the book corner for the children to share with each other and to take home to share with their families. These books can be bought through educational publishers, borrowed from libraries, or created with the support of parents and older siblings in your setting.
* *CDs and websites with poems and songs in different languages* – These should be available, also with headphones. Again, these could be purchased or downloaded from YouTube or made within your school community.
* *Role play areas* – These can include everyday objects from a range of cultures, ensuring children have access to both familiar and less familiar utensils: for example, chopsticks in the home corner; afro combs in the hairdresser's; saris in the clothes shop. It is of course vital that adults in the setting are familiar with any cultural or religious impact of these objects before they are used, to avoid causing upset or offence by them being misused. You should avoid including any religious texts or icons in free play areas, for example.
* *Maps of the world pinpointing places the children have visited or lived in* – These can build on children's knowledge and understanding of the world as well as enabling children to take pride in their experiences.

The importance of providing first-language support

The use of a child's first or dominant language is of great support in the acquisition of any additional language. Continuing to use their dominant language ensures the cognitive aspects of learning continue whilst the child's use and understanding of English is 'catching-up' with their use of their first language.

Although providing individualised bilingual support in every child's first language is unrealistic financially and logistically, in most settings there are activities which can help support the first language of the learner in the classroom:

* When talking with parents or carers of bilingual learners, it is imperative to clarify the most effective support they can offer their child at home is to communicate in their first language – sharing books, teaching writing, exploring the world and to reassure them that this will not inhibit their learning of English.
* If you have a large number of children in your school or setting speaking one particular language, it may be possible to secure a teacher or teaching assistant proficient in that language to work alongside pupils and to facilitate parent meetings and dual language resources.

- You may be able to secure the support of parents with some availability during the day to support first-language learning in the class.
- Many Local Authorities have a central interpreter resource facility – or at the least they may offer a translation service to support communications between home and school or resources.
- School or classroom 'buddies' who share a common language – it is important not to feel intimidated if you cannot understand the conversation they are having; focus on the rewards of a confident learner who feels supported.
- Many schools now use iPads or computers in the classroom with specialist language software or constant access to 'Google Translate' or similar to support classroom interactions between teacher and child or between the children. This strategy also gives status to the bilingual learner as other children will be eager to sit next to them to have the opportunity to also utilise the device.

How children acquire an additional language

From the moment we are born, and indeed even before we are born, we participate in the process of learning to communicate through speech. This process is complex and involves a range of factors: the need to communicate drives us to establish recognisable patterns in our behaviour. Our interactions with those close to us and our ability to 'tune into' the language around us helps us to gather the skills and develop receptors to enable us to organise patterns in the language we hear and to begin to make our own meanings clear. Our brain helps us to establish pathways to organise apparently random grammatical rules in order to clarify meaning through interactions. Chomsky's research into language acquisition and his development of the hypothetical brain tool of the Language Acquisition Device (LAD) is helpful here (Chomsky 1965), as are Vygotsky's cultural communicative theories on the crucial value of interactions to encourage and formalise meaning through speech.

For children learning a new language, these pathways are already established in their brains from learning their first language. These children are learning alternative linguistic labels for the meanings they are already familiar with that their brains can already organise (NALDIC 2016).

Jim Cummins developed a very useful model to consider how the development of learning English as an additional language is inextricably linked to learning their first language. His research concluded that children's ability to switch between two or more languages showed a 'common underlying proficiency' (CUP) for organising language: 'Conceptual knowledge developed in one language helps to make input in the other language comprehensible' (Cummins 2000: 39). In other words if a child understands the concepts around floating and sinking from experience and discussion in their first or primary language, it is fairly straightforward for them just to learn a new label for this process, rather than develop an understanding of the process and language simultaneously. This advocacy for children to continue to learn and talk in their family language is crucial when planning for inclusion.

Cummins (2001) has also developed an influential model of how this acquisition of a second language develops. He is clear that children initially require the Basic Interpersonal Communication Skills (BICS) during the first two years of learning an additional language. These are the social interactions necessary to be part of an interactive community. Gradually, the learner will develop their language fluency to Cognitive Academic Language Proficiency (CALP). At this state, the learner is able to use the language functionally, but now needs more complex structures and vocabulary to enable them to articulate and analyse more complex ideas through the English language. This stage is likely to last for at least five to seven years before fluency is secured.

Understanding BICS and CALP can help us as practitioners to plan for learning beyond the initial stage of acquiring social English:

> The ability of pupils for whom English is an additional language to take part in the national curriculum may be in advance of their communication skills in English. Teachers should plan teaching opportunities to help pupils develop their English and should aim to provide the support pupils need to take part in all subjects.
>
> (DfE 2013)

Supporting bilingual learners in the mainstream classroom

As Maslow's Hierarchy of Needs shows, all children need to feel valued and safe and secure in order to thrive and progress (Maslow 1943). Including children in the mainstream classroom is an important aspect of this process. For children to feel safe and valued, they need to feel part of the class community. It is therefore important to keep children within the mainstream classroom wherever possible. As soon as you withdraw a child for an intervention, they may be identified as different and separate from their peers and thus any positive effect on their self-esteem is negated. The National Association for Language Development in the Curriculum (NALDIC) recommends specialist support within the classroom wherever possible alongside the class teacher and the other children, rather than withdrawing children for regular language interventions (NALDIC 2016). In this way, children will be able to draw on the models of spoken language around them, as well as engaging in whole class tasks. The class teacher should be able to plan with any specialist teacher or teaching assistant to exchange details on what content is to be taught and how to support the bilingual learners to access the curriculum most effectively.

There may be some interventions that are best provided away from the busy classroom environment, but it is best that these interventions are minimal and staff should be mindful about what the children may be missing when taken away from the regular classroom routines.

Stages of English learning

The Department for Education (DfE) defines a learner's 'first language' as the language to which a child was initially exposed during early development and continues to be exposed

Table 4.1 Gravelle's 'Framework for planning'

	What do learners bring to the task?	What does the task demand of them?	What support needs to be planned?
Social			
Cognitive			
Linguistic			

in the home or in the community. For almost all EAL learners, this means that if they are an EAL learner when they start school at 3–5 years old, they will be an EAL learner throughout their education and their life.

In order to categorise and support development for each child on this continuum, it is useful to look at Hilary Hester's *Stages of English Learning* (Hester 1990). It is important to note that each child's development does not relate to age and each child may not follow the exact same path. The descriptions refer to both the social (BICS) and linguistic/cognitive aspects of learning a language. Many schools and local authorities use these stages to plan for the needs of each learner and to track individual progress.

When planning activities to support bilingual learners, it is helpful to consider Gravelle's 'Framework for planning' (Gravelle 2000). Table 4.1 offers a useful model to remind us that we are planning to support the child's social, as well as cognitive and linguistic development.

This simple framework does not need to be a formal detailed written plan for every session but it should instinctively become part of the thinking and planning process to ensure all aspects of the child's need are considered.

Stage 1: New to English

During Stage 1, Hester describes that the child may remain silent for some time, as they are likely to be 'tuning in' to the language heard around them. They are likely to begin to use English words to label objects and to use gestures to make themselves understood. They may be reluctant to interact with English-speaking adults and will be more responsive in play situations with their peers.

In addition to the generic inclusive practices outlined above, children entering school at Stage 1 need plenty of practical 'hands on' experience alongside confident and articulate speakers.

Provision to support children at Stage 1: New to English

In talking

- Provide first-language support wherever possible
- Plan time and opportunity for the child to watch and listen to activities without pressure to join in or respond verbally
- Use child-led role play to encourage peer interaction and contextualised language development
- Sing and use rhymes with strong repetitive patterns of language
- Provide opportunities to play games and work on practical art and DT activities in mixed ability groups to encourage informal conversations
- Use pictorial routine charts – with repetitive instructions reinforced by adults
- Provide a listening area with stories and rhymes in English and own languages
- Ensure quiet, safe places for the child to go to when feeling overwhelmed or to just sit and listen to the language surrounding them, e.g. story tents or book areas

In reading

- Offer texts in the child's first language
- Provide dual language texts with repetitive and strongly patterned texts and clear illustrations, to read/share in school and to take home
- Ensure story character toys or puppets are available to inspire rehearsing and retelling of stories
- Provide graphic novels for older children
- Use sequencing pictures to retell stories and interactive and participatory phonics activities

In writing

- Allow children to draw ideas before attempting writing
- Use role play to prepare and experience stories
- Make own dual language books based on familiar repetitive texts with adult scribing ideas with child, e.g. Brian Wildsmith's *The Cat Sat on the Mat* detailing the cat's growing disdain as a variety of other animals join her. This text works very well for adapting and developing children's own stories and illustrations.
- Plan interactive and participatory phonics activities, e.g. Jolly Phonics rhymes, actions and images 'The ssssnake is in the grass'

Scenario 2: Ania

It is Ania's first day at school. She is 4¾ years old. Her mother braids her hair in exactly the way she likes it best and Ania puts on her brand new shiny black shoes. Her mother helps her with the stiff buckles. Finally, she is starting school. As Ania approaches the classroom door, she is bombarded with excited noise and colour. Her mother helps her hang up her coat and hugs her goodbye. Ania is led to a carpet by a large smiling lady. She sits down and a small boy next to her starts to cry. The large lady with the smile holds a huge book with a picture of a bear on it. Ania loves stories. Her mother reads to her every morning over breakfast. In Polish. As the lady begins to read, Ania is confused. She cannot understand the words. The lady is smiling and the other children begin to join in with the story. Ania doesn't understand the words; she doesn't know when to join in; she doesn't know what the children are saying. After the story, the children go to different parts of the room to play. Ania stays on the carpet. She is suddenly feeling quite alone. She is scared and feels she does not belong. Ania longs for school to be over. Perhaps she will never belong . . . .

Reflection

Consider how Ania's feelings are the same as a monolingual child starting school for the very first time. How does the fact that Ania cannot yet communicate in English affect her start of school? Reflect on what you have learnt from this chapter so far and reflect on your own experiences of your first day at school and consider how you might prepare more effectively to help Ania settle into school.

Stage 2: Becoming familiar with English

At this stage, the child is becoming more confident when speaking to their peers in English and becoming familiar with key phrases they have heard frequently. They may be more confident in articulating need and can understand more than they can independently articulate.

Provision to support a child at Stage 2: Becoming familiar with English

Activities for children at this stage of their English acquisition should include those already listed at Stage 1 and might additionally include:

In talking

- Opportunities for children to hear and communicate with children and adults who speak English fluently
- Simple partnered language games, e.g. as part of a topic on food: 'I like . . . but I don't like . . .' to support experience of common grammatical structures
- Story telling with partners
- Low-risk drama activities in pairs and small groups, e.g. freeze frame where the children select a significant moment from a book or story and pause that moment very much like a photographic still

In reading

- Read books to the children with clear and vivid images clearly displayed
- Offer opportunities to play with story boxes (Bromley 2002) with other children, to retell the stories and to begin to tell their own stories
- Encourage independent reading of short poems and rhymes the child is becoming familiar with. These could be typed up and laminated with supportive illustrations.
- Encourage the child to read repetitive or cumulative stories, e.g. *The Enormous Turnip*
- Reading their own books, which they've made in class

In writing

- Writing in first language actively encouraged
- Shared and guided writing of simple and repetitive statements – made into simple books for the child to read and take home, e.g. 'I can . . .' book
- Drawing simple sequencing stories/comic strips with teacher scribing story in English

Scenario 3: Minal

Minal has recently arrived in England from Turkey. Her mother sent her to live with her aunty near the seaside where she felt Minal would be safer and have more opportunities. She enjoys speaking English to her friends in the local park. She has learnt many phrases in English from the songs she loves to listen to on YouTube and the American TV shows she loves to watch. She is starting school in Y4 midway through the school year. Minal was a good student in her home in Turkey where she played striker in the school's football team. She is a fluent reader in Turkish and enjoys reading her mum's magazines.

Reflection

Consider how to build on Minal's skills and aptitudes alongside supporting her English language development. How might you know these details about her life? Why do they help you?

Stage 3: Becoming confident as a user of English

By this stage, Hester describes a child who is confident when speaking in most social situations. They can read and write in English, but find it difficult to differentiate between types of English 'voice' in non-fiction writing. They sometimes prefer to talk in their first language when the concepts being studied are complex.

Stage 3: Becoming confident as a user of English

In addition to the provision outlined in Stage 2, the role of the adult is to ensure that the child is continuing to use their experience and knowledge in both languages. Activities to support Stage 3 could include:

In talking

- Record children's own stories in their first language and in English to share with younger/less experienced pupils
- Encourage children to prepare and perform puppet shows
- Allow children to hear, collect and tell jokes
- Model language of different non-fiction registers through shared writing with real audiences for outcomes, e.g. class blogs for parents, persuasive letters to the head teacher, instructional texts for younger children

In reading

- Read a wider range of fiction and non-fiction to the children – continuing to ensure illustrations/diagrams are clear and vivid
- Broaden the range of texts in first language and English
- Use films as texts with strong themes and characters

In writing

- Make own non-fiction books following the teacher's model
- Use writing frames to help structure own non-fiction writing
- Rehearse writing ideas through film plotting and making

Stage 4: A very fluent user of English in most social and learning contexts

It is important to continue to consider the requirements of bilingual learners at this stage. Although their language needs are not obvious, there is still a need to ensure that children are developing their skills in the more nuanced ways first language users employ particularly in wider environments.

Stage 4: A very fluent user of English in most social and learning contexts

In talking

- Establish more formal talk situations such as debates and presentational talk for assemblies
- Discuss inferences in guided reading
- Encourage the child to recite poetry in their first language and English
- Ask them to explore and collect colloquialisms

In reading

- Encourage reading aloud to younger or less experienced readers
- Plan performance poetry activities
- Use drama activities to deepen knowledge and understanding of text, e.g. hot seating

In writing

- Encourage writing in role
- Use activities such as making posters to share information
- Encourage the child to write an autobiography or diary, or keep a blog or vlog

Scenario 4: Ania in the future

Ania is now in Y6 – she speaks English very fluently now. She doesn't even sound Polish at all anymore. At home, her mum speaks to her in Polish and she replies usually in English. She doesn't even consciously switch between her languages. It is automatic. Occasionally, she forgets the Polish word for something and her mum is wistful.

> ### Reflection
>
> Consider how Ania has changed over the years. What experiences do you think have helped her grow in confidence in her English speaking? Do you think that she still needs any specific EAL support? What ongoing provision might be helpful to her?

Conclusion

This chapter has sought to outline what it means to be a bilingual learner. It has detailed the vital links between language and identity and has looked at how we acquire language effectively. It has also reviewed some examples of provision that practitioners may consider when designing an inclusive setting where all learners can work alongside one another and where language difference can be celebrated. All children need to feel safe and valued and understood. All children can learn most effectively when they feel their voice is worth listening to: 'If you talk to a man in a language he understands, that goes to his head. If you talk to him in his own language, that goes to his heart' (Nelson Mandela).

References

Arnot M., Schneider, C., Evans, M., Liu, Y., Welply, O. and Davies-Tutt, D. (2014) *School Approaches to the Education of EAL Students.* The Bell Foundation

British Council (n.d.) *EAL Nexus Online*: https://eal.britishcouncil.org/teachers/eal-learners-in-uk (accessed June 2016)

Bromley, H. (2002) Meet the Simpsons, *Primary English Magazine*, 7(4): 7–11

Chomsky, N. (1965) *Aspects of the Theory of Syntax.* Cambridge, MA: MIT Press

Conteh, J. (2015) *The EAL Teaching Book*, 2nd edn. Sage Learning Matters

Cummins, J. (2000) *Language, Power and Pedagogy: Bilingual Children in the Crossfire.* Clevedon: Multilingual Matters

Cummins, J. (2001) *Negotiating Identities: Education for Empowerment in a Diverse Society*, 2nd edn. Los Angeles: California Association for Bilingual Education.

DfE (2013) *The National Curriculum in England Key stages 1 and 2 Framework Document.* DfE

DfE (2015) *National Statistics: Schools, Pupils and their Characteristics*: https://www.gov.uk/government/statistics/schools-pupils-and-their-characteristics-january-2015 (accessed July 2016)

Gravelle, M. (2000) *Planning for Bilingual Learners an Inclusive Classroom.* Stoke on Trent: Trentham Books

Gravelle, M. (2005) *Bilingual Learners: Bilingualism, Learning and Inclusion*: www.scribd.com/doc/34761285/Bilingual-Learners-Bilingualism-Learning-andInclusion-M-Gravelle-2005 (accessed June 2016)

Hester, H. (1990) *Stages of English Learning*: https://www.clpe.org.uk/library-and-resources/useful-resources/stages-english-learninghttps://www.clpe.org.uk/sites/default/files/Stages%20of%20English%20Learning%20Hilary%20Hester.pdf

Jenkin, M. (2014) What Makes a Language Attractive – Its Sound, National Identity or Familiarity? *The Guardian*, 17 July: https://www.theguardian.com/education/2014/jul/17/what-makes-a-language-attractive (accessed 10 March 2017)

Maslow, A. H. (1943) A Theory of Human Motivation, *Psychological Review*, 50(4), 370–396

NALDIC www.naldic.org.uk/ (accessed June to August 2016)

Savva, H. (1991) Bilingual by Rights, in *Language and Learning 5*. Birmingham: The Questions Publishing Company

Thornborrow, J. (2004) Language and Identity, in *Language, Society and Power*. Routledge

Val, A. and Vinogradova, P. (2010) *What is the Identity of a Heritage Language Speaker?*: www.cal.org/heritage/pdfs/briefs/what-is-the-identity-of-a-heritage-language-speaker.pdf (accessed May 2016)

Chapter 5

Supporting children who are highly able

Jenny Fogarty

This chapter explores:

- What do we mean by highly able?
- How do we know a child is more able?
- What barriers exist for highly able children?
- Effective inclusive practices for the highly able child.

The aim of this chapter is to explore, discover and discuss what we mean when we say a child is highly able. Historically, educational settings may have described children as 'gifted and talented'; however, new research is showing that this term is too limited in its scope. The chapter will explore the range of definitions linked to this topic, from 'gifted and talented', 'highly able', 'academically more able', or 'students with high learning potential'. The chapter will consider the extent to which this classification is perceived as a barrier and how perception and recognition itself can be the biggest barrier to including this group of children in the classroom. A discussion around identification strategies in school will be explored along with key aspects of good practice. By broadening your understanding of this specific type of need, your understanding of inclusion is also developed; many feel that these children represent the 'lucky' ones, who seem to excel in many areas of the curriculum and for whom traditional barriers do not exist. However, research shows that the lack of recognition for these pupils can lead to demotivation and underachievement, and in some cases, exclusion from the education system completely.

What do we mean by highly able?

In order to support highly able children effectively in the classroom, to ensure they remain interested in their learning and well motivated, it is important to first define what is meant by this term. For many practitioners in education, 'highly able' has replaced the more familiar term of 'gifted and talented'. The Department for Education (previously Department for Children, Schools and Families) defined gifted and talented children as 'Children . . . who have one or more abilities developed to a level significantly ahead of their year group (or with the potential to develop these abilities)' (DCSF 2008, p.1).

Traditionally, gifted and talented children have been interpreted by educational settings as those showing an aptitude for grasping concepts easily and quickly in academic subjects (being 'gifted'), and those who excelled in such skills as sport, music, or performing arts (being 'talented'). These gifts or talents are often seen in relation to their peers and/or in comparison to age-related learning expectations. Many educational settings introduced a range of programmes and support for children they deemed to be gifted and talented, that focused on additional maths and literacy provision or extracurricular support in areas where a group of children in a school shared the same gifts or talents. It is possible to see where this could be problematic: if a child's aptitudes are not recognised as part of this particular group of subjects, they may be overlooked and, similarly, if a school does not have the resources to support a specific interest, it may be ignored and the children not provided with the opportunity to develop that aptitude.

As a result, it is becoming increasingly common for the term 'highly able' to be used in place of 'gifted and talented', as the former is broader in understanding and interpretation. Since 2010, schools are no longer required to identify children as part of the National Register of Gifted and Talented (The Sutton Trust 2012) and as a result, schools are now in a position to identify particular strengths in individual children. Highly able children, therefore, can be defined similarly as those children who excel or achieve significantly above the level expected for their peers in particular subjects, areas of the curriculum or interests. In this way, in developing a fully inclusive model of meeting the needs of a highly able child, you can consider what a highly able child may look like in a broader sense. Children may be considered highly able when:

- They are achieving significantly beyond the level expected for their age in all areas of learning. They are 'all-rounders'.
- They show a high level of achievement in one particular area of knowledge or skill, e.g. reading, cricket, algebra.
- They show potential to develop a high level of achievement in a particular area (Potential Plus UK 2015; The Sutton Trust 2012).

The definition outlined above is deliberately left open to interpretation, in line with current thinking. The terms 'most able', 'academically more able' and 'high learning potential' all reflect more recent research in this area of education, that focuses on general characteristics and potential for achievement, rather than specific measurable outcomes for children. Levels of achievement may be measurable through data and statistics, test scores, SATS outcomes, intelligence testing, and so on. However, often it is the professional judgement of those working with these children which will determine who is highly able. There can be the concern that those who are identified as highly able in one context may not be viewed that way in another and this itself can be considered a barrier, as will be explored later in the chapter.

Working with highly able children

When working with a group of children, how do you know which children are highly able? Think about the characteristics and behaviours they exhibit:

- Are they the most confident speakers or more hesitant?
- Can they empathise with their peers and socialise well, or do they prefer to work independently?

- Do they show a particular strength in one subject or area, or are they good 'all-rounders'?

You may soon find that your assumptions about highly able children are challenged. Often children who may not have been part of the 'gifted and talented' agenda previously, can show traits of highly able children; for example, a child who is able to work in an unexpected or creative way when solving a problem, or the child who relishes the opportunity to lead others, guiding and managing a group for a shared goal.

How do we know a child is more able?

As an inclusive practitioner, it is important to recognise the variety of needs that children in our settings may have. Identifying children who are highly able is as important as identifying any other type of special educational need, or disability. There is no checklist of characteristics or behaviours that practitioners can use to identify highly able children. Previously, if children scored above a certain level on standardised tests or exams, they were often labelled as 'gifted and talented' but this form of identification only tells us part of the story. Achieving well on tests indicates ability in certain areas, but you need to take the broader definition of 'highly able' to be more representative of the needs seen in educational settings. Identification of highly able children is down to the individual judgement of professionals in their setting and, generally, this has always been the case. In 2008, the Department for Children, Schools and Families asserted that 'Teachers' observation and informal assessment play an essential part in recognising high potential' (DCSF 2008, p.6).

Children with SEN and/or disability and high ability

When working in an inclusive learning environment, it is necessary to consider that those children who may have a special educational need or disability in one area, may also be highly able in another. For example, there are many examples of children with dyslexia, which is a neurodiversity condition that impacts on a child's literacy capacity. However, a child who may struggle to read may be highly able in other areas of learning. Prominent examples include the late world-famous boxer Muhammed Ali, actress Whoopi Goldberg, the Norwegian Prime Minister Erna Solberg and international businessman Richard Branson. Similarly, there are those people with a disability who show high ability, a prominent example being Professor Stephen Hawking. When considering those competing in the Paralympics, once the barriers to them engaging in their sports are removed, they are capable of exceptionally high levels of achievement. As educational practitioners, it is important to consider the potential for high ability in all learners, regardless of any pre-existing special educational needs or disability.

As a practitioner in an educational setting, ensuring effective relationships with the children in your care underpins all elements of inclusion and building effective relationships with highly able children is no exception. The challenge with identifying highly able children is that their additional needs are not immediately obvious and may indeed take months or years to be realised.

By developing a confident and robust professional judgement, founded on positive and secure relationships, children can be identified as showing highly able traits. By considering a range of characteristics, this will help to support practitioners in making these decisions. When working with children you must always stop and consider 'Who are the learners and what do they know?' This will help you to plan effective and engaging lessons and activities that stimulate them to learn more and make sustained progress.

When considering highly able learners, establishing what they know is crucial and it can be easy to assume that it is the children who are first at finishing their tasks that are showing the most potential for learning. These 'fast-finishers' can appear as highly able and, indeed, may well be. However, not all children who complete tasks quickly are highly able and practitioners must consider the quality of the work being produced, not just the quantity. This broader, more holistic understanding is in line with the definitions discussed in this chapter. Any assumptions about highly able children – for example, 'Ali always finishes his maths sums first, so I will give him ten more' – need to reconsidered. By looking closely at the work produced and the steps taken to achieve the learning taken, you can consider if children really *are* more able, or if they are simply keen to finish any task given to them in order to receive praise from the teacher for its completion.

Similarly, the established ways of assessing whether or not a child is highly able can, and do, still offer some helpful guidance. The most frequently used assessment tool is that of formal intelligence or intelligence quotient, usually referred to as 'IQ'. An individual's IQ is determined by dividing an individual's mental age x 100, by their chronological age. A score of 100 is considered to be average for the population and there are a range of ways that the mental age or intelligence can be calculated. However, IQ is only one indicator amongst a number of possible characteristics of high ability and is related to particular cultural contexts. That is to say, IQ scores are based on the concept of intelligence held by most Western psychologists and are a measure of an individual's 'ability to carry out abstract problem solving' (Gardner et al. 1996, p.2), where by solving these problems an individual's cognition skills capacity can be measured. A more advanced ability to problem solve could therefore be considered a characteristic of a highly able child.

Some examples of the type of test questions

1. Rearrange the following letters to make a word and choose the category in which it fits.

    RAPETEKA

    A. city   B. fruit   C. bird   D. vegetable

2. Which number should come next in this series?

    25,24,22,19,15

    A. 4   B. 5   C. 10   D. 14

3. Which word does not belong?

    A. apple   B. marmalade C. orange   D. cherry   E. grape

4. At the end of a banquet, 10 people shake hands with each other. How many handshakes will there be in total?

    A. 100   B. 20   C. 45   D. 50   E. 90

5. The day before the day before yesterday is three days after Saturday. What day is it today?

    A. Monday   B. Tuesday   C. Wednesday D. Thursday   E. Friday

(IQ Test Labs 2015)

The ability to demonstrate logical and abstract reasoning skills is one that is particularly highly prized in Western society and, as such, the concept of having a high IQ is considered to be a desirable characteristic. However, as previously discussed, having a more rounded and wider understanding of ability is useful in developing your inclusive practice and the concept of intelligence has moved on in this area, albeit with much debate surrounding it.

Multiple intelligence

Howard Gardner's concept of multiple intelligences was developed to recognise that there are myriad ways in which intelligence can be defined and it is necessary for a broader understanding to become valued as well (1993). There are a range of ways of assessing an individual's predisposition to a range of alternative intelligences developed by Gardner. The range of intelligences include: musical-rhythmic, visual-spatial, verbal-linguistic, logical-mathematical, bodily-kinaesthetic, interpersonal (working with others), intrapersonal (preferring to work alone and reflective), and naturalistic (plants, animals and the environment).

A discussion about multiple intelligences has been common in educational settings in the last decade and initiatives to support practitioners to appeal to these intelligences may be in place in your setting. There are a range of online tests and questionnaires available to determine a person's predisposition to a particular type of intelligence. An example of the type of question would be:

Rate how far you agree with the following statements:

1. I pride myself on having a large vocabulary.
2. Using numbers and numerical symbols is easy for me.
3. Music is very important to me in daily life.
4. I always know where I am in relation to home. (Literacyworks 2016)

However, it is necessary to consider the extent to which the original theories may have been distorted or adapted for commercial interest. That is, many resources have been designed for schools to buy in, in order to provide a solution to a perceived 'problem' of how to cater for children who demonstrate interests and aptitudes beyond the scope of the curriculum. It is therefore wise to exercise caution to ensure that 'pseudoscience' is not given an unworthy place in the classroom (Bennett 2013).

Knowing that children will manifest their ability in a range of ways – not just through their success in literacy and mathematics – means it may be more useful to us as educational practitioners to consider whether you provide opportunities for children in your settings to demonstrate these aptitudes. For example, does your setting give opportunities for children to learn by working alone (intrapersonal), learning through doing (bodily-kinaesthetic) or exploring ideas through discussion (verbal-linguistic)? Again, by developing a more rounded perspective of intelligences, children's highly able characteristics can be explored.

A discussion on intelligences has touched on how social perceptions can emphasise certain characteristics as having more value than others, leading to some children being identified as highly able more easily, i.e. those with a high IQ. Another challenge when identifying highly able children can be the assumptions that practitioners make to value certain types of behaviours linked to particular backgrounds. In some instances, educational settings may reflect current perceptions in society of what is considered valuable. Children who have greater access to what the significant social theorist Bourdieu describes as 'social capital' (Field 2008) may be more likely to be recognised as highly able by teachers and educational practitioners. Children whose parents actively enrich their educational experiences – for example, through trips abroad, visits to museums and art galleries, sports events and access to a range of reading material – may show more potential to be highly able and this may be more easily recognised. This recognition occurs because they seem to fit with an educational setting's perception of what it means to be highly able. It can be interpreted that these children are being identified as highly able, when they are actually just the most well-adjusted to dominant expectations of the current UK education system. Ofsted (2015) has acknowledged that identification of highly able children from less affluent backgrounds can be easily overlooked, as they have not had the opportunities to develop talents and skills, and their educational settings are making assumptions about their capacity, based on their more limited experiences.

It is therefore important for practitioners to ensure that these assumptions are exposed and acknowledged in order to widen identification of highly able children. Taking time to build the positive professional relationships that must exist in the truly inclusive class-room is key to revealing the hidden highly able. It will also be important for practitioners to recognise that highly able children may have talents and skills from a range of alternative opportunities, including those from other cultures of which the setting has little experience. By using the range of expertise and capabilities in the local community, further understanding can be developed within an educational setting which will benefit all who learn and work there.

Learning-rich environments

Read the following examples of children in a classroom and consider the characteristics and behaviours they are displaying. How would you support them in your setting? Do you consider them to be highly able? What next steps could you take?

Alex is 5 and the youngest in her family. She was nervous about starting school but soon found refuge in the maths corner of her kindergarten class where she was confident to make number patterns, counting in multiples of 2, 5 and 10. When working with other members of her class, she becomes withdrawn and reluctant to give her ideas but is much happier working one-to-one with an adult who helps to write her answers for her. She is working on longer multiplication questions and when asked how she gets to the answers, describes and draws the patterns she sees in her head.

Daryl struggles to complete tasks in English and Maths lessons. His writing is neat but spellings are tricky for him and numbers leave him confused and upset. He lives with his mum and his grandmother and he is eligible for free school meals. Approaching his eighth birthday, he was chosen from his class to go to a 6-week after-school art class with a visiting artist. Everyone was amazed at the stunning drawings he could achieve and the artist told everyone who would listen how well Daryl responded to his coaching and guidance.

Ben often ends up outside the head teacher's office. By the age of 10, he has nearly given up on school. Nothing he is taught interests him and he finds it much easier to make jokes with his friends, which means he is often in trouble. He knows that teachers think he is naughty but he doesn't care any more. What he does care about is his dance crew on a Saturday morning, but no one has ever asked him about that. He practises his moves for hours every night but is worried his dad is going to stop him going if he keeps getting into trouble at school. He has the opportunity to go to America in the summer for an international dance competition and he can't wait.

When identifying children who are highly able, it is necessary to consider any perceived gender bias that may inform your professional judgements. Ofsted (2015) have raised their concerns that highly able boys are underperforming compared to highly able girls, which would lead practitioners in educational settings to focus their attention on ensuring highly able boys are given the support they need to succeed. However, this should also be treated with caution: 'There is no research to suggest that boys are inherently more gifted than girls, but significant research to show that boys are twice as likely to be seen as gifted than girls' (Stephen and Warwick 2015, p.126).

It is necessary to question why these assumptions have been established in order to ensure that educational settings are providing equal access to support for highly able children.

If, somewhere along the way, a bias has developed towards identifying male learners as gifted or highly able and yet they are not performing as well compared to their female counterparts, it may be right to question whether this identification or these labels were correctly applied in the first place. Were these boys actually more able or was the commonly held notion that girls are outperforming boys responsible for driving up the numbers of boys identified as highly able in order to redress the balance? Whatever the cause, it remains the case that as practitioners you have a professional responsibility to treat all your learners as equals, regardless of gender or family background. When you identify highly able learners as such, the rationale is to provide inclusive learning opportunities for them, to support them to thrive and enjoy education and to eliminate any barriers that may exist, which will now be considered.

What barriers exist for highly able children?

In order to effectively support children who are highly able in educational settings, it is important to take time to reflect on to what extent being highly able presents barriers to full inclusion. The portrayal of highly able children in the media and general social consciousness is one that itself creates the biggest barrier for these children, that of perception. Many people fail to perceive being highly able as problematic; indeed, the opposite can be said to be true. For some, the concept of additional support for highly able children is elitist and Stephen and Warwick discuss how some practitioners may view these children as being 'blessed twice over' (2015, p.11). Any additional advantages given to these children may be seen as unfair, since they already have the perceived advantage of being highly able. This chapter will now explore how being highly able can be a disadvantage, in order to fully determine how they can best be included in the classroom. Many of these barriers have been outlined by research undertaken by Potential Plus UK (2015), formerly The National Association for Gifted Children.

The educational barriers that exist for children who are highly able centre around the lack of challenge they experience in their learning opportunities. If lessons are lacking in challenge for highly able children, they often find work too easy and become demotivated and bored. Repeated examples of this can occur where a child's ability or aptitude in a subject exceeds that of their teacher and a complex relationship dynamic is formed. Some teachers can become fearful of highly able children and feel threatened that their knowledge is being undermined in the classroom and any weaknesses may be exposed. This fear can result in decisions being made to stretch the highly able child in ways that may not be appropriate, for example placing young children in classes above their chronological age, in order to give them work that is deemed to be more challenging. Often educational settings have limited experience or resources to support children who are highly able and simply do not know how to support children who are excelling in the classroom.

Boredom and lack of motivation can become barriers for highly able children in themselves, not just as a result of lack of challenge. If children are not developing their learning in ways that are interesting and stimulating to them, they can easily become disinterested in the school system as it does not recognise their capabilities. Always completing activities first, completing them in ways that seem uninteresting, or lack of opportunities to develop in areas that children excel, can all lead to feelings of antipathy and disengagement. Prolonged periods of boredom can result in children switching off from lessons, teachers and peers, and children even becoming disruptive. There have been many cases where children who display challenging behaviour do so as a direct result of the boredom they experience in class, because they are highly able and this has not been recognised. By displaying behaviour that is challenging, they may develop a pattern of behaviour where seeking attention, even if it is negative, is preferable to being overlooked or dismissed altogether.

For some children who are highly able, they may experience challenges related to socialisation and forming friendships. Where children are highly able, this difference compared to their peers, similar to the wide range of special educational needs addressed in other chapters, marks them out as different. For some children, the difference associated with being 'clever' can isolate them from their peers as other children can struggle to interact with children with this difference. Other children may feel intimidated by the potential of highly able children and seek to undermine them, which could, in the worst cases, trigger a pattern of bullying or social isolation. Similarly, children who are highly able can often isolate themselves, as they can become frustrated when their peers cannot relate to them in a way that they understand. A lack of understanding by highly able pupils and their peers needs to be addressed by the skilful teacher in order for children to benefit from the enhanced cognitive development gained from social interaction, as pioneered by Lev Vygotsky (1986). Social development is often seen as one of the most significant benefits of the school system designed currently and, as such, any factors that limit opportunities for children to socialise should be acknowledged. Indeed, for many practitioners, overcoming barriers to social development is at the heart of inclusive practice.

For some highly able children, failure is an experience that is relatively unknown to them, particularly in classrooms where they are not challenged and are used to being successful. However, highly able children will be aware of others' failures, but without experiencing it for themselves a fear of failure can easily be developed. Failing, and persevering after failure to make continued improvements, is a necessary part of the learning experience and many practitioners feel that educational settings provide the safe space in order for children to learn what it means to fail and how to overcome the negative emotions associated with failure, in order to continue to improve. If highly able children have never experienced this, either at home or in a classroom setting, it is understandable that an anxiety around failure can occur. This anxiety can be paralysing and can prevent highly able children from ever embracing new challenges, particularly when their own identity is strongly linked to their ability to succeed. For many highly able children, their ability to succeed easily compared to their peers is recognised and rewarded, and this contributes to their feelings of self-worth. A situation where they might find something difficult, or even fail at something, should therefore be avoided in order to maintain these positive feelings, not only for the highly able child themselves, but also for those around them, that value their high ability.

Katy's story

Katy was excited to start school. In the Early Years, she excelled in all areas of learning, picking up concepts and ideas quickly and seemingly with little effort. She was the first in her class to write her name, count to 10 and always finished first any activities given to her. During a spelling lesson one day, her class teacher asked the class how to spell 'school'. Confidently, she put up her hand and was chosen to give her answer. 'S-C-O-O-L' she sounded out. Immediately, her friend,

Helen, sat opposite her, shouted out, 'Oh no! Katy's got something wrong! It's got an H in it, H for Helen!' As Katy realised her mistake, the shame crept up on her and she felt her cheeks begin to burn. The class laughed along with Helen and her teacher moved on quickly saying, 'Good try Katy but yes Helen, its S-C-H-O-O-L.' From that point on, learning changed for Katy. Rather than having a go, she preferred to hang back, waiting for others to go before her. Whenever she felt ready to try and give her answer, she would remember how hot she felt and her cheeks would begin to tingle, in anticipation of another mistake. Katy became so consumed by this fear that she became reluctant to try anything new and needed reassurance from her teachers before she began a new activity. She became more withdrawn and didn't like to draw attention to herself in case she made a mistake again.

How do you think the episode in the spelling lesson changed Katy's attitude to learning? Why do you think this might be? How does Katy's embarrassment affect the way she approaches new tasks? What impact might this have on her learning, if it were to continue?

Fixed and growth mindset

The work of American psychologist Dr Carol Dweck (2006) has been transformative in developing practitioners understanding of how mindset contributes to sustained success. The fear of failure that many highly able children experience can be attributed to their perceived 'fixed' mindset, whereby they believe their skills and attributes are fixed and cannot be developed. For highly able children, they need to continue to prove themselves over and over, in order to assure those around them that their highly able characteristics remain. However, if highly able children can develop a 'growth' mindset, where learning can be developed through effort, regardless of their starting point, challenges can be embraced more readily and improvements made. Developing a 'growth' mindset is seen as key to future success as it embraces challenges, with all their associated potential for failures, and sees all experiences as opportunities for learning, including failure itself. Characteristics of those with a 'growth' mindset include those who:

- Embrace challenges
- Persevere in the face of setbacks
- See effort as the route to mastery
- Seek out, and learn lessons from, criticism
- Find inspiration from the successes of others.

For educational settings, many lessons can be learned from Dweck's work in order to support and develop a 'growth' mindset culture for all children, not just the highly able.

Related to a fear of failure and the anxiety caused by this, is the stress associated with perfectionist tendencies exhibited by some highly able children. Research conducted by

Potential Plus UK revealed worrying levels of emotional stresses for highly able pupils related to their ability to set themselves unobtainable goals. These 'high levels of perfectionism' (Potential Plus UK 2015, p.17) can be as a result of the fixed mindset exhibited by highly able children where, if they do not achieve 100 per cent of their goal, they consider themselves to be a failure. Often, they find it challenging to recognise small, incremental achievements and as such can become increasingly stressed and anxious about achieving their bigger goal. For some highly able children, this can be a very narrow perception of their own achievements, particularly if they show an aptitude in a specific area. All other achievements, not linked to their aptitude, do not hold value for them, particularly if they are not recognised or rewarded by the adults around them. The stress and the mental health concerns linked to these perfectionist traits should not be underestimated, as the emotional well-being of highly able children can be one of the biggest barriers to them reaching their full potential.

Removing barriers to achievement

As a practitioner in an educational setting, why is it important to consider barriers that exist for highly able pupils? To what extent do these barriers influence the practice in educational settings? When working with a group of children, have you considered any barriers to achievement they might be experiencing? How do you know they are barriers?

Effective inclusive practices for the highly able child

By reviewing the identification approaches and barriers that exist for highly able children, you can begin to develop your understanding of the holistic nature of this type of need. It is no longer the case that educational settings can categorise children by the number of points they score on a specific test or how they complete an activity compared to their peers. In this chapter, it has been established that to identify children, secure professional relationships underpin a holistic judgement about their ability in the context in which they excel and you need to avoid assumptions or pre-conceptions, which may exist as barriers in themselves.

By including more able children in the classroom, they can make their own unique contribution to the learning environment, along with their peers. However, there are a number of strategies that practitioners and leaders in educational settings can adopt in order to support their full inclusion.

In order to develop an effective whole school inclusive ethos, opportunities should be provided to enrich the learning experience of highly able children by all those involved in delivering the education. Ideas such as 'gifted and talented clubs' are seen as exclusionary and potentially a waste of precious school resources. By providing clubs and extracurricular opportunities that meet the needs of all learners, it is vital that the needs of all learners are established and an overview of these needs across the setting is established. By regularly updating this overview, the talents, skills and dispositions of the highly able children can be tracked and appropriate support can be put in place. Drawing on the range of expertise available in a community can be an effective way to support existing staff to meet the needs of highly able learners. However, developing a whole school approach means that every practitioner in the educational setting takes responsibility for including every child in that setting. It is no longer the responsibility of the 'gifted and talented co-ordinator' to ensure the needs of highly able learners are met and resources to support highly able children should be applied fairly and in a transparent way.

The role of transition between settings can support this by utilising the skills of practitioners who are experienced in supporting children of an older chronological age, combined with the practitioners in the existing settings who can adapt the learning to meet the learners' emotional needs. An effective example of this is seen where sports coaches from secondary schools work with their primary colleagues to team-teach and develop skills for all children. By not providing an 'elite' group, all children are included by the sports coach and will have a range of experiences to stretch and challenge those children who are highly able in this area. Not only does this provide excellent opportunities for the highly able child, it also serves to provide professional development for educational practitioners in order to eliminate barriers between them and the highly able.

Strategies to support the highly able

Whilst it is important to recognise the importance of a personalised approach to provision for highly able children, the following represents a range of examples of the type of support possible:

- Identification of a mentor or coach who shares a similar ability or aptitude to guide and support development in that area, e.g. sport
- Shared activities and collaboration with children in other settings
- Enriched curriculum activities where the teachers and practitioners clearly state their high expectations for the highly able child
- Effective differentiation of learning tasks which may include sharing resources from classes older than the chronological age
- Providing opportunities for children to develop and share personal projects and passions within the curriculum
- Development of enrichment programmes where highly able children can expand their learning beyond the traditional curriculum
- Parent support programmes where parents and carers of highly able children can be given advice and guidance to nurture and develop the interests and aptitudes of their child

---

Part of developing the whole school ethos is the development of a growth mindset culture in which learning develops and thrives, as discussed previously (Dweck 2006). This is developed in an educational setting by the assessment for learning agenda pioneered by Shirley Clarke (2008, 2014) where children are encouraged to take ownership for their learning within a learning culture underpinned by a growth mindset attitude. For highly able children to take responsibility for developing their learning, identifying their own next steps and ensuring they are suitably challenged, educational practitioners can support highly able children to create meaningful learning experiences. In a climate where failure is embraced as an important and valuable part of true learning experiences, the anxieties associated with this for some highly able learners can subside. By integrating this within a whole school

approach this is effective inclusive practice for all children, whilst recognising the particular benefits this could have for the highly able.

Some strategies adopted by schools promoting a growth mindset culture and advocated by Clarke (2014) include the reduced use of stickers and rewards for attainment, focusing instead on the effort needed to undertake tasks. By simply rewarding the 'top of the class' (whatever that class may be), it encourages children to be extrinsically motivated, meaning that they complete tasks for the reward or sticker. For the highly able child, this can result in a plethora of stickers, stars, certificates and trophies for tasks that have required little or no effort on their part, simply because they achieved a certain standard that for them was not challenging. Supporting children to become intrinsically motivated, to enjoy the process of learning in itself and not because of the expected rewards, highly able children can set their own challenges to develop linked to their own interests and areas they excel at, therefore reducing opportunities for boredom in the classroom.

This whole school approach also extends to practitioners' approach to differentiation in the setting. According to the Training and Development Agency for Schools, 'Differentiation is the process by which differences between pupils are accommodated so that all students have the best possible chance of learning' (TDAS 2007).

To support highly able children effectively, differentiation needs to take into account the areas in which your children are showing their ability in order that tasks and activities can be closely matched to their next steps. This may require practitioners to view differentiation in a more individualised way, meeting the needs of the individual child rather than grouping children into the traditional 'top, middle, bottom'. Not only can this labelling be damaging to the children in the groups, it also does not reflect the changing needs of children and the extent to which some children can excel in tasks or activities, not necessarily in every subject. Below are some examples of differentiation strategies that have been adapted for highly able children to illustrate how this could work in an educational setting:

- *Differentiation by outcome* – Highly able children may choose the type of final outcome they produce linked to their strengths and aptitudes. An example of this could be for a highly able creative writer; as part of an extended writing project, they may choose to write a book for a specific audience giving a clear purpose and meaningful outcome for their endeavours.
- *Differentiation by support* – Highly able children benefit from the additional support of adults in the setting as much as other children but are often overlooked. For example, by pairing the teacher with a highly able child to complete a specific task that they are good at, such as a joint art project, the highly able child benefits from quality, one to one feedback to improve and develop their skill. Not only does this improve the quality of the work for the child, it also demonstrates how the teacher values their skill.
- *Differentiation by task* – Highly able children may be given a task that is different to their peers altogether, reflecting their own interest and ability. This is particularly useful when the highly able child is competent in a skill, e.g. multiplication, and further practise and recall of their times tables would be demotivating and detrimental. In this instance a completely different task, such as an open-ended investigation that would require application of multiplication, may be more challenging and appropriate.

To effectively include the highly able child in an educational setting, it is necessary for all educational practitioners to consider their own, and their institution's, understanding and definition of what it means to be highly able. By considering a broader view of the terminology, you are able to identify and, in turn, support those children who are achieving significantly higher outcomes than their peers, in a range of interests, skills and endeavours. This chapter has explored a range of considerations you need to make in educational settings when identifying highly able children, along with a discussion of the barriers that exist for these children. By acknowledging these, the chapter has begun to outline some strategies that can be used in educational settings to include highly able children, in order for *all* children to be fully included in the classroom and enjoy the rich and broad learning experiences that this results in.

References

Bennett, T. (2013) *Teacher Proof* Oxon: Routledge

Clarke, S. (2014) *Outstanding Formative Assessment: Culture and practice* Oxon: Hodder Education

Clarke, S. (2008) *Active Learning Through Formative Assessment* Oxon: Hodder Education

DCSF (Department for Children, Schools and Families) (2008) *Identifying Gifted and Talented Learners: Getting Started* Available at: http://webarchive.nationalarchives.gov.uk/20130401151715/ http://www.education.gov.uk/publications/eOrderingDownload/Getting%20StartedWR.pdf [Accessed July 2016]

Dweck, C. (2006) *Mindset – How you can fulfil your potential* London: Constable & Robinson

Field, J. (2008) *Social Capital: Key ideas* Oxon: Routledge

Gardner, H. (1993) *Frames of Mind* London: Fontana Press

Gardner, H., Kornhaber, M. and Wake, W. (1996) *Intelligence: Multiple perspectives* Fort Worth, TX: Harcourt Brace

IQ Test Labs (2015) *IQ Tests and Intelligence* Available at: www.intelligencetest.com/ [Accessed July 2016]

Literacyworks (2016) *Assessment: You're your strengths* Available at: www.literacynet.org/mi/assessment/findyourstrengths.html [Accessed September 2016]

Ofsted (Office for Standards in Education) (2015) *The Most Able Students* Available at: https://www.gov.uk/government/uploads/system/uploads/attachment_data/file/408909/The_most_able_students_an_update_on_progress_since_June_2013.pdf [Accessed July 2016]

Potential Plus UK (2015) *Too Much Too Soon: The emotional and mental health issues of the UK's high learning potential children* Available at: www.potentialplusuk.org/file_upload/files/too%20much%20too%20soon.pdf [Accessed July 2016]

Stephen, M. and Warwick, I. (2015) *Educating the More Able Student* London: Sage

The Sutton Trust (2012) *Educating the Highly Able* Available at: www.suttontrust.com/wp-content/uploads/2012/07/Educating-the-Highly-Able-Report.pdf [Accessed July 2016]

TDAS (Training and Development Agency for Schools) (2007) *Professional Standards for Teachers: Core* Available at: https://www.rbkc.gov.uk/pdf/standards_core.pdf [Accessed July 2016]

Vygotsky, L. S. (1986) *Thought and Language* Cambridge, MA: MIT Press

Chapter 6

What it means to have a disability or special educational need

Gianna Knowles

This chapter explores:

- What is meant by the term 'disabled'
- The SEN Code of Practice 2014
- Medical models and social model of disability and SEN
- Support available for disabled children in educational settings.

> ## What does the term 'disabled' mean to you?
>
> - When you think about the term 'disabled', what does it mean to you?
> - How many conditions can you think of that a person might have that would lead them to being defined as being 'disabled'?
> - Do you regard yourself as being disabled?
> - If you answered 'yes' to this question, do you feel that being disabled has had a *more positive* or *more negative* impact on your life than others around you?
> - If you answered 'no' to this question, have you considered how you may through age or other circumstances become disabled?
> - You may have a close family member who is disabled; if this is the case, what insight has this given you into how disability is generally viewed in the UK?

The Disabled Living Foundation (DLF) states that there are 'over 6.9 million disabled people of working age' in the UK, 'and 10 million disabled people in Britain, of whom 5 million are over state pension age' (DLF 2016). It is also states that there are '770,000 disabled children under the age of 16 in the UK' (DLF 2016), which is the equivalent of one child in twenty. As practitioners working in educational settings, it is therefore the case that some of the children we work with will be disabled. However, while there are government and medical definitions that define the term 'disabled', in other areas of society disability is seen as a contested term and the notion that someone is 'disabled' as a social construct. That is to say, those who deem themselves 'able-bodied', label others who have different mental, physical and sensory abilities to what they regard as 'normal' or typical, as impaired and disabled

(Reaume 2014). Further to this, these differences, rather than being celebrated simply as 'differences', are seen as something to be corrected. There is a growing understanding that it is the view the able-bodied have of 'disabled people as pitiable, tragic victims' (Reaume 2014, p.1248) that causes the barriers that often prevent disabled children and adults in engaging in day-to-day activities, rather than the disability itself. As Slorach writes: 'disability is a complex phenomenon, reflecting an interaction between features of a person's body and features of the society in which he or she lives' (Slorach 2016, p.17). These are challenging ideas which this chapter will examine in more detail.

Defining disability

The Equality Act 2010 defines disability in Britain in the following way: 'you're disabled under the Equality Act 2010 if you have a physical or mental impairment that has a "substantial" and "long-term" negative effect on your ability to do normal daily activities' (Gov.uk 2016a). Where the definition of 'substantial' means it might take longer 'than it usually would to complete a daily task', for example, getting out of bed and getting dressed. 'Long-term' is clarified as meaning that the disabling condition affects the child or adult for twelve months or more (Gov.uk 2016a). So, if we take the example of having an accident and breaking a leg, it is likely this will be a short-term impairment in terms of being able to do daily tasks, and it would be reasonable to expect that the condition would be temporary and that once recovered, the adult or child would be able to go about life as usual. However, if the accident caused more severe or longer-term damage to the leg, the person may be deemed disabled.

Some conditions which would deem a person to be disabled are present from birth. For example, cystic fibrosis, autistic spectrum conditions and cerebral palsy. In some instances, someone might have a condition that develops later in life and over time becomes progressively more disabling, for example, Parkinson's disease, Alzheimer's disease, motor neurone disease, or osteoarthritis. These are conditions that gradually impact on a person's capacity to undertake daily tasks, although early signs of these conditions often go unnoticed and, in the case of some of these conditions, symptoms can be treated by drugs which will mitigate some of the condition's impact on mobility and lifestyle. However, as progressive conditions, they will eventually have a considerable impact on a person's capacity to complete daily tasks and, therefore, those with progressive conditions can be classed as disabled. Similarly, being diagnosed with HIV infection, cancer, or multiple sclerosis would also mean someone automatically met, from the day of diagnosis, the definition of disability under the Equality Act 2010. Some of these conditions mainly affect adults; however, HIV infection, cancer, or multiple sclerosis can affect children, as can other progressive conditions. In this way, we can see how the law makes a distinction between conditions people may be born with and those they may go on to acquire, either through illness, ageing, or accident and how both conditions present from birth, or acquired later in life, may mean an adult or child is deemed to be disabled.

The Special Educational Needs and Disability Code of Practice: 0 to 25 years

Practitioners working in educational settings will be familiar with the *Special Educational Needs and Disability Code of Practice: 0 to 25 years* (hereinafter, SEN Code of Practice) (DfE 2015). This document discusses disability in the following ways:

> Many children and young people who have SEN may have a disability under the Equality Act 2010 – that is 'a physical or mental impairment which has a long-term and substantial adverse effect on their ability to carry out normal day-to-day activities'. . . This definition includes sensory impairments such as those affecting sight or hearing, and long-term health conditions such as asthma, diabetes, epilepsy, and cancer.
>
> (DfE 2015, p.16)

The SEN Code of Practice also makes the important point that there is a distinction between disability and Special Educational Needs (SEN), stating that while children may have conditions such as those outlined above, which fall under the disability definition: 'children and young people with such conditions do not necessarily have SEN, but there is a significant overlap between disabled children and young people and those with SEN' (DfE 2015, p.16). The distinction being:

> A child or young person has SEN if they have a learning difficulty or disability which calls for special educational provision to be made for him or her . . . if he or she . . . has a significantly greater difficulty in learning than the majority of others of the same age.
>
> (DfE 2015, p.15)

So, in this way, a child may be deemed to be disabled because they have cystic fibrosis, but this may have no bearing on their capacity to learn. Whereas a child who is deemed to have an SEN may be able to undertake routine day-to-day tasks, but struggle because their behaviour can be challenging, struggle to socialise and make friends, or find reading, writing and mathematics challenging. They may also find it more difficult than might be typically expected of a child of their age to grasp new ideas or concentrate for sustained periods of time (Gov.uk 2016b).

Therefore, having explored the government's definition of disability we know we are thinking about long-term conditions that impact on:

- Vision (for example blindness or partial sight)
- Hearing (for example deafness or partial hearing)
- Mobility (for example walking short distances or climbing stairs)
- Dexterity (for example lifting and carrying objects, using a keyboard)
- Learning or understanding or concentrating
- Memory
- Mental health
- Stamina or breathing or fatigue
- Social and other behaviours, characteristics associated with autism spectrum conditions, attention deficit condition or Asperger's syndrome (ONS 2015).

The World Health Organization's definition of disability

Our exploration of what the term 'disability' means has focused on how the term is used in the UK. The World Health Organization (WHO) provides the following international definition:

- Disabilities is an umbrella term, covering impairments, activity limitations, and participation restrictions
- An impairment is a problem in body function or structure
- An activity limitation is a difficulty encountered by an individual in executing a task or action
- While a participation restriction is a problem experienced by an individual in involvement in life situations.

There are many similarities between this definition and the previous definitions we have explored, that is, the concept of disability is centred on notions of 'impairment' and 'limitations'. However, the WHO does also make the point that:

> Disability is thus not just a health problem. It is a complex phenomenon, reflecting the interaction between features of a person's body and features of the society in which he or she lives. Overcoming the difficulties faced by people with disabilities requires interventions to remove environmental and social barriers.

That is to say, the notion of disability as a social construct is becoming increasingly internationally recognised.

Source: WHO 2016

Scenario 1: Carrie

Josie Long, the head teacher of St Mary's Primary School in North London, has just popped into the staff room at lunch time to let the Special Needs Coordinator (SENCo) know that they are anticipating welcoming a new child. Carrie is 9, she likes stories, dancing and painting and has Down's syndrome. The conversation between Josie and the SENCo has been overheard by some of the other teachers and teaching assistants in the staff room.

One of the teachers remarks, 'I hope she's not put in my class, the last thing I need is another child who can't read or write, refusing to do things and throwing tantrums if things don't go their way.'

Adriana is a teaching assistant who has worked with children with Down's syndrome in her previous job. She's surprised and upset by the teacher's comment.

Adriana's previous school provided her with training to ensure she could support the children she worked with, and she knows that first and foremost whoever is working with Carrie needs to know about Carrie as a little girl – what she likes to do, what she can do, what she is capable of. Adriana also knows that, just like all children, no two children with Down's syndrome will be alike and while there are certain characteristics that children with Down's syndrome share, how these characteristics present will vary from child to child.

Adriana remembers how, in her training, they were told that Down's syndrome is a genetic condition that occurs through the presence of an extra chromosome in a baby's cells; it is not an inherited condition and usually occurs because of a chance happening at the time of conception. The impact of Down's syndrome will vary from child to child and will have the effect of delaying the development of cognitive functions relating to reading, writing and maths. 'But', thinks Adriana, 'by the age of 9, both Carrie and her family will know a lot about what Carrie can do and the strategies that work for Carrie to help her learn and enjoy school.' Adriana remembers that one of the things they will need to find out from Carrie and her parents is any routines Carrie finds particularly helpful in supporting her at school. She knows it can be characteristic of Down's syndrome that Carrie may respond better to an environment that is ordered and consistent, so she knows what to expect and what is likely to happen next and if any changes to the day's usual timetable have had to be made. 'Mind you', thinks Adriana, 'most children and adults like to know what's happening and if it's going to change, whether they have Down's syndrome or not.'

Adriana also knows that Carrie may also use self-talk as a way of talking herself through what she needs to do and to express her feelings in a world that can sometimes be very confusing, particularly as she gets to grips with her new school and is making new friends. Adriana remembers children with Down's syndrome are sometimes seen as being stubborn. In her training, she was taught that stubbornness and a seeming refusal to co-operate may indicate that the child doesn't fully understand what is expected of them, or that they are feeling the situation is getting out of their control. She remembers that the best way to deal with this is to try and find out what the problem is.

Adriana gets on well with St Mary's SENCo and, given what she has just heard in the staff room, thinks it would be a good idea if she has a word with her to suggest some training for the staff, before Carrie arrives (with reference to advice from the Down's Association 2016).

Medical models and social models of disability and SEN

So far, this chapter has explored a number of definitions of disability and, as has already been noted, the definitions discussed, be they disability as defined by UK law or as outlined by the World Health Organization, describe disability in terms of 'impairments', with 'negative-effect on ability', 'limitations' and 'restrictions'. As Slorach writes, 'For most people the term [disability] refers to a range of limitations in the mental or physical functioning of individuals – an approach reflected in most of current disability-related legislation in Britain and elsewhere' (2016, p.11). Approaching disability in this way can be termed as the *medical model* of disability – that is, expressing disability through categorising people by how some people are different from what might 'normally' be expected to be the usual range of physical and cognitive abilities a person should have. This approach adheres to the idea that there is a usual norm of physical and cognitive attributes a person should have and a particular trajectory of development a child should pass through, from birth to adulthood. Such development is often expressed in terms of 'stages', whereby a child is expected to reach certain developmental milestones at a particular age. Failure to meet these milestones suggests that something is 'wrong' with the child; as SCOPE states, 'the medical model looks at what is "wrong" with the person' (SCOPE 2016).

An alternative view to the medical model is what is known as the *social model* of disability: 'The social model of disability says that disability is caused by the way society is organised, rather than by a person's impairment or difference' (SCOPE 2016). The medical model looks at what is 'wrong' and, sometimes, offers ways to 'fix' the problem, which, in turn, 'creates low expectations and leads to people losing independence, choice and control in their own lives' (SCOPE 2016), as the rest of society focuses on what the disabled person cannot do – rather than what they can. The social model of disability also underlines the fact that it is those who deem themselves 'able-bodied' who are limiting and restricting the lives of the disabled. It is the majority able-bodied community who have defined 'ability' and 'disability' and built an environment that only the able-bodied can access. They have created an educational and work environment that is accessible only to the able-bodied and defined this as the 'normal' way in which life should be lived and enjoyed and that to do so requires a body that can function in a 'normal' way. In this way, artificial social, as well as physical, barriers have been constructed that prevent those deemed disabled from enjoying the same access to the lifestyles expected by the able-bodied. Not only this, but the able-bodied have also socially constructed an idealised version of the 'normal' body in terms of how the body should look. As Goodley writes, 'ableist processes create a corporeal standard, which presumes ablebodiedness, inaugurates the norm and purifies the ableist ideal' (Goodley 2013, p.640). Therefore, disabled children and adults are marginalised by able-bodied society, because their bodies do not fit social norms of how bodies should look and function.

In rejecting these notions of 'disability' that focus on impairments and difficulties, the social model of disability seeks to remove the barriers that restrict life choices for disabled children and adults since, when these artificially created barriers are removed, many disabled children and adults can exercise choice and control over their lives and live independently.

Support for disabled children in educational settings

While many disabilities are usually identified soon after birth – if not before – some, such as autistic spectrum conditions, may not be fully recognised until a child attends an Early Years setting or school. Similarly, any SEN a child may have might not become apparent until a child enters a formal learning situation such as school. However, the SEN Code of Practice is clear that it is important any needs are 'picked up at the earliest point' to ensure support is 'routinely put in place quickly, and . . . parents . . . know what services they can reasonably expect to be provided with' (DfE 2015. p.11). In line with our discussion about the social model of disability, the SEN Code of Practice, as well as outlining what constitutes an SEN or disability, also notes that 'Our vision for children with special educational needs and disabilities is the same as for all children and young people – that they achieve well in their early years, at school and in college, and lead happy and fulfilled lives' (DfE 2015, p.11).

A further fundamental principle of the current SEN Code of Practice is the requirement that the children and parents are fully involved and their wishes taken into account, through regular meetings, about support that is in place for the child:

> Children and young people and their parents or carers will be fully involved in decisions about their support and what they want to achieve. Importantly, the aspirations for children and young people will be raised through an increased focus on life outcomes, including employment and greater independence.
>
> (DfE 2015, p.11)

A widespread criticism of the previous arrangements in place for children with disabilities or an SEN was that it was hard to get a statement, and any transitions often meant starting from scratch again.

Summary of the SEN Code of Practice

- It is a fundamental principle of the SEN Code of Practice that children, parents and families have quick and easy access to professionals who can assess and establish if a child has a disability or SEN.
- Once a disability or SEN is indicated, the child or young person and their family will work with educational health and social services representatives to establish the child's Education and Health Care plan (EHC).
- The child and family can expect joint planning and commissioning of services to ensure there is close co-operation between education, health services and social care so all aspects of the child's needs are supported.
- The services Local Authorities (LA) must provide to ensure 'joined-up' provision for a child must be published by the LA through what is known as the 'local offer'.
- The LA local offer must set out in one place information about provision they expect to be available across education, health and social care for children and young people in their area who have SEN or are disabled, including those who do not have EHC plans.
- Most LAs set out their local offer on a dedicated part of their LA website.
- Young people and parents of children who have EHC plans have the right to request a Personal Budget, which may contain elements of education, social care and health funding.
- Any support accessed by children, young people and their families must be negotiated in participation with children, their parents and young people.
- It is a principle of the SEN Code of Practice (DfE 2015) that children and families are included in decision making and that there should be control for children, young people and families over the support and collaboration accepted from education, health and social care services.

- All support accepted should focus on inclusive practice and remove barriers to learning for the child or young person.
- Parent Carer Forums should be established in every local area.
- Families may receive help from an independent supporter, who will be recruited locally and trained to support families through the assessment process.

Source: DfE 2015

Activity – research the local offer in your Local Authority

All Local Authorities (LAs), are required to make information easily available to children, young people and families about their local offer of support for children and young people with disabilities and SEN. Most LAs have this information on their website. Search your LA's local offer online. It should include information about:

- How to request an assessment for an Education and Health Care plan (EHC)
- Arrangements for identifying and assessing children and young people's needs
- Education provision available, such as nurseries, playgroups, schools and colleges and support services like educational psychologists and SEN services
- Children's and adult health services, including GPs, therapists and hospital services
- Social care services, such as short break services and children's and adult disability services, including child care and leisure activities
- Travel and transport arrangements
- Transition support to help movement between different phases of education and life, from home to school at five, from primary to secondary school, from school to higher education, training or work
- Financial support that may be available, including the Disabled Student Allowance (DSA)
- Arrangements for resolving disagreements and for mediation.

Educational Health Care (EHC) plans and Personal Budgets

Once it has been agreed a child should receive an EHC, it will also be decided the Personal Budget that will be available to them. The Personal Budget is there to buy the support a child may need to enable them to achieve the best learning and well-being outcomes possible for them. It is a principle of the EHC and provision of Personal Budgets that the child and their family are involved in planning the spending of the Personal Budget.

Once the Personal Budget has been agreed it can be looked after by the local authority, school, or college. This is called an 'Arrangement' or a 'Notional Budget'. In other instances, the family, or child as they get older, can manage all or part of the Personal Budget themselves. The money to do this will come from a Direct Payment. In some instances, a Third Party Arrangement will be set up to manage the Personal Budget for the child; for example, if the child is a Looked After Child under the age of 16. Once a child becomes 16, they can ask for their own Personal Budget, at the end of the school year in which they become 16 (Kent.gov.uk 2016).

What does an EHC look like?

Usually the EHC is set out in the sections outlined below.

- *Section A* outlines the views and interests of the child and the aspirations of the child and their family. This section is sometimes labelled 'All about me' and will supply information about what the child likes to do, their health, schooling and friendships. Where appropriate, it must also have information about how to communicate with the child and how to engage them in decision making and outline the child or young person's history.
- *Section B* outlines the child's disability or special educational needs and the educational provision that needs to be made for them.
- *Section C* details any health care needs that the child may have relating to their SEN or disability.
- *Section D* outlines any particular social care needs which relate to their SEN or disability, including any child in need or child protection plans which may be in place.
- *Section E* discusses 'the outcomes sought for the child, over varying timescales, covering education, health and care as appropriate. This section should distinguish between outcomes and provision. The provision should help the child or young person achieve an outcome; it is not an outcome in itself. The principles require LAs to facilitate the development of the child or young person to achieve the "best possible" educational and other outcomes' (IPSEA 2016). This will include:

  o   How achievement of these outcomes will be monitored, including reviewing the EHC
  o   Transition review arrangements in place to ensure continuity between different settings a child might move between – for example, moving from one school to another
  o   The setting and monitoring of shorter-term targets which the Early Years provider or school might set.

- *Section F* details any additional support the child may need in the educational setting, including how many hours of support, the type and frequency of support, including where it is secured through a Personal Budget.

- *Section G* outlines any health provision reasonably required by the child and who will provide it; 'For example, occupational therapy and physiotherapy or other therapies, medical treatments and delivery of medications, a range of nursing support, specialist equipment, wheelchairs and continence supplies' (IPSEA 2016).
- *Sections H1/2* detail any social care provision the child may require; for example, adaptations to the home, transport needs, holidays and respite care. These sections will also include respite provision for parents who have a disabled child.
- *Section I* indicates the education setting that will best meet the needs of the child, be that a school or any other type of provision.
- *Section J* deals with what the Personal Budget is and how it can be best used to support the child.
- *Section K* outlines who provided the advice and information in writing-up the EHC and copies of all the advice and information gathered during the statutory assessment process should be attached to the EHC plan as appendices.

Source: Examples of completed EHC are available online at IPSEA 2016.

Scenario 2: Carrie

Adriana finds Roshan, St Mary's SENCo, after school and says she has heard about Carrie joining them soon. Adriana explains she has experience of working with children with Down's syndrome and would be happy to share her experience with other members of staff.

A couple of days later Roshan asks Adriana if she would like to support Carrie and her teacher when Carrie joins the school and 'yes, could Adriana do some staff training about Down's syndrome and supporting children with DS, at the staff meeting in three weeks?'

One of the first things Adriana organises is a home visit to Carrie. She takes with her the school's Welcome Pack, which is prepared for all children new to the school. It includes a booklet with pictures of the adults who work in the school, and the school building, cloakrooms, toilets and classrooms. It has pictures of children doing activities throughout the day – being in the playground, in assembly, hanging up their coats, learning in their classrooms and eating their lunch. Each picture has a caption, so Carrie and her family can go through the book whenever she wants.

Adriana has been able to have a telephone conversation with the school Carrie is currently attending and has been forwarded a copy of Carrie's EHC, so St Mary's already know a lot about how to support Carrie with her learning. During the visit, Adriana talks to Carrie and Carrie's mum about aspects of the EHC and how these will happen for Carrie at St Mary's. They have a long chat about Carrie's dancing and Carrie shows her photographs of her at dancing and of shows she has been in. Carrie is not very keen on the colour of the St Mary's school uniform, but she says she knows she'll get used to it. She also says she does not like PE because she does not like having to get changed, so Adriana makes a note of this – to remind her to think about a strategy for supporting Carrie at these times. Carrie's main concern is that she won't have her friend Jacqui with her and what will she do for friends? This is something else Adriana already has a plan for, since this is something that worries most children and adults when they are in a new situation and St Mary's has a well-organised friendship support strategy.

Carrie has a speech therapist who visits her at school and the same speech therapist will also visit her at St Mary's, so this provides some continuity. Adriana agrees with Carrie and her mum that Carrie's new class will be told about Carrie's condition and Down's syndrome before she arrives, and that Carrie will make an initial visit in the next two weeks.

Overall, things went well for Carrie joining her new school – there were a few times in the first half-term when not everything went according to plan, particularly one day when both Carrie's teacher and Adriana were unexpectedly absent on the same day, which upset Carrie as no one had thought to explain to Carrie what was happening. In discussion with Carrie's mum, St Mary's adopted a system that had worked well at her previous school. They developed an online home–school system to share information between home and school, about what has gone well and anything that has not gone so well both at home and at school. It's also easy to upload pictures to the system.

Source: Advice from the Down's Association 2016

Conclusion

To some extent, the largely deficit thinking and understanding about what the term 'disability' means that was inherited from the late nineteenth and first half of the twentieth centuries has been changing over the past few years. Arguably, there has been a positive impact on both wider societal perceptions of disability and how schools and educational settings work with disabled children and their families. The media coverage of 2012 and 2016 Paralympic Games is a good indication of how children and adults with disability are having an increasingly higher profile in mainstream society. In this way, the focus on disability is shifting from the deficit model of what a disability might mean in terms of what the child, or adult, *can't do*, to what they *can do*, this *can do* idea being the much celebrated theme of Channel 4's trailer for the 2016 Paralympics (Catchpole 2016). Catchpole, who is disabled, writes, 'as a film, it is pretty phenomenal. It's witty, slick, doesn't prettify disability, and the music is brilliant' (Catchpole 2016). Indeed the trailer, which depicted disabled athletes, dancers and musicians performing to high levels, was widely praised, both in terms of showing what disabled people *can do* and because the achievements depicted are, by any standards, certainly worthy of note.

However, in discussing the trailer and its theme of 'there's no such thing as can't' (Catchpole 2016), Catchpole reminds us that those shown in the trailer will, just as anyone who excels in their chosen field, have put much effort and practice into what they are excelling in. She is concerned that using terms such as 'superhero' in relation to Paralympians has a wash-back effect on other disabled children and adults for whom 'living well and happily with a disability is, I'd argue, about accepting the can'ts you have to accept, whether they are imposed by your own body or society, and navigating them in the best way you can' (Catchpole 2016). She goes on to write that 'creating a view of disabled people as magical creatures who might look impaired but actually – ta dah! – are as capable as anyone else, if not more so' (Catchpole 2016), creates a situation where society can feel good about what has already been achieved and forgets that there is still much to do to remove barriers to learning and participation, for those who are disabled and are *not* Paralympians, in day-to-day activities and experiences.

Therefore, having raised some of the key points around the subject of disability and including disabled children in schools and educational settings, the next two chapters look in more detail at a range of specific disabilities and neurodiversity conditions. Chapters 7 and 8 discuss dyslexia, dyspraxia, ADHD and autism, and explore how schools and education settings can continue to develop their practices to better support children with these conditions.

References

DfE (Department for Education) (2015) *Special Educational Needs and Disability Code of Practice: 0 to 25 years Statutory guidance for organisations which work with and support children and young people who have special educational needs or disabilities* DfE

DLF (Disabled Living Foundation) (2016) *Key Facts* www.dlf.org.uk/content/key-facts [accessed 24 July 2016]

Down's Association (2016) *About Down's Syndrome FAQs* www.downs-syndrome.org.uk/ [accessed 24 July 2016]

Catchpole, L. (2016) I love Channel 4's paralympics advert. But we can't all be superheroes www.theguardian.com/commentisfree/2016/jul/20/channel-4-paralympics-advert-disabled-people-not-all-superhuman [accessed 24 October 2016]

Goodley, D. (2013) Dis/entangling critical disability studies, *Disability & Society*, Vol. 28, No. 5, pp. 631–644 Routledge

Gov.uk (2016a) *Definition of Disability under the Equality Act 2010* www.gov.uk/definition-of-disability-under-equality-act-2010 [accessed 24 July 2016]

Gov.uk (2016b) Children with special educational needs and disabilities (SEND) https://www.gov.uk/children-with-special-educational-needs/overview [accessed 24 July 2016]

IPSEA (Independent Parental Special Educational Needs Advice) (2016) EHC plan checklist file:///C:/Users/knowl/Documents/SIP3[5]/MS%202016/Chapter%207%20GK/ipsea-ehc-plan-checklist-2015-april.pdf [accessed 25 July 2016]

Kent.gov.uk (2016) Personal budgets for Special Educational Needs (SEN) www.kent.gov.uk/__data/assets/pdf_file/0006/18735/IASK-personal-budgets-for-Special-Educational-Needs.pdf) [accessed 25 July 2016]

ONS (Office for National Statistics) (2015) *Harmonised Concepts and Questions for Social Data Sources Primary Principles* ONS

Reaume, G. (2014) Understanding critical disability studies, *Canadian Medical Association Journal*, Vol. 186, No. 16, p. 1248

SCOPE (2016) *The Social Model of Disability* www.scope.org.uk/about-us/our-brand/social-model-of-disability [accessed 24 July 2016]

Slorach, R. (2016) *A Very Capitalist Condition*. London: Bookmark Publications

WHO (World Health Organization) (2016) *Disabilities* www.who.int/topics/disabilities/en/[accessed 14 September 2016]

Chapter 7

Inclusion and neurodivergency

Gianna Knowles

This chapter explores:

- What is meant by the term neurodiversity and what it means to be neurodivergent
- Aspects of neurodivergency often recognised as: dyslexia, dyspraxia and ADHD
- How to remove barriers to learning for children with neurodivergent approaches to learning.

What is neurodiversity?

In discussing disability in Chapter 6 of this book, we explored what is meant by the term 'disability' and the tensions between medical and social models of disability. In discussing disability, we also explored how disabled children and adults can face barriers to their well-being and achievement because they are seen, usually by the able-bodied community, as being limited by their perceived disability. While, as Slorach writes, through 'successive innovations in medicine, science and technology' (Slorach 2016, p.11), disabled children and adults have been able to lead increasingly independent lives, this does not necessarily mean that they have also been able to take full advantage of the education provision on offer or to be accepted into the world of work. There are still barriers that prevent disabled children from achieving in educational settings, and there are many workplaces that still marginalise disabled workers, despite laws prohibiting discrimination. That barriers to learning and other forms of discrimination still exist is due more to the perceptions of the able-bodied, about the disabled, rather than because disabled children and adults are unable to learn or work.

Slorach and others (Goodley 2010; Silberman 2015) discuss how there has come to be a dominant notion of 'normal growth' and 'normal development' (also explored in Chapter 1), such that any physical or cognitive characteristics that do not seem to meet these criteria are seen as 'impairments' (Slorach 2016, p.12). Indeed, the current definition of disability in the UK states, 'You're disabled under the Equality Act 2010 if you have a physical or mental impairment that has a "substantial" and "long-term" negative effect on your ability to do normal daily activities' (Gov.uk 2016). However, increasingly, there is a growing realisation that the concept of 'normal' is artificial. It is helpful to be able to determine the particular support and help children and adults need, because of particular physical and cognitive characteristics they have – be that support medical, social, or educational. But to regard certain behaviours or characteristics as impairments and therefore limiting on what we might expect a child or adult to be able to do, does, of itself, act as a barrier to that individual's well-being and capacity to achieve.

In this way, the term 'neurodiversity' shows us that just as humans are diverse in terms of race and gender, so too are they diverse in their cognitive functions. Silberman defines neurodiversity as 'the notion that conditions like autism, dyslexia, and attention deficit hyperactivity disorder (ADHD), should be regarded as naturally occurring cognitive variations with distinctive strengths' (Silberman 2015, p.17). That is to say, it has been a dominant idea that there are 'normal' brains that should work in one particular way, and if an individual has a 'normal' brain they will learn in a linear, measurable and expected way, where their progress in learning will be in line with others of a similar age. In contrast, someone deemed to be dyslexic, for example, has an impaired or abnormal brain and will not be able to follow the same, prescribed developmental path.

Neurodiversity, on the other hand, argues that no two brains are alike and all have natural variations specific to the individual. Therefore, it is more useful to think about 'typical' cognitive function and 'atypical' to describe behaviours and characteristics of cognitive functioning that are expected, depending on the age and experience of the individual: 'Like biodiversity, which is seen as critical to the health of ecosystems, advocates of neurodiversity assert that neurological variation is not only natural, but is central to the success of the human species' (McGee 2012, p.12). This is an idea echoed by Murray who writes, 'Perhaps this diversity can make us stronger as a species, as communities . . . brains vary, and this can lead to variations in cognitive style which can be disabling, but also seem to play a role in some extraordinary abilities' (2016).

Defining and diagnosing specific conditions within neurodiversity

Having explored what the concept of neurodiversity might mean, the rest of this chapter will discuss in more detail a number of specific conditions that fall under the neurodiversity umbrella. The conditions discussed here – dyslexia, developmental coordination disorder (often discussed as dyspraxia) and ADHD (attention deficit hyperactivity disorder) – are by no means all the conditions we could look at. However, they are three of the most common that teachers and practitioners work with in educational settings.

The challenge with discussing conditions that fall under the neurodiversity umbrella is that, unlike a condition such as cystic fibrosis, where there is a much clearer understanding of exactly what cystic fibrosis is, the same is not true of neurodiversity conditions. When professionals, such as doctors, child psychologists and others, are involved in assessing children and deciding whether or not they have a particular neurodiversity condition, they will often refer to either the *ICD 10* or the *DSM-5*. The *ICD 10* is the *International Statistical Classification of Diseases and Related Health Problems 10th Revision*, issued by the World Health Organization (WHO 2010) and the *DSM-5* is the American Psychiatric Association's *Diagnostic and Statistical Manual of Mental Disorders – 5* (APA 2013). The advantage of these documents is that they provide an international and broadly agreed way of discussing and determining a range of physical and cognitive health and well-being conditions.

However, particularly with the *DSM-5*, there is disagreement with the way certain conditions are defined, particularly those relating to neurodiversity. Many, including professionals, object to the term 'disorder', since, as we have already discussed, the notion of 'normal' or 'typical' is, to a greater extent, a social construct. All characteristics and behaviours are along a continuum: some children and adults may have characteristics, or behave in ways, that present as atypical in particular situations but be completely typical in others. Therefore, in discussing neurodiversity conditions, we need to be aware that being able to label or define a condition is only part, albeit often a very helpful part, of the picture. For those working in educational settings with children who have a neurodiverse condition – or seem to have a proclivity for one – the important thing is to find ways of supporting them in their learning and achievement.

Dyslexia

The main presenting characteristic of what is termed 'dyslexia' is usually when a child is not making the same gains in developing reading, writing and spelling skills as their peer group. What is common to most children with dyslexia is that they find aspects of literacy challenging; however, no two children with dyslexia will have the same profile, in terms of what it is about reading, writing and spelling that is challenging for them (Reid 2013). What can be frustrating for the child and for those working with the child – and a reason that an assessment for dyslexia may be delayed – is that a child may learn to read in a typical way, but find spelling very challenging. Therefore, because the child can read, this will mask other aspects of literacy that are a challenge for them and, for this reason, children with dyslexia are often incorrectly labelled as 'lazy', or reprimanded, for example, for not learning their spellings, rather than being provided with the proper support to help with the specific area of challenge.

Typical indicators of dyslexia

Dyslexia will present differently in different children and the points below are offered as guidance in terms of characteristics that may indicate dyslexia – it is not a checklist for diagnosing a child as being dyslexic.

General possible indicators of dyslexia

The child may:

- Have family members who have been diagnosed as having dyslexia
- Understand new learning easily and be able to verbalise ideas, but their literacy levels will not be at the same level as their understanding
- Struggle to remember and carry out three instructions in a sequence, or learn sequences such as days of the week or the alphabet and/or have difficulties understanding time and tense
- Seem to lose concentration quickly and be excessively tired after a day at school
- Become easily anxious or frustrated and lack confidence

Specific literacy indicators

The child may:

- Have a good understanding of what is being read, but struggle to decode the words themselves, including finding it difficult to recognise or remember sounds (phonemes) in words, or substitute alternative words to the one in the text
- Be slow or hesitant when reading and not want to read aloud, or read a word once then seem to not recognise it later
- Find spelling challenging and be reluctant to write
- Write letters and numbers the wrong way round and have poor handwriting
- Find copying challenging and very tiring

Specific mathematics indicators

The child may:

- Find mental arithmetic and learning times tables very difficult; they may also struggle with mathematics terminology, for example, knowing when to add, subtract, or multiply.

Processing indicators

The child may:

- Struggle to understand sequences and patterns
- Muddle left and right
- Have difficulties with organisation

This list is not an assessment for dyslexia, it outlines characteristics and behaviours which, if a number of them are present, may require further investigation. Some of the items on the list may be due to a range of factors, so it is important that someone with expertise in the field follows up any initial observations.

Source: Adapted from Reid 2013

It must be remembered that 'dyslexia occurs within a continuum and . . . there can be shared overlapping characteristics between dyslexia and other specific learning difficulties' (Reid 2013, p.2), for example, with developmental coordination disorder and dyscalculia, so where it is recognised that a child seems to be experiencing challenges with their learning, these challenges may have a number of root causes. In this way, the term 'dyslexia' can be seen more as a 'convenience term' (Reid 2013), because it collects together under it a range of different types of difficulties, rather than being able to define a specific area of challenge. However, it can be helpful for children, families and educators to know if dyslexia is present, as it provides a starting point for devising an individualised programme to support a child with their learning.

In thinking about dyslexia, it is helpful to bear in mind two things. Firstly, being able to read, write and spell correctly is a discrete technical skill and while it is an important means of transmitting knowledge and understanding, it is not the knowledge and understanding itself. Secondly, it is important for social and educational reasons that a child can learn to read, write and spell correctly and aspects of these skills will present different challenges to different children with dyslexia. However, where the learning intention is *not* literacy – that is, the point of the learning activity is *not* to develop reading and writing skills – there are many other ways children can be engaged with learning.

Strategies to support a child with dyslexia

Collecting information

- Information can be presented through discussion and an increasingly wide range of audio and visual platforms, which do not have to be print based. Similarly, in terms of recording knowledge and understanding, children can use electronic, audio and visual ways of communicating and recording what they know.

Reading

- Where the learning must be print based – because it is a literacy activity, for example – some children find the use of colour helpful in working with the print. Some children respond well to coloured 'overlays' through which they can read the print. Others respond better by having the text printed, or copied onto coloured paper, or key words highlighted in various colours, clearly printed, with wide spacing.
- It can also help if any printed material is reinforced with additional audio and/or visual support.
- Before beginning to read, it may help to provide some context about what the print is about; if it is a story, explain the key characters and where the story takes place. While not wanting to 'spoil' surprises in the story by explaining those 'up front', reading the text to the child first – or pair-read with the child – will help, checking for comprehension along the way. If the child is just focusing on decoding the words, this may get in the way of comprehending what the print is conveying.
- Use picture clues to help with understanding the print.

Writing

- Lined paper and tablets
- Mind maps and writing frameworks to structure ideas

In addition, many children benefit from more structure.

Mind mapping

A mind map is a way of organising information and ideas visually, usually transforming something linear into a 'picture' or graphic representation. The special arrangement of the visual clues can show text relations, and represent other aspects of the organisation of the text. For example, if the text is a story, it might show the relations between characters and the order events happen in. In an instructional text, it would help to show the order in which instructions might be completed in.

Often the central theme is positioned in the middle of the page, from which several related main text ideas radiate out (Merchies and Van Keer 2016). In this way, the map represents the overall meaning of the text and the individual elements within it.

Some individuals prefer to deal with information in a traditional linear way – that is, how this book is presented, where you start reading at the beginning of a chapter and usually read through to the end. Others prefer to see the 'overall picture' of what the information looks like and the relationships between the different aspects of information being presented: 'The design and content arrangement of mind maps . . . can enhance text processing and learning' (Merchies and Van Keer 2016, p.129). As we have seen, different brains process and understand information in different ways; therefore a mind map is a way of presenting text-based information in a different format, requiring alternative processing procedures to linear-based text. The mind map draws on the 'interconnectedness of the verbal and visual system' (Merchies and Van Keer 2016, p.129) in the brain to support processing the necessary information.

Report writing – panda twins born in China's Sichuan Province

Simple mind map

This is an example of a simple mind map to help a child comprehend and respond to the information in the report below.

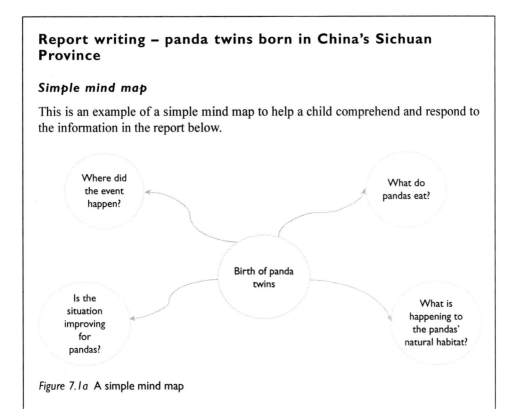

Figure 7.1a A simple mind map

Information presented in a linear format

Twin panda cubs, a male and a female, were born at a breeding research base in China's south-west Sichuan province on Tuesday. Mother Chenggong gave birth to the cubs early morning. CCTV showed footage of the newborns crawling in an incubator. It said they were both in good health.

Giant pandas, an endangered species, are in decline because of human activity destroying the areas in which they live in the highlands in south-western China. Pandas survive almost entirely on a diet of bamboo. However, according to the World Wildlife Fund, a 2014 census found 1,864 giant pandas living in the wild, almost double the number of the late 1970s (adapted from an online Reuters (2016) article).

Complex mind map

The mind map below is more complex, asking the child to research further information and form an opinion based on the information they have collected.

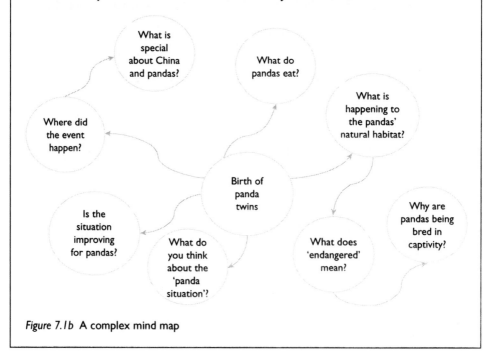

Figure 7.1b A complex mind map

Developmental coordination disorder – DCD and dyspraxia

Developmental coordination disorder (DCD) is the term used by the *DSM-5* (APA 2013) to describe 'a condition where a child has difficulties in learning everyday motor skills, which cannot be explained by physical, sensory or intellectual impairment' (Movement Matters 2016). DCD is often used interchangeably with the term 'dyspraxia', which can be misleading. Unlike dyspraxia, 'DCD has an internationally agreed definition' (Movement Matters 2016), which dyspraxia does not.

The Dyspraxia Foundation defines dyspraxia as:

> . . . a form of developmental coordination disorder (DCD) . . . affecting fine and/or gross motor coordination . . . DCD is often regarded as an umbrella term to cover motor coordination difficulties, dyspraxia refers to those people who have additional problems planning, organising and carrying out movements in the right order in everyday situations. Dyspraxia can also affect articulation and speech, perception and thought.
>
> (Dyspraxia Foundation 2013)

The Dyspraxia Foundation states that a child who has dyspraxia shows atypical characteristics with fine and/or gross motor coordination. Gross motor skills are those that relate to the coordination of the whole body – walking, running, jumping and rolling over, for example. Fine motor skills use the small muscles of the fingers, toes, wrists, lips, and tongue and are to do with picking things up, holding objects – spoons and forks, for example – and, where the lips and tongue are concerned, talking. Further indicators of possible dyspraxia may be when children experience challenges, 'with self-care, writing, typing, riding a bike and play' (Dyspraxia Foundation 2016).

Children who may have been diagnosed as having the more specific condition of developmental coordination disorder will display many of the characteristics and behaviours of the children we have just discussed; however, DCD, it is argued (Movement Matters 2016), relates specifically to atypical development with motor skills, whereas dyspraxia is a wider term that also encompasses 'many non-motor difficulties . . . memory, perception and processing as well as additional problems with planning, organising and carrying out movements in the right order in everyday situations. Dyspraxia can also affect articulation and speech' (Dyspraxia Foundation 2016).

Children with dyspraxia may also experience challenges with 'memory, perception and processing' (Dyspraxia Foundation 2016). As with dyslexia, the term 'dyspraxia' is no one thing and no two children who have dyspraxia will present in the same way; it is more a term that covers atypical characteristics and behaviours that relate to the physical and cognitive functions listed and may include 'attention, emotional self-regulation, anxiety, short term and working memory challenges' (Skills for Action 2016). Dyspraxia is thought to be caused by 'the way in which the brain forms connections . . . between different parts of the brain when learning a new skill' (Skills for Action 2016).

There are a number of medical and neurological conditions that can also impact on gross and fine motor skills; for example, cerebral palsy, muscular dystrophy and hemiplegia. So, as with any atypical behaviours or characteristics a child displays, it is important to have an expert opinion to determine what exactly seems to be happening for the child.

Possible indicators of dyspraxia

Children in the early years

Particular care in ascribing specific conditions to very young children is always cautioned since children develop at different rates, for all sorts of reasons. However, if a child is particularly late in reaching developmental milestones such as rolling over, sitting, standing, walking and speaking, then these indicators along with others listed here may signal dyspraxia.

Other indicators of dyspraxia in young children might include being unable to run, hop, jump, or catch or kick a ball, and other gross-motor skills such as dressing. Children with dyspraxia may struggle with concepts such as 'in', 'on' and 'in front of', and with activities such as putting together jigsaws. They may find it difficult to make and keep friends and be anxious or easily distracted.

Children in KS1 and 2

As children with dyspraxia get older, they will still be challenged by the indicators already discussed and they may have developed strategies to help them avoid certain situations, like doing PE, for example. Other indicators might be that the child:

- May have trouble with maths and writing structured stories
- Experiences great difficulty in copying
- Writes laboriously and immaturely
- Is unable to remember and/or follow instructions and is generally poorly organised.

Sources: Dyspraxia Foundation 2016; Skills for Action 2016

Scenario 1: Paolo

In PE, the children are doing gymnastics and working on different types of jumps and jumping in and out of hoops on the ground. Paolo, age 5, can jump up and down, but he is struggling to jump 'into' the hoop. Some other children initially found this challenging too, but through trial and error they have seemed to naturally workout how to jump into and out of the hoop. Paolo gets frustrated and blames the hoop.

The teaching assistant knows Paolo is likely to struggle with this activity and goes over to support him. She asks Paolo's friend to come and be Paolo's partner and starts by asking them to step into the hoop from opposite sides and 'bump tummies'. She gives them lots of praise and encouragement and they all laugh when the boys do 'bump tummies'. The laughter has reduced Paolo's anxiety and frustration and he is much happier to work with his friend and the TA on the activity.

'Research shows visually fixing on a target helps with motor planning' (Skills for Action 2016), and now Paolo has a better sense of where he is aiming for. After a few more jumping attempts, including jumping with linked arms with his friend, Paolo is successful in jumping into the hoop by himself. He is delighted with his success, as are his friend and the TA, and 'this brief burst of elation helps the brain to register the connection between the intended action, the motor plan and the successful achievement of the goal' (Skills for Action 2016).

Attention deficit hyperactivity disorder (ADHD)

Recognising ADHD

ADHD is defined as being present where there is a triad of inattention and/or hyperactivity-impulsivity behaviours:

- *Predominantly inattentive type* – This is characterised by the capacity to be easily distracted and unable to ignore distractions other children can 'screen out'. The child struggles to stay on tasks, does not seem able to organise themselves, or listen and pay attention, and may make frequent mistakes in any independent learning activity they are engaged in.
- *Predominantly hyperactive-impulsive type* – Characteristics of this form of ADHD include restless 'fidgety' and 'chatty' behaviours, struggling to remain seated and impulsively calling out, struggling in turn-taking and constantly interrupting.
- *Combined inattention and hyperactivity type* – This is the most common type of ADHD and will combine both the inattentive and hyperactive, impulsive behaviours.

For it to be confirmed that ADHD is present the child must have been exhibiting several of the symptoms listed before they are 12 years old (Kutscher 2014), and the *DSM-5* recommends before age 7 (Kutscher 2014). Many children will exhibit some of these behaviours at some point, but for a child with ADHD their behaviour will 'interfere with overall life functioning, and occur in at least two settings (such as home, school)' or at an activity club, such as dance, or football, for example (Kutscher 2014, p.53).

Sources: Kutscher 2014; RCP 2016; ADHD Foundation 2016

While the predominant characteristics of ADHD are inattention and restlessness and the need to be 'off and doing' things, rather than sitting down, when a child with ADHD is engaged in an activity that they are interested in, then they do have the capacity to pay attention and be less restless. For example, a child may be engaged in playing with a particular toy, or at a games console in the same way a more typical child will. However, if a child with ADHD is engaged in an activity they find less interesting, they will be seemingly less attentive and more easily diverted by environmental distractions, by other children in the class being engaged in a different activity to the one they are doing, by something going on outside in the playground, or by thinking about something they watched on television the previous night.

However, current thinking suggests these behaviours may not be due to being inattentive, and occur because the child cannot 'screen-out' general distractions in the way other children can. That is, ADHD can be defined 'as a deficiency of inhibition, not a deficiency of attention span' (Kutscher 2014, p. 53). Kutscher (2014) calls this being 'brakeless' – that is, the child cannot stop, or put the brake on in certain situations. Therefore, if we think of ADHD in this way, the main presenting characteristics of ADHD might look like this:

- Inattention – unable to stop being distracted
- Impulsive – unable to stop internal thoughts and ideas
- Hyperactive – unable to stop acting on distractions and internal ideas (Kutscher 2014).

Kutscher discusses how children with ADHD fail to apply the brakes, or are uninhibited in some behaviours, where others would 'hold back', because the frontal and pre-frontal lobes of the brains of the child with ADHD are 'under-functioning' (Kutscher 2014, p.56). The frontal and pre-frontal lobes are the parts of the brain that stop the system from being flooded by sensory information and allow time (which might be only a few seconds, if that) in which options can be considered before taking action.

Self-regulating mechanisms

The inability to inhibit – often seen as the classic defining characteristic of ADHD, is the lack of the ability to inhibit or stop certain behaviours. The capacity to be unable to 'put the brakes on' means that children with ADHD may not be able to stop certain behaviours and this will have a knock-on effect on other self-regulating behaviours; some of these are discussed below:

- *Foresight* – This concerns the ability to predict the future, which includes planning for the future and understanding the consequences of actions. This becomes less easy to manage as the child grows older: many young children have not yet developed foresight, but as children get older and become young adults, the need to be able to plan for the future becomes more important.
- *Hindsight* – This is about the capacity to learn from our mistakes. Without hindsight, we are likely to keep repeating the same mistakes, rather than learning from them and avoiding the same mistakes in the future.
- *Self-talk* – We work through our choices by thinking things through. For very young children, this can actually involve speaking aloud. However, without the capacity to think about and 'weigh up' the pros and cons of the choices on offer, the choices that are made will be impetuous, rather than rational, and therefore may end up being the wrong choices.
- *Working memory* – This is the capacity to manage different aspects of information all at once. For example, in order to make a decision, it is necessary to 'self-talk' the possible outcomes of the decision and to draw on foresight and hindsight to think through what might happen if this decision is made and what happened last time.

- *Prospective memory* – Kutscher calls this a relatively newly formed term for the ability to 'remember to remember' (Kutscher 2014, p.57). For example, a child may have homework and typically children will plan doing it into their week and other activities, but will first have to remember that it actually needs doing.
- *Problem solving* – This is particularly challenging for a child with ADHD, since again being able to solve problems also requires planning, foresight and hindsight.

Strategies to support children with ADHD

Supporting children with ADHD

As with all children, the best way of supporting them is to find out something about the child. Indicators of neurodiversity conditions, such as the indicators listed above, are useful starting points when talking to a child about what they would like help with.

Some schools and educational settings use the 'passport' technique to help the child record what they are good at and what help they need. They carry their 'passports' with them, so adults new to working with them will know how best to support the child.

Below are some ideas for what a passport might contain:

- I am very good at football, I am the striker for our team and I support Manchester United.
- I can concentrate for a while and then I can get distracted. Sometimes I may appear to not be listening. I learn better if my learning is in five- or ten- minute 'chunks', and I can do something active between each chunk, like sending me on an errand, or letting me run round the playground.
- I might shout out answers or interrupt the teacher because I am worried if I wait for the teacher to notice me, I may have forgotten the answers. It helps if the teacher tells me she is going to ask me a question. Or the question she is asking, I am not expected to answer.
- It can help if I can talk to someone like a teaching assistant, as it means I don't have to hold in my ideas/words for too long.
- It helps to provide instructions individually to me so that I have to focus in on what is being said. Sometimes a card or visual clues can be helpful.
- I can concentrate better if I have clear instructions and there aren't too many instructions all in one go.

- I know I have ADHD and sometimes the other children laugh at me, particularly when some adults don't understand how to help me concentrate or stop calling out. However, sometimes teachers choose someone to run around the playground with me, and then I'm really popular and people want to help me.
- When I have to go somewhere new, or meet new people, it really helps if someone tells me what to expect and practices with me what might happen and what I could say.

Source: www.wellatschool.org/help-at-school-adhd

Treating ADHD with drug therapy

While ADHD can be managed through a range of behaviour and family support strategies, in some instances children with ADHD are prescribed medication: 'The most commonly prescribed drugs are methylphenidate (Ritalin) and dexamphetamine (Dexedrine)' (Young Minds 2016). However, the medication for ADHD can have side effects and should only be given to children after it has been prescribed by and is managed by a specialist and 'should always be taken as part of a treatment package based on the child's individual needs' (Young Minds 2016).

Scenario 2: Somy

Somy is a very bubbly, outgoing and bright 10-year-old girl. However, she sometimes does silly and potentially dangerous things to make her friends laugh, and sometimes her friends fall out with her because she's too noisy and impetuous and they get in trouble with her when she annoys the teacher.

However, the school have recently worked hard with Somy to help her and the adults and children around her sort out strategies that help her learn and enjoy school. When presented with choices, like what to do at playtime, Somy's friends will help her make decisions about games they might play, rather than doing the first thing she thinks of, which can be running in to join a game of football without being invited or asking to join in the usual way. This upsets others and has caused fights.

Somy is very good at maths and often used to shout out the answers to questions the teacher asked. Now she sits with a TA, or has her own mini whiteboard so she can tell the TA the answer, or write it down, rather than calling out. Now that the school has recognised how good she is at maths, she is given more challenging work which keeps her occupied, whereas before she would race through the work and get bored and disruptive. She has also earned the respect of the other children for her high ability in maths.

Written work is more challenging for Somy and she can become easily distracted. Breaking up the task and giving her focused tasks to complete in short time frames, usually about five minutes, can help Somy. She also works better if she is very clear about what is expected of her and will often concentrate for longer if she works on a computer. The school have also devised an agreed range of 'break-out' activities Somy can do, once she completes a task. These can vary from taking messages to other classes to feeding the school's pet rabbits. She also likes the school's buddy reading initiative, where older children share books with younger children.

No two children who have a neurodiversity condition will manifest their needs in the same way. While there are certain indicators in a child's behaviour that will suggest a dominant condition, children may show characteristics across a range of conditions. As with all aspects of inclusive practice, the most important things is for those working with the child to try a range of strategies to find those that work for the child and support the child in their learning. While initially this may require trial and error, once strategies which do support the child have been found, it is important that this information is accessible to all concerned with the child and that the information is passed on as the child moves through the school or to another school. It is also important for the school or educational setting to work closely with the child's family as they will have very detailed experience, knowledge and understanding of the child and will know what 'works' and what the child finds upsetting or frustrating.

References

ADHD Foundation (2016) What is ADHD www.adhdfoundation.org.uk/whatisadhd.php [accessed 14 August 2016]

APA (American Psychiatric Association) (2013) *Diagnostic and Statistical Manual of Mental Disorders*, 5th ed. American Psychiatric Publishing

Dyspraxia Foundation (2013) Dyspraxia in children www.dyspraxiafoundation.org.uk/dyspraxia-children/ [accessed 14 August 2016]

Dyspraxia Foundation (2016) What is dyspraxia? www.dyspraxiafoundation.org.uk/about-dyspraxia/ [accessed 12 August 2016]

Goodley, D. (2010) *Disability Studies: An Interdisciplinary Introduction.* Sage

Gov.UK (2016) *Definition of disability under the Equality Act 2010* www.gov.uk/definition-of-disability-under-equality-act-2010 [accessed 24 July 2016]

Kutscher, M. L. (2014) *Kids in the Syndrome Mix of ADHD, LD, Autism Spectrum, Tourette's, Anxiety and More!: the one stop-guide for parents, teachers and other professionals*, 2nd ed. Jessica Kingsley Publishers

McGee, N. (2012) Neurodiversity contexts, *American Sociological Association* 11(3), 12–13 Sage Publications

Merchies, E., and Van Keer, H. (2016) Mind mapping as a meta-learning strategy: Stimulating pre-adolescents' text-learning strategies and performance? *Contemporary Educational Psychology* 46(2016), 128–147

Movement Matters (2016) *FAQs* www.movementmattersuk.org/dcd-dyspraxia-adhd-spld/developmental-disorders-documentation/frequently-asked-questions.aspx [accessed 12 August 2016]

Murray, F (2016) *Neurodiversity and Mental Health* www. medium.com/@Oolong/neurodiversity-and-mental-health-bed479fa74c6#.4glj0qh8z [accessed 11 August 2016]

Reid, G. (2013) *Dyslexia and Inclusion*, 2nd ed. Routledge

Reuters (2016) Panda twins born in China's Sichuan province www.reuters.com/article/us-wildlife-pandas-idUSKCN10K1EH [accessed 12 August 2016]

RCP (Royal College of Psychiatrists) (2016) *Attention Deficit Hyperactivity Disorder (ADHD) in Adults* www.rcpsych.ac.uk/healthadvice/problemsdisorders/adhdinadults.aspx [accessed 14 August 2016]

Silberman, S. (2015) *Neurotribes: The legacy of autism and the future of neurodiversity*. Allen and Unwin

Skills for Action (2016) *Developmental Coordination Disorder/Dyspraxia* www.skillsforaction.com/DCD-and-dyspraxia [accessed 12 August 2016]

Slorach, R. (2016) *A Very Capitalist Condition*. London: Bookmark Publications

WHO (World Health Organization) (2010) *International Statistical Classification of Diseases and Related Health Problems*, 10th revision www.who.int/classifications/icd/en/ [accessed 14 August 2016]

Young Minds (2016) Getting help www.youngminds.org.uk/for_parents/worried_about_your_child/adhd/support [accessed 14 August 2016]

Chapter 8

Supporting the inclusion of autistic children

Nicola Martin and Damian Milton

This chapter explores:

- What is the autism spectrum?
- How autism is about a different way of thinking
- Autism and sensory processing and stress and anxiety
- Autism, social interaction and Theory of Mind
- Autism, communication and language
- Managing transitions for autistic children
- Strategies to support the inclusion of autistic children.

This chapter aims to reflect that autism is a spectrum condition, that every individual is different and that people change over time. Authentic views of people on the spectrum and their families underpin discussion of autism theory and its relationship to practice. While the focus is on education (at any age), good practice recommendations embedded in this chapter apply in other contexts and could also help to foster inclusive practice for people without an autism diagnosis.

Autism is usually identified by observational forms of diagnosis involving the child and the family. Girls are often diagnosed later than boys and the spectrum is wide, encompassing nonverbal people, with and without additional learning disabilities, as well as highly successful employed graduates. As children grow into adults, characteristics associated with autism may become less obvious and support requirements will change. Identification of autism in adulthood is becoming more common, although the issue of who pays is contentious and post-diagnostic support is usually minimal. Principles associated with good autism practice will be relevant across the lifespan.

This chapter aims to foster an empathic understanding of what it might be like to be autistic with a view to helping practitioners to create autism-friendly learning environments. Autistic people and their families are increasingly present in all forms of media and this is a bit of a mixed blessing. Scare stories about what might cause autism gained prominence around the MMR vaccination debate and the consequences have been problematic (not least because of the rise of measles, due to the decrease in vaccinations). Contrary to what the papers say, there isn't an autism epidemic. However, the number of people being identified as being on the autism spectrum is increasing, primarily because of a changing recognition of what autism is and what it means to be autistic. Once thought to be a rare condition, the definition of autism was widened by the introduction of the notion of the 'autism spectrum' (Wing and Gould 1979). Estimating the numbers of autistic people within society is thus not an easy task, yet a figure of more than one in a hundred is cited by the National Autistic Society (UK's leading autism charity). As public awareness is increasing and while access to diagnosis in adulthood is patchy at best, many older people have identified with what they have heard or seen, and have 'self-identified'. Historical under-identification of girls and women (who are thought often to present more subtly than males on the spectrum) appears to be being rectified to an extent. Family life often revolves around the requirements of the autistic child or children and families may need practical non-judgemental backup from a range of services. Practitioners are also reminded that parents are in it for the long haul, while teachers and other professionals are just passing through.

The Children and Families Act (CFA) (2014) was conceived with the aim of joining up access to health, social care and education services for young people up to the age of 25 identified with Special Educational Needs and Disabilities (SEND). Only those with the most complex requirements access a full Educational Health and Care Plan (EHCP). Usually additional intellectual impairment as well as autism would be the trigger, but schools and colleges do have responsibility for pupils and students who do not reach the EHCP threshold and still need help. Transitions are notoriously problematic for people on the spectrum, so the extension to age 25 is good news. Although progress to further education and employment is specified, this rather implies that university has not been considered as a possible option, even though the number of students with autism in higher education is on the increase.

Pupil and parental engagement are central to the principles which underpin the CFA. Practical means by which all autistic children and young people can make their views known need to be found, including those who communicate unconventionally for adults. The Autism Act 2009 and the Adult Autism Strategy (2010), similarly aim to take a more joined-up view of support. Access to Work funding exists to help with employment and the Disabled Student Allowance is still in place in higher education. However, at the time of writing, all disability benefits are under threat, graduates on the autism spectrum are frequently unemployed, and the Autism Act and Adult Autism Strategy have not necessarily had the impact that was anticipated. People on the spectrum are increasingly advocating for themselves and organising, often via the Internet. Research informed by the principle 'nothing about us without us' enables policy makers to flex their empathy muscles a little bit and see the world to a greater extent through the eyes of autistic people. We also have the 2010 Equality Act – lest we forget.

Traditionally, the education of autistic people has been dominated by behavioural and cognitive approaches, some of which have been criticised, particularly by autistic authors (Milton 2014). A recent increase is apparent in strategies based on relational or developmental concerns and focusing more on working with identifying requirements arising from autistic learning styles, rather than attempting to remediate perceived skills deficits. Some of these approaches are reviewed here. The authors emphasise an inclusive, person-centred ethos and urge readers to keep individuality in mind. If you have met one autistic person or child, you have met one autistic person or child.

A recent study in the preferred use of language by various stakeholders within the wider autism community found that autistic people generally had a preference for identity-first language, whilst parents and professionals tended to like being 'on the spectrum' (Kenny et al. 2015). Both terms are used here and the unpopular words ('deficit' and 'disorder') are avoided, unless directly quoted.

What is the autism spectrum?

Autism is clinically defined as a neuro-developmental disorder, signified by deficits in social interaction and communication, coupled with the presence of repetitive behaviours and adherence to routines (WHO 1992; APA 2014). Some autistic people have significant learning disabilities. A 'spiky profile' is usual, with some showing significant areas of interest and ability and other areas of difficulty. Widening diagnostic criteria has led to an ever-growing number of verbally articulate people being diagnosed. In recent decades, a welcome rise of autistic writers, scholars and self-advocacy groups has led to informed critique of traditional notions of autism and what it means to be autistic.

A different way of thinking

Central to the majority of accounts of autism are descriptions of autistic cognition; in particular, explanations for the repetitive behaviours and routines which form part of the diagnostic criteria. A number of theoretical models have been devised in order to try and explain such observed patterns, the most significant being theories regarding executive functioning, a weak drive toward central coherence, and monotropism (Baron-Cohen 2008; Milton 2012b).

The term 'executive functioning' is used by psychologists when referring to the employment of planning or problem-solving abilities in order to attain a goal. Autistic people are often thought to have difficulties with executive function, as well as in switching attention between tasks. However, within areas of interest and strength, many are able to show skills associated with executive functioning, suggesting that differences exist in the way autistic executive processing operates. Happe (1994) theorised that executive functioning did not adequately explain areas of strength found within the autistic cognitive profile, such as an eye for detail, as evidenced by higher than average performance on tasks such as the block design task (Shah and Frith 1993). Differences are not necessarily deficits and the use of the expression 'executive function deficit' as a catch-all has been criticised by autistic scholars who reject the deficit model.

A weak drive toward central coherence was highlighted by Happe (1994) and associated with difficulties processing overall contextual meanings, whilst simultaneously having strengths in processing aspects or details within an overall context, something Vermeulen (2015) refers to similarly as 'context blindness'. However, many autistic people can demonstrate that they process gist meanings and conceptual abstractions, so the notion of 'a weak drive to central coherence' is not always applicable. Autistic scholars such as Dinah Murray, Mike Lesser and Wenn Lawson developed the term 'monotropism' to describe a different way of looking at autistic cognition and processing (Murray 1992; Murray et al. 2005; Lawson 2010). Monotropism is characterised by atypical distribution of attention and interest. Accordingly, the amount of attention available to a child or adult is limited and differing cognitive processes compete for this scarce resource. Murray and colleagues (2005) suggest that many autistic people prefer to concentrate attention on a small number of interests. Social interaction, language use and shifting attention are all tasks that require the broad use of attention and interest and challenge many people on the spectrum: 'We suggest that the uneven skills profile in autism depends on which interests have been fired into monotropic superdrive and which have been left unstimulated by any felt experience' (Murray et al. 2005: 143).

The 'spiky profile' is a term frequently associated with autistic people and reflects a strikingly uneven pattern. Higher levels of ability and confidence are often associated with areas of special interest which is hardly surprising because of the tendency to focus on these in depth (Kenny et al. 2015), and autistic scholars caution against terms like 'low' or 'high' functioning, as their use does not reflect the 'spiky profile'. Such a label can result in the needs of more verbal autistic people and the strengths of those who are less verbal going unrecognised, highlighting again the need to communicate with autistic individuals on their terms. Whilst specialist interests are very common across the spectrum, it is a myth to think that 'savant skills' are common or only found amongst autistic people (Arnold 2010). Grandin (1995) argues that autistic interests and ways of thinking can be utilised as the basis of employment and meaningful occupation. Utilising a child's interests within a learning environment can also be highly motivating and calming as well as a source of joy.

Scenario 1: Michael

Michael is 9 years old and he loves everything about Lego. He likes building with it, sorting it, counting it, drawing it and even writing stories about his Lego people. He has a teacher who thinks he should be interested in things that are not Lego. His mum and dad and his little sister think Lego is just fine. They are impressed by Michael's ability to create with Lego.

Lego is Michael's main interest. His teacher has a plan. If he completes the work she sets him, although he finds it tedious and unmotivating and takes what feels to Michael like large amounts of time, then he can play with a Lego man for five minutes.

However, she has decided he cannot take a Lego man into assembly because if Michael did this, everyone else would want to. Michael does not like the teacher's plan and his mum did not appreciate Lego being described as an 'obsession' in the Annual Review. Michael was very happy to get Lego from everyone in the family for his birthday.

Working with a child's interest

From what we have already learnt about autism, it is clear from this scenario that Michael's teacher is struggling to understand that she needs to communicate with Michael *on his terms* about his interest in Lego. A more supportive and inclusive approach for Michael would involve the teacher using Michael's interest in Lego to motivate and support him in undertaking the learning and other school activities she has planned for him.

Many children find going into a large assembly hall with lots of other children and adults intimidating, noisy and overwhelming. Failing to understand what Michael, in particular, needs to support him through situations he finds challenging will cause Michael upset. It may also make the teacher feel frustrated that she is seen as being unable to 'manage' the situation. By understanding that Michael's behaviour is not an act of defiance against the teacher, and perhaps through seeking advice, she will find more appropriate ways of supporting Michael. As the National Autistic Society says, what autistic children need is 'effective supporters will be endowed with the personal attributes of calmness, predictability and good humour, empathy and an analytical disposition' (NAS 2016).

Sensory processing

Sensory sensitivities have been reported by autistic people for many years (Grandin 1986). However, the inclusion of sensory processing differences into diagnostic criteria for the first time in the most recent edition of *Diagnostic and Statistical Manual of Mental Disorders (DSM-V)* (APA 2014) has been controversial, because sometimes non-autistic people have sensory issues too. Experiences of sensory processing can vary greatly between differing accounts by autistic people, with both 'hyper' and 'hypo' (or under) sensitivity to sensory stimuli. Sensory responses vary between individuals and may be context specific. Sensory fragmentation or a difficulty in integrating incoming sensory information, is commonly described by autistic people, with some reporting 'synaesthesia' and sensory information becoming entangled (Tammet 2006).

The more obvious sensory modalities are sound, sight, smell, touch and taste, but things like perception of one's own body position and balance and interpreting feelings of pain or temperature, difficulty with coordination and motor-planning may also pose challenges. There is a high incidence of dyspraxia amongst the autistic population. Struggling to process incoming sensory information can lead to overload, affecting levels of stress and potentially creating anxiety. A general low-arousal approach can be effective, as can sensory aides such as noise-cancelling headphones (Caldwell 2014). There is no credible evidence for the effectiveness of techniques looking to 'desensitise' autistic people. It is also worth remembering that heightened sensory experiences can be a source of fun for some. It is necessary to understand what is going on for the individual; a 'one size fits all' approach will not do.

Scenario 2: Michael

Michael's teacher has taken his Lego away. He is now 10 years old and Lego is still his main interest. Michael is in the playground and everyone is running about. It is really hot and sunny, and the sunlight is reflecting off the shiny surface of the fence. Another boy is scraping a stick along the railings. Three children are swerving close to Michael playing aeroplanes. Nobody invites him to join in and he has his hands over his ears and his hood up, even though it is hot. He is not very happy and is just trying to keep out of the way.

Michael puts his hand in his pocket and – oh joy! – Lego man is there. He sits on a bench in a quiet place and holds Lego man close to his face and wobbles him by his eye. That feels better. Michael's Teaching Assistant comes up to him and takes Lego man away because he's not supposed to have Lego in the playground. She says he can have him back at the end of the day if he 'joins in nicely for the rest of playtime'.

A number of sensory audit tools have been produced, some with input from autistic people (Attfield et al. 2012). It's worth looking at some of these resources. It would also be helpful to try and empathise with the experience of someone who has sensory sensitivities when trying to design learning environments.

Learning environments and sensory stimulation

Look around the setting in which you work. Is it:

* Noisy, crowded, chaotic and extremely visually stimulating?
* Are people racing about?
* Is it unpredictable?
* Would it be helpful to create some more tranquil, ordered and predictable spaces?
* Who might benefit?
* Is this just an 'autism thing' or might it help others too?

Research ways in which learning environments can be designed to support children who can find them noisy and overwhelming places.

Stress and anxiety

'Everyday experiences' can become highly stressful and anxiety-raising for some autistic people, whose senses become overwhelmed in their struggle to deal with an excess of information. Emotionally meaningful information may make overload more likely. The result can be a response often described as a 'meltdown', which presents as a sort of emotional outburst. An autistic child or adult may also react by 'shutting down' and being under-responsive while focusing attention on whatever is causing them stress, at the expense of being able to process more general information. Panic attacks are not uncommon. When an individual is in a state of ongoing chronic stress, it does not take much to 'tip them over the edge', and so autistic people are often already managing extremely well with high levels of stress and anxiety before additional demands on their attention are added. When meltdown, shutdowns and panic attacks appear to have no apparent environmental antecedent, it's worth exploring whether the autistic child or adult has experienced a build-up of stressful events before the 'presenting incident'. The term 'challenging behaviour' can be very unhelpful when applied to autistic people, especially when there may be a lack of understanding and respect for why an autistic child or adult may need to be acting in the way that they are.

A low-arousal approach is often effective as a means of reducing potential stressors and overload. However, low arousal does not mean 'no arousal', as some sensory experiences can be fun and conducive to learning. A calm empathic approach is vital, both to reduce the risk of meltdown or shutdown and when intervening. Identifying and reducing external stressors is an appropriate response if a meltdown or shutdown has occurred and, ideally, to avoid them happening in the first place. These factors will be particular to the individual and may well involve the behaviour of other people. An attempt to engage with something predictable and comforting to the autistic child or adult can be helpful once calm has been restored. Intervening without understanding in an authoritarian way when someone is already agitated is unethical and likely to be ineffective. An opportunity to reflect on an incident may be possible when the autistic child or adult is calm, but will not be helpful otherwise.

Social interaction

The idea of Theory of Mind (ToM) attempts to theorise and explain the difficulties autistic people experience around interacting socially with others. ToM is explained in terms of the ability to empathise with other people and imagine what they might be thinking and feeling, in order to comprehend and predict their actions. Wing (1996) suggested that autistic people have impaired 'social imagination' (linked to aforementioned 'context blindness'). For Hobson (2002), ToM forms the basis of symbolic thought and the development of imagination.

Milton (2012a) poses an alternative argument which suggests that rather than seeing the breakdown in interaction between autistic and non-autistic people as solely located in the mind of the autistic child or adult, a 'double empathy problem' exists between the two parties, largely due to the differing perspectives of those attempting to interact with one another. Drawing upon the sociological theories of Erving Goffman and Harold Garfinkel, Milton (2012a) suggests that the social subtext of a social situation is never a given, but negotiated in practice in the interactions between people. When people of widely differing dispositions (both biologically and culturally) interact, both will have a difficulty in under-standing the other. This theory is particularly pertinent when considering the teaching of social skills and social rules in explicit ways. As much social life is understood tacitly, mutual understanding and rapport needs to be built, rather than simply imposing a normative interpretation of social contexts and interactions onto autistic people (Milton 2014). As Williams has written:

> I had virtually no socially shared nor consciously, intentionally expressed, personhood beyond this performance of a non-autistic 'normality' with which I had neither compre-hension, connection, nor identification. This disconnected constructed facade was accepted by the world around me when my true and connected self was not. Each spoonful of its acceptance was a shovel full of dirt on the coffin in which my real self was being buried alive . . . .
>
> (1996: 243)

Given differences in ways of processing information, various social contexts can become very tricky to navigate, even without additional communication difficulties or learning disabilities. Gaining mutual rapport and a flow within social interaction is not the sole responsibility of one child or adult. Empathy is a two-way street and it would be very helpful if people tried to see things from the perspective of the autistic child or adult. Rather than interpreting autistic people as being overly 'rigid' in their manner and pursuit of interests, such tendencies could be understood as providing predictability and stability in an otherwise chaotic and fragmented experience. When considering the need for predictability, unfor-tunately other children and adults can be very unpredictable and can increase stress and anxiety. Gentle and structured play may help build interactions between autistic pupils and their peers. Rather than assuming that the autism creates a number of problems in need of fixing, a child-centred pedagogy could be focused on helping the autistic child to gain recognition of themselves and their own capacities. At any age, working with the autistic child or adult and not against their autism, is more likely to be productive and is undoubtedly more humane.

Communication and language

Building communication is a two-way process, involving shifting relationships, tacit under-standing, and changing social environments. Given different ways of thinking and processing sensory information, it is little wonder that many autistic people struggle with aspects of communication, including the assumed need for making eye contact, or conversational turn-taking. Jordan and Powell (1990) argue that superficially 'good' language skills can mask more subtle difficulties in communication.

Visual communication aides can help some individuals but not every autistic child or adult learns well from visual materials, particularly those which are symbolic and abstract in nature. In an educational context, it is easy to become overly reliant on one system of communication which may not suit everybody. The Picture Exchange Communication System (PECS) could help some learners in the educational setting while others do not relate to it well. Pupils can grow out of PECS and settings may well be slow to phase the approach out once it has become redundant. It is possible to overload an autistic child or adult by trying out too many communication systems at one time. Conversely, visual reference points may also provide aids to comprehension for learners who are not on the autism spectrum, so their use in an educational setting may be appropriate within a broader framework of universal design for learning. When PECS goes wrong, it is usually because the setting is slow to adapt and insists on continuing with the symbols after they have ceased to be useful to the individual. For example, in the case where a teacher stated 'Gerry dragged me by the hand to the fridge, opened it and pointed at the juice. I insisted that he go back to the board and fetch his PECS symbol, and then I gave him the drink as a reward', it is clear that the teacher was missing the fact that the child had moved on, and no longer needed the PECS symbol to make his wishes known.

Transitions large and small

Transitions between activities can be stressful, especially if they are poorly managed. Big transitions, such as moving from one phase of education to another, or navigating a parental divorce, can be extremely anxiety provoking. Sharing information between educational establishments requires co-operation and ensuring that an approach which is suitable for the individual is employed. Visual references may be included in a transition passport document, for example, which may record interests and favoured activities, likes and dislikes, strengths and difficulties. Leaving school may be a time when a young person decides to leave their autism diagnosis behind them and confidentiality must be respected if this is the decision that has been made.

Scenario 3: Michael

Michael is now 16 and is going to an open day at the local sixth form college where he hopes to take A levels. There is an 'ice-breaking exercise' in a large hall with over a hundred other students and five members of staff. For about the first five minutes, everyone has to stand in a circle and throw a ball to someone and say their own name – this seems like half an hour to Michael. After that, they have to throw the same ball and say the name of the person they are throwing the ball to (except if this is the third throw or the last person had a 'b' in their name or a ponytail). If any of these conditions apply, they have to stand on one leg, but it's not clear why or how the ball starts being thrown about again. It's quite a heavy, fast-moving ball which some people throw quite hard, but it is required that everyone joins in even if it is a very unpleasant experience. Some people are laughing and that's a bit confusing.

This does not seem to have anything to do with A-level choices and it is not clear how long the activity will last. Michael hopes he will never have to do this again. He has prepared a list of questions to ask a member of staff, but doesn't know who to ask or indeed which people are staff. It's very hot. Suddenly, the game is stopped by someone who blows a whistle really loud and says 'Right, take twenty minutes, and then make your way to the other building to meet and greet the staff and iron out any outstanding issues.'

Michael walks out and realises he did not know what time he was supposed to go to the other building, or where it was, or what he was supposed to do. He thought there were at least three other buildings. Michael went into the toilet and locked himself in a cubicle to think.

Removing barriers to participation

In any social situation there will be autistic children and adults. The college did not need to be told that Michael, who is autistic, would be visiting them on their open day to consider how they might organise the day to meet a range of young peoples' needs.

For all the young people who attended the open day and enjoyed the activities they participated in, there will have been a significant number, autistic or not, who would have found the ice-breaker activity challenging.

Society is becoming increasingly aware that children and adults respond to social situations in a range of ways and therefore must be provided with a range of ways which allow access to and participation in social situations.

In order to support Michael and other attendees at the open day the college might have provided:

- 'Ambassadors' to meet attendees and explain the different events scheduled for the day

- More explicit information, with a timetable of activities and information about where to go for advice on the different courses the college offers
- Quiet places to go to, and
- Specific people to contact who can answer particular enquiries.

Universal Design for Inclusive Learning

Intervening with understanding has been emphasised within this chapter. Inclusive practice is about including everyone and fostering a sense of belonging and community. It is not about treating all learners the same, but it is about equality of opportunity. Some autism-focused interventions will be discussed briefly here, but these also have the potential to reduce barriers for other learners within a framework of Universal Design for Learning (UDL) (Milton et al. 2016).

Autism-focused examples of UDL

A useful distinction can be made between interventions and overarching frameworks. Rigid adherence to a specific intervention may not meet the diverse requirements of all the learners in a given setting and, in practice, a fairly eclectic approach is common. UDL is a framework, as are approaches such as SPELL and REAL, which seek to provide a set of principles rather than a box of tools.

REAL principles (Reliability, Empathy, Anticipation and Logic) can help things to run smoothly for everyone (Hastwell et al. 2013). No one thrives in chaos, and reliability fosters a sense of security. Seeing the world through the eyes of the learners will enable practitioners to anticipate what is likely to work well and situations which should be avoided, such as unpredictable changes. Logical communication increases understanding and feelings of safety. Techniques such as the use of visual timetables could enhance clarity. REAL owes much to Maslow's hierarchy of needs (1954), and is based on the same assumption that learning is only possible if learners feel a sense of safety and belonging.

The National Autistic Society describes the SPELL approach, which is similar to REAL. SPELL stands for Structure, Positive (approaches and expectations), Empathy, Low arousal, and Links. Knowing the usual order of events in a day increases predictability and makes it easier to be more flexible within a framework. Positive expectations are based on an empathic understanding of the learner and building on natural strengths and interests enhances motivation. Utilising in-depth interests within the curriculum, rather than as add-on motivators, contributes to the creation of a positive atmosphere. Understanding is checked constantly within SPELL and links between learning experiences are made explicit rather than implied. Calm and order are essential components of an anxiety-reducing situation and attention should be paid to the potential for sensory overload. Noise, busy colourful displays, bright lights, strong smells and general clutter can be distracting and aversive.

The SPELL framework is complementary to other approaches, including REAL and TEACCH (Treatment and Education of Autistic and related Communication Handicapped Children.). A TEACCH classroom would include visual approaches to routine, as well as areas for quiet focus, rather than having every wall covered in bright displays. The Picture Exchange Communication System (PECS) can be usefully incorporated into a TEACCH classroom. Visual timetables to make routines predictable, and other visual prompts, can help autistic pupils and, for example, some for whom English is an additional language.

What does Universal Design in a mainstream classroom look like?

The setting is a mainstream classroom which includes many neurodiverse learners as well as refugee children and those for whom English is an additional language. Some of the pupils' parents do not speak or read English.

Classroom displays are designed for sharing information with as many pupils and parents as possible; therefore the written word is used minimally and images are used extensively in a structured and predictable way to help everyone to understand what is going on. Displays include visual timetables which are changed each day.

TEACCH principles underpin the approach and it is not just useful to disabled pupils. An emphasis on order and structure and multiple approaches to supporting and developing communication are also evident here.

A circle of friends and buddy systems in which peers provide a support network can benefit learners who are socially isolated and create a co-operative atmosphere in class. It is important to be careful not to coerce people into false friendships. Remember too that peers may still be together at age 11 or 15, so the way the intervention is introduced might create difficulties further down the line. Do not say 'Be very nice to Andrea. She is special because she is autistic and she has got no friends.'

Social stories (Gray 1994) were developed to help people understand their own feelings and those of others via personalised comic strip conversations. These could be utilised to help explore social situations and conventions from different perspectives. On a cautionary note, Reynhout and Carter (2006) questioned the extent to which skills learnt via social stories are maintained, as navigating social life is not achieved via acquiring a set of measurable competencies.

An eclectic approach which is built on an understanding of the requirements of the individuals operating within an educational setting is likely to be more inclusive than the adoption of a set of techniques which may well not be right for everyone. A framework such as SPELL or REAL and the principles of UDL act as a reminder to consider carefully everything we do as practitioners and to intervene with understanding and with a view to creating a learning environment in which everyone thrives and everyone belongs.

Working with autistic children

In working with autistic children, the key points to remember from this chapter are:

- Good autism practice is good inclusive practice and an autism-friendly classroom can benefit everyone. Universal Design for Learning is a positive approach which involves planning for inclusion from the beginning.

- Interventions are often utilised in an eclectic manner and it is important to intervene only with understanding and within a framework that fosters belonging and well-being for all learners.
- Insights from people who are themselves on the autism spectrum are an essential aid to understanding autism.
- Remember to respect the learning style of the individual – work with the autistic child and not against their autism.
- Be mindful of individuality and that people change over time. (Families are individual too.)
- Diagnosis is not necessarily a goal in itself, as it will not automatically lead to services.
- Work out how the autistic person is processing information rather than making assumptions.
- Stress can be very disabling – reduce input when people are over-stressed.
- Collaborate for consistency of approach.
- Utilise interests as an intrinsic part of the learning process.
- Avoid the deficit model of autism – think about what the child *can do* and how to enable that to happen.

References

APA (American Psychiatric Association) (2014) *Diagnostic and Statistical Manual of Mental Disorders, 5th edition (DSM-V)*. Washington, DC: APA.

Arnold, L. (2010) The medium is the message. Accessed at: www.ucl.ac.uk/cpjh/Arnold (22 November 2010).

Attfield, I., Fowler, A. and Jones, V. (2012) Sensory Audit for School and Classroom. Autism Education Trust. Accessed at: www.aettraininghubs.org.uk/wp-content/uploads/2012/05/37.1-Sensory-audit-tool-for-environments.pdf (17 March 2017).

Baron-Cohen, S. (2008) *Autism and Asperger Syndrome: the facts.* Oxford: Oxford University Press.

Caldwell, P. (2014) *The Anger Box: sensory turmoil and pain in autism*. Hove: Pavilion Press.

Grandin, T. (1986) *Emergence, Labeled Autistic*. Novato, CA: Academic Therapy Publications.

Grandin, T. (1995) *Thinking in Pictures*. New York: Vintage.

Gray, C. (1994) *Comic Strip Conversations: illustrated interactions that teach conversation skills to students with autism and related disorders*. Arlington, TX: Future Horizons.

Happe, F. (1994) *Autism: an introduction to psychological theory.* London: UCL Press.

Hastwell, J., Harding, J., Martin, N. and Baron-Cohen, S. (2013) *Asperger Syndrome Student Project. 2009–12. Final Report, June*. University of Cambridge Disability Resource Centre.

Hobson, P. (2002) *The Cradle of Thought: exploring the origins of thinking*. London: Macmillan.

Jordan, R. and Powell, S. (1990) Teaching autistic children to think more effectively. *Communication*, Vol. 24, pp. 20–23.

Kenny, L., Hattersley, C., Molins, B., Buckley, C., Povey, C. and Pellicano, E. (2015) Which terms should be used to describe autism? Perspectives from the UK autism community. *Autism*, Vol. 20(4), pp. 442–462.

Lawson, W. (2010) *The Passionate Mind: how people with autism learn*. London: Jessica Kingsley.

Maslow, A. (1954) *Motivation and Personality*. New York: Harper Collins.

Milton, D. (2012a) On the ontological status of autism: the 'double empathy problem'. *Disability and Society*, Vol. 27(6), pp. 883–887.

Milton, D. (2012b) *So What Exactly is Autism?* [resource linked to competency framework]. Autism Education Trust. Accessed at: http://www.aettraininghubs.org.uk/wp-content/uploads/2012/08/1_So-what-exactly-is-autism.pdf (14 March 2017).

Milton, D. (2014) So what exactly are autism interventions intervening with? *Good Autism Practice*, Vol. 15(2), pp. 6–14.

Milton, D., Martin, M. and Melham, P. (2016) Beyond reasonable adjustment: autistic-friendly spaces and Universal Design. In D. Milton and N. Martin (eds), *Autism and Intellectual Disabilities in Adults*, Vol. 1. Hove: Pavilion, pp. 81–86.

Murray, D. (1992) Attention tunnelling and autism. In P. Shattock and G. Linfoot (eds), *Living with Autism: the individual, the family and the professional*. Durham conference proceedings, pp. 183–193; obtainable from Autism Research Unit, School of Health Sciences, The University of Sunderland, Sunderland SR2 7EE or the National Autistic Society.

Murray, D., Lesser, M. and Lawson, W. (2005) Attention, monotropism and the diagnostic criteria for autism. *Autism*, Vol. 9(2), pp. 136–156.

NAS (National Autistic Society) (2016) About autism: strategies and approaches. Accessed at: www.autism.org.uk/about/strategies.aspx (17 March 2017).

Reynhout, G. and Carter, M. (2006) Social Stories™ for children with disabilities. *Journal of Autism and Developmental Disorders*, Vol. 36(4), pp. 445–469.

Shah, A. and Frith, U. (1993) Why do autistic individuals show superior performance on the block design task? *Journal of Child Psychology and Psychiatry*, Vol. 34(8), pp. 1351–1364.

Tammet, D. (2006) *Born on a Blue Day: inside the mind of an autistic savant*. New York: Free.

Vermeulen, P. (2015) Context blindness in autism spectrum disorder: not using the forest to see the trees as trees. *Focus on Autism and Other Developmental Disabilities*, Vol. 30(3), pp. 182–192.

Williams, D. (1996) *Autism: an inside-out approach*. London: Jessica Kingsley.

Wing, L. (1996) Autistic spectrum disorders. *British Medical Journal*, Vol. 312(7027), p. 327.

Wing, L. and Gould, J. (1979) Severe impairments of social interaction and associated abnormalities in children: epidemiology and classification. *Journal of Autism and Childhood Schizophrenia*, Vol. 9, pp. 11–29.

WHO (World Health Organization) (1992) *The International Classification of Mental and Behavioural Disorders: Clinical descriptions and diagnostic guidelines, 10th edition (ICD-10)*. Geneva: WHO.

Children and Families Act 2014

https://councilfordisabledchildren.org.uk/sites/default/files/uploads/documents/import/Children AndFamiliesActBrief.pdf (accessed 17 March 2017).

Equality Act 2010

https://www.gov.uk/guidance/equality-act-2010-guidance (accessed 14 March 2017).

Martin, N. (2008) REAL services to assist university students who have Asperger syndrome. *NADP Technical Briefing 10/08*.

SEN Code of Practice (2015)

https://www.gov.uk/government/uploads/system/uploads/attachment_data/file/428744/SFR14-2015_Main_Text.pdf (accessed 17 March 2017).

http://integratedtreatmentservices.co.uk/our-approaches/speech-therapy-approaches/spell-framework/ (accessed 14 March 2017).

https://www.teacch.com/ (accessed 17 March 2017).

www.pecs-unitedkingdom.com/ (accessed 17 March 2017).

Tomlinson, J. (1996) *Inclusive Learning: the Report of the Committee of Enquiry into the postschool education of those with learning difficulties and/or disabilities, in England*. Accessed at: www.csie.org.uk/resources/tomlinson-96.pdf (14 March 2017).

Chapter 9

Children who have suffered loss and grief, including bereavement

Edlene Whitman

This chapter explores:

- What do we mean by loss, grief and bereavement?
- How many children are affected by bereavement?
- What are the emotional processes children experience and their conceptual understanding of loss and death?
- Common feelings and behaviours in response to bereavement
- Separation, divorce, forces children and families who are transitory
- How can school support? Key aspects of good practice and resources
- Guidance for schools and educational settings in supporting children who are bereaved by the death of a parent.

This chapter looks at loss through bereavement, separation and relocation. We consider how children are emotionally affected by loss, and how adults can support them in dealing with this. Robert Kastenbaum (1972) suggests that adults like to think of childhood as 'the kingdom where nobody dies', but children are very aware of death from an early age. Some children may experience loss due to the death of a family member or friend, while others experience the loss of separation from significant people or home due to relocation, maybe even through seeking refuge in another country. Children are also aware of loss through media platforms which stream news and events directly, instantly and graphically into their homes, computers and phones (Doka 2000).

Children in armed forces or diplomatic service families may relocate quite regularly and others may 'lose' a parent due to relationship break up or divorce. Young children are especially vulnerable to divorce, often manifesting their response to the situation through challenging behaviour, psychological distress and academic problems (Furstenberg and Allison 1989). According to the Office for National Statistics (2013) almost half (48 per cent) of couples divorcing in 2013 had at least one child aged under 16 living in the family. The effects of loss, separation and grief are similar, and therefore it is appropriate to link them in this chapter which seeks to help those working with children feel more confident about supporting them as they cope with loss. The founder of Winston's Wish, a charity that provides support, training and resources for children and families suffering bereavement says:

> The more that educators, counsellors, school administrators, parents and anyone else who works with children and adolescents realize this, the more equipped they will be to

help young people cope with grief and incorporate loss in their lives in ways that are mentally and physically healthy.

(Stokes 2004)

What do we mean by loss, grief and bereavement?

Loss can be defined as the fact or process of losing something or someone, or the feeling of grief after losing someone or something of value. Grief can be defined as the feeling of intense sorrow experienced as a result of loss, while bereavement is the condition of being without the significant person.

Scenario 1: Sarah's story

When Sarah's father died suddenly, she was just 15 and it changed her life in more ways than one. Her father's work took the family to many places but they had been settled for over six years and Sarah couldn't remember living anywhere else. She had loyal friends, a great school and a good life, a secure house with plenty of freedom and no money worries.

Just before New Year, Sarah's dad was admitted to hospital and while Mum played it down, the children continued life as normal, expecting Dad to recover and return home soon. But two weeks later, he died. Sarah was able to say goodbye to him but she was confused because, in her grief and desire to keep life as normal as possible, Mum didn't talk to her much. Five years on, there are still unanswered questions, things that remain unspoken. Occasionally details emerge, a small piece in the jigsaw but the big picture is still elusive.

In the immediate aftermath of Dad's death, life was a blur, seen through a veil of tears and a mist of confusion. Sarah had a few days off school during which her friends kept in contact. Within days though, they were leaving the tied house that was owned by the company Dad had worked for, on the move again, and effectively homeless. An evening out to say goodbye to friends and then before she knew it, the family was back in London, Sarah had lost her father, her home, her friends and her school.

Sarah and her mum stayed with her aunt and uncle for a while. Sarah shared a room with her cousin, and shared her cousin's friends and her life. She joined her cousin's school, in the same year group and the same classes. Some of the subjects were different, she had been studying dance, and now she was studying food technology. She missed her friends, the freedom to come and go as she chose and not having to worry about money. She was living in someone else's home, following someone else's rules and living someone else's life.

After a while, the magnitude of the situation hit Sarah and she became depressed and the school arranged some counselling which proved a lifeline. Later, Mum got a job and they moved to their own home, but life had changed forever, and so had the future.

How many children are affected by bereavement?

There is no official data collected on the number of children affected by the death of a parent, sibling, carer, or other significant person, so the following figures from the Child Bereavement Network are therefore estimates:

- Seventy-eight per cent of 11–16 year olds in one survey said that they had been bereaved of a close relative or friend.
- In 2014, 23,200 parents died in the UK, leaving dependent children, i.e. one parent every 22 minutes, leaving around 40,000 newly bereaved dependent children aged 0–17.
- By the age of 16, around one in twenty young people have experienced the death of a parent.
- In the last national survey in 2004, around 3.5 per cent of 5–16 year olds in the UK had been bereaved of a parent or sibling, i.e. around 309,000 school-age children.
- In a survey of primary schools in Hull, over 70 per cent had a child on their roll who had been bereaved of someone important to them in the last two years.
- The incidence of childhood bereavement in youth offenders is ten times higher (41 per cent) than the national average (4 per cent). We might question whether this has contributed to their situation.

Children may also experience the death of siblings, close friends, grandparents and significant others. An Institute of Education study found that grandparents provide over 40 per cent of childcare for parents who are at work or studying and over 70 per cent of childcare at other times (Dex and Joshi 2004). More children live in extended family households, with a third of grandparents sharing their home with a dependent grandchild (Grandparents Plus n.d.). Mortality rates also vary by social class and geography, so children living in disadvantaged areas are more likely to be bereaved. The Childhood Bereavement Network also notes that mortality rates among disabled young people with complex health needs are higher than general, so young people attending special school are more likely to be bereaved of a friend. Children growing up in forces families are also more likely to experience the loss of a parent on active service. In 2011, Ofsted found that service children were generally susceptible to social and emotional disturbance while a parent was on active deployment and that moving regularly also had an impact on their performance at school and their well-being (Ofsted 2011).

What are the emotional processes children experience and their conceptual understanding of loss and death?

Bowlby reminds us that we need special people in our lives for social and emotional development and therefore the loss of this person 'can have profound effect on a child and may lead to anxiety, depression and insecurity later in life' (Rathbone 1996, p.18). How a child or young person responds to someone dying will depend on their age and understanding, the relationship they had with the person who died, and how that person died. Every child is different, so we need to consider individual needs, experience, age and stage of development, and therefore responses will vary according to the range and intensity of behaviours. Children and young people grieve just as deeply as adults but they show it in different ways. They learn how to grieve by mirroring the adults around them, and rely on adults to provide them with what they need to support them in their grief.

Common feelings and behaviours in response to bereavement

Child Bereavement UK is a charity which supports families and educates professionals when a baby or child dies or is dying, or when a child is facing bereavement. They provide excellent materials and resources as well as valuable guidance and advice from which some of the following is derived. It is useful to understand that 'puddle jumping' is a type of in-built safety valve that prevents young children being overwhelmed by powerful feelings, dipping in and out of their grief, intensely sad one minute, then playing happily the next. However, as children get older, this instinctive 'puddle jumping' becomes harder and teenagers may spend long periods of time in one behaviour or another. A young person will not 'get over' their grief, but with time and appropriate support, they will hopefully learn to live with it: 'a child jumps in and out of puddles of grief, but an adult is deep in a river, being swept along with the current, finding it very difficult to get out' (Adams 2011).

Children and young people's responses to bereavement by age and stage

Pre-school children, age 0–5

What are they thinking?

- Very young children can't understand about death, but they do know that someone they love is missing.
- They may believe death is temporary or reversible and struggle with the concept of forever.
- They may think death is like sleeping and ask 'when will they come back/wake up', 'why did they go away', 'why can't I visit them in heaven?'
- Young children tend to take this literally and may see the world as part-real and part-fantasy.
- They may worry about who will care for them and fear abandonment.
- They may think they can bring someone back if they are 'good' or make up ideas to fill gaps in knowledge, i.e. 'magical thinking'.

How are they feeling or behaving?

- They may pull away, cry, search for the missing person.
- They can sense the mood around them and may be clingy or afraid of strangers.
- They are egocentric, see themselves as the cause of events around them.
- They may be irritable, aggressive, or regress, e.g. bed-wetting or thumb-sucking, or have feeding or sleeping problems.
- They may play at being dead, trying to make sense of the world around them.
- Not having the language to communicate how they are feeling, they may show it in their behaviour.
- They may 'puddle jump' in and out of their grief, between sadness and normality.

How can adults help?

- Provide reassurance and comfort – the world can become a very scary place for a child. Perhaps provide something that feels or smells like the missing person and try to keep to routines as far as possible.
- Distract them and give gentle explanations, using very concrete terms to acknowledge and explain what has happened, avoiding euphemisms like 'gone away'/'to sleep'/'to heaven'.
- As children grow, they need more information to help them make sense of the situation and they may need repeated explanations and information given in different ways. Don't assume they understand.
- Find out what has been said at home and respect the beliefs of the family to avoid confusion.
- Provide a supportive and safe environment where it's okay to ask questions and share feelings and encourage adults to role model their emotions.
- Give opportunities to express feelings through play and creativity.
- Understand that 'puddle jumping' is a safety valve and give them time and space, rather than trying to 'cheer them up'.

Primary school children, age 5–11

What are they thinking?

- They begin to understand that death is final, permanent, universal and unavoidable.
- They may see it as something a bit 'spooky', a spirit, like a ghost, angel, or skeleton.
- Children with family pets may have experienced loss already and know that a beloved pet will not be coming back.
- They may be curious about specific details of what happens after death.

How are they feeling or behaving?

- They may display physical symptoms – headaches, tummy ache – as manifestations of emotional pain; stress-related conditions such as eczema or asthma may be exacerbated.
- They may be withdrawn, feel sad, lonely, depressed, angry, guilty, insecure, clingy.
- They may have nightmares, fear of abandonment and worry about the future, such as where they will live.
- They may be the 'perfect' child, brave and in control, or want to be very grown up, taking over the role of caregiver, or they may have behaviour, learning or friendship issues.
- They may feel overwhelmed, and/or worry that they are to blame for the death and react by withdrawing or losing interest in everything.

How can adults help?

- Realise that regression is instinctive, not chosen behaviour.
- Allow them to feel angry and find safe ways of dealing with their feelings, e.g. stress ball or physical activity.
- Maintain consistency with the usual boundaries around acceptable behaviour.
- Adults need to show their feelings and emotions to show children it is okay to do so.
- Beware of expecting too much of them, e.g. 'man of the house now'.
- Rather than trying to cheer them up, it's probably best to give them some time and space.
- Involve them in arrangements and include them in the planning if possible.

Adolescents, age 11+

What are they thinking?

- Death may challenge their developing ideas about themselves and their future leading them to question their faith or understanding of the world.
- Understanding the finality of death, and the impact it has had and will have on their future, e.g. not sharing milestones with a parent.
- They want to be grown up and independent, but also need support, and find it hard to balance the two.

How are they feeling or behaving?

- They may reflect on the meaning and purpose of life, or not want to reflect, and hide their feelings.
- They may be withdrawn, sad, feel lonely, confused and depressed. Life can lose purpose and meaning. They may become apathetic or develop a 'what's the point?' attitude, resisting support.
- The death of someone important may make them feel different, at a time when they want to be the same as everyone else.
- Relationships with others are becoming increasingly important, and any loss can lead to feelings of anger or severe distress. They may spend more time with friends or withdraw from the family to be alone. But they can feel that friends just don't understand and they then struggle to maintain social groups.
- Influenced by social media, they may prefer to share feelings online or through their mobile phones rather than face to face.
- They may become very hard-working to compensate for feelings of guilt, or they may 'act out' in anger, impulsively or recklessly, e.g. substance misuse or fighting.
- They may become dependent or regress to a younger age, exhibiting insecurity and low self-esteem, but they may show maturity and wisdom beyond their years with real empathy for others going through difficulties.
- They can feel completely overwhelmed by powerful feelings and emotions that they do not understand or expect, and cannot control.

How can adults help?

- Treat them as individuals with their own specific needs. Ask them what they need and involve them in discussions around plans for their support. Encourage them to take responsibility and make choices from a range of options.
- Provide information they need to understand what has happened, why and the implications for their lives. Be honest.
- Let them know you are there if and when they need you without putting them under pressure, and don't be offended if they prefer to speak to someone of their own age group, or other adults, so remind them who else they can go to.
- Provide activities to ease the pressure – talking and spending time with other bereaved young people can help, e.g. creating a memory collage.
- Be consistent around behaviour expectations so they feel safe and there is continuity even when life feels very far from normal.
- Highlight positive attitudes and worthy attributes.
- Be prepared to seek additional professional help if necessary.

Children with SEN

What are they thinking?

- All children struggle with the concept of death and its permanence but children with learning difficulties may find this particularly difficult to grasp and benefit from simple, practical examples to illustrate the difference between dead and living things.

How are they feeling or behaving?

- They long for things to be the same as they were before.
- In some cases, they may never come to a complete understanding of the finality of death, believing that the dead person has gone away and will return one day.
- Many of the feelings and actions are the same as those for young children.
- For children with SEN, it is about their needs and development, not their age.

How can adults help?

- Don't underestimate their ability to understand and cope with tough things in life.
- Find creative ways to communicate without words if needed.
- If using words, use the real ones, e.g. 'dead' and 'dying', not euphemisms.

Supporting bereaved children

The activities and ideas below will be helpful for all children and may be especially helpful to those with additional needs:

* Acknowledge any death because to ignore what has happened implies that this is an unimportant event and denies the existence of the person who has died.
* Use as many real-life examples as you can, e.g. pictures of funerals and coffins to aid understanding.
* Try to include the child with the helpful rituals of death, such as condolence cards or attending the funeral. If this is not appropriate, give them an opportunity to say goodbye with their own simple ceremony.
* Pre-grief work is especially important to help prepare for an expected death. A well-thought-through visit to a hospice or hospital may help, or use video or TV programmes that depict someone seriously ill and then dying. Many hospices have bereavement services (St Christopher's Hospice 2010).
* Use stories to help explain what happens when something or someone dies.
* Help children express emotions and reassure them they are normal and necessary. Looking at photographs or watching videos of the person who has died can facilitate expressions of sadness or anger.
* Offer opportunities for safe ways to express frustration and anger. Reassure that being angry is okay; children may be able to release some of their anger through using paint, clay, shredding newspaper, or by hitting objects in a soft play area.
* A memory box of tangible reminders chosen by the child or listening to recordings of the voice or favourite music of the dead person may help the visually impaired.
* Create a timeline with photographs of significant events and then build the deceased's life story.

Separation, divorce, forces children and families who are transitory

As Yvonne Gabell observed 'One event in a child's life may lead to multiple loss' (Gabell 1996). The death of someone important can be devastating for any child but, for service families or other families who move around a lot, perhaps on short term-contracts, or travellers, or refugee families, there are additional challenges. The disruption to their schooling due to moving house, or even country, leaving familiar surroundings, and friends, can be stressful and isolating for the children and their families.

Having to change school in mid-term adds to the stress, as they may face difficulties integrating into a new school, and having to make new friends, breaking into established relationships. They may have to move several times before eventually settling and every time they change school they must explain their situation all over again – for some, this may be too difficult and they choose to keep quiet. Friends and staff can inadvertently say hurtful or inappropriate things, which add to their grief. Child Bereavement UK (CBUK 2011) provides valuable advice for supporting forces families and Gypsy and traveller families. Gypsies and travellers die on average 10–12 years earlier than the mainstream population, are more likely to experience the premature death of a child (17 per cent compared to just under 10 per cent of the wider population), and have a high suicide rate, particularly amongst young men.

When someone close dies, children from these groups may lose not just their own family unit but also their belonging to a much wider one. Their identity is often very bound up with the role of the parent and if that person dies, this may cause them to rethink their place in the world. Teenagers especially may feel a huge sense of loss around who they thought they were and struggle with what feels like a whole new identity.

Children whose parents may work abroad, or are away for long periods, may find it difficult to accept that the person who has died is never coming back and this makes it more difficult for them to deal with the reality.

Death in action or through violence is often totally unexpected, sudden and traumatic, heightening the sense of shock and disbelief. Visiting the scene after a traumatic death can help those affected to make some sense of what has happened and to start to answer 'how' and 'why'. The opportunity to do this is limited if the death happens in some far-away and dangerous place. Without answers to those questions, a child may make up their own story based on unhelpful fantasies – their 'magical thinking'. For any grieving child, school can offer space and time to escape from overwhelming emotions found at home.

How can school support? Key aspects of good practice and resources

> For a child, or young person, whose life has been turned upside down, the routines of school life can give a sense of normality. Everything else may have fallen apart but school and the people within it are still there, offering a sense of security and continuity.
>
> (CBUK 2011)

The death of a child is always distressing, whether expected or not. Children in school may have life-limiting, or even terminal illnesses, for which the school and family will have a management plan. This may apply more often for children attending special educational needs settings. However, when the time comes, it is always a shock.

Case study: Daryl's story

Daryl was a normal, fun-loving, cheeky, popular, energetic 6-year-old playing in the garden in the summer holidays with his brother and sister, when suddenly he collapsed. An ambulance came but sadly Daryl was pronounced dead at the scene, having suffered a major heart attack.

It was by chance that the head teacher of his school was tidying up in her office, taking advantage of the peace and quiet of the holidays, when she picked up a voicemail from the local authority safeguarding team, informing her of Daryl's sudden death. It was a shock – she couldn't believe it and needed to understand what had happened. Unbeknown to the school, Daryl had an underlying heart condition, diagnosed and treated as a baby, but not thought to be a continuing worry, so Mum had not told the school about it. She wanted him to grow up like any other active little boy.

The head teacher carefully worded a message which she sent to all staff. It was important that they heard about it as soon as possible, from her, before they picked it up on the grapevine, since many of them lived in and were part of the local community. Staff were equally shocked and needed to know what to do and how to react.

As soon as possible, the head teacher contacted the family, to give her condolences and to talk about how the school would respond at the beginning of term. It was also important to consider the needs of Daryl's siblings and his friends in school.

While staff tried to come to terms with their own feelings, they knew that they needed to plan for the start of term and how they would handle the first day. It was agreed that the head teacher would break the news to Daryl's class first and then to the whole school in assembly, following which each teacher would spend time talking with their class and giving them time to absorb the news in their own way. The family was consulted at every stage to ensure that they were happy with what was being said and how it was being handled.

The local authority provided support through the human resources and psychology teams. The school's family worker and learning support mentor were key roles in providing support to staff, children and families, making good use of the resources of local services too, such as a local hospice that provided bereavement counselling and training.

There are two elements to how a school can support children suffering grief, loss or bereavement. The first is 'after the fact', that is, the response to the event itself, how to work with the family, communicating effectively and drawing upon the available services. The second is about providing children with some understanding of death and providing all children with an environment where they can learn about loss and feel safe and secure to express their feelings and emotions.

In January 2013, South Whitehaven Children's Centre was acknowledged by Ofsted as a model of good practice in this area (Ofsted 2013), as they provided a 'sensitive, responsive, empathic approach' to enable children to express their feelings, acknowledge their loss and develop skills to cope with their changed lives.

Their children's bereavement group provided a safe and protected space where children felt safe to talk and express their grief, and where they felt listened to. It also provided parents and carers with opportunities to share their experiences, where they had time, a listening ear and opportunities to grow and heal at their own pace.

South Whitehaven's eight-week course uses play therapy, art, music and massage to help children and families learn that all emotions are acceptable, including laughter and fun, as well as time for reflection and acknowledgement of the pain.

The staff are skilful and astute, realising there is no universal route to supporting someone through bereavement, and therefore they also provide one-to-one support if preferred. This has implications in terms of training for staff in schools. The resources section below provides some useful contacts which can help schools to train staff.

The following is a possible timeline for dealing with the death of a parent and can be used as a starting point for developing a programme suitable for your own school or setting (Winston's Wish 2011b).

Guidance for schools and educational settings in supporting children who are bereaved by the death of a parent

Short-term

- The school is informed of the death of a parent.
- The child and family are consulted on how to tell the rest of the school.
- The head teacher seeks advice from the local authority, Child Bereavement UK and Winston's Wish, and contacts the family to express sympathy and support.
- School staff are informed.
- A strategy for telling the rest of the children is established.
- Staff are reminded about other children in school who have suffered bereavement and for whom this may be especially difficult.
- Governors and key parents may support by being around at home time.
- Information is given to teachers on how to manage various responses and where to seek additional support.
- Staff discuss how to respond to the child on return to school – what to say and how to behave.
- The child's class given a chance to focus on feelings and ask questions.
- The Class Teacher (CT) is supported by key staff, e.g. family worker, learning mentor.
- CT (and other key staff) visit the family at home to explain what the school is doing and the plan for return.

Medium-term

- When the child returns to school, they are met by CT and given some time to adjust to being back.
- The child is given the chance to identify an adult supporter.
- The child is given permission to dip out of lessons whenever needed for the next few days and seek out chosen supporter.
- The child is supported as they share with the class what has been agreed.
- Class mates are advised that the child wants people to talk about it and understand when they cry sometimes.
- Time is set aside at the end of the day to review with CT how things have gone and any changes for the next day.

Long-term

- In consultation with the family, agree how the school will mark the funeral – who will attend and whether the school will close.
- Other members of the school may wish to contribute memories.
- In agreement with the rest of the staff, arrange a system for the child whenever the pressure of grief builds up, e.g. 'time out' to visit their supporter.
- Ensure the family knows about local and national child bereavement services.
- CT compiles a 'calendar of memories' – noting any significant sensitive dates, e.g. the anniversary of the death, birthday, Father's Day, etc. This calendar can follow through the school and on to next school.
- Staff need heightened sensitivity to issues, e.g. if the death was in a fire, then be aware that studying the Great Fire of London might be difficult.

In terms of curriculum and teaching programmes, there are some obvious links, such as in religious education where children can learn about the traditions and beliefs of different religions. This helps them to see that there are different ways to respond to death and bereavement. Children can visit places of worship and hear from faith leaders about what they believe and about what happens when someone dies. For example, most Christians believe in some kind of heaven but this may vary according to denomination, while Muslims may believe that death is just moving on to another part of the journey of existence. The London Borough of Bromley Agreed Syllabus for Religious Education includes a module for children in Year 5/6 to explore emotions connected with loss and leaving, including religious teaching concerning death and the afterlife. It also looks at what has changed during the year, such as new teacher, friends, new home, etc.

In science, children learn about life and living processes, so it seems appropriate for them to look at what happens at the end of life, too. Looking at a dead bird or insect can help them to understand that it has no feelings or senses any longer, nor does it suffer pain. This can help children to accept the permanence of death.

In English, there are many opportunities to read stories about death and loss and to discuss them. Some suggested books are listed in the resources section. Children can also be encouraged to write letters, poems, stories, journals or diaries, or captions for pictures that they may create.

In Personal, Social, Health Education (PSHE), there is an opportunity to think about feelings and emotions and how we respond to different situations, helping children to recognise that it is okay to have feelings, and to express them (Winston's Wish 2011a). The Social and Emotional Aspects of Learning (SEAL) programme which was widely used by schools, and is still used in many, provides an excellent framework for helping children to look at emotions and relationships (DfES 2005). It is worth seeking out, although it has been officially archived by the UK government.

Memo from a grieving child

Please:

- Keep me informed of what is going on
- Be honest with me, even if you have to say 'I don't know'
- Speak in simple language with no euphemisms
- Let me be involved in the grieving process with others – don't exclude me
- Let me cry alongside you
- Let me be able to comfort others
- Assure me that I am loved and safe and will be taken care of
- Accept what I do or say without judgement – don't compare me with others
- Let me be able to say goodbye
- Allow me to talk about the person who has died
- Give me the structure, discipline and routine that will help me recover
- Help me keep the memories alive (Perkins, 2007).

Useful resources

Websites

- Winston's Wish – www.winstonswish.org.uk
- Child Bereavement UK – www.childbereavementuk.org/
- CRUSE bereavement care – www.cruse.org.uk/
- Childhood Bereavement network – www.childhoodbereavementnetwork.org.uk

Books for adults

A Teachers Handbook of Death, by Maggie Jackson and Jim Colwell, 2001, Jessica Kingsley.

Childhood Bereavement: Developing the Curriculum and Pastoral Support, by Nina Job and Gill Frances, 2007, National Children's Bureau.

Grief in Children: A Handbook for Adults, by Atle Dyregrov, 2008, Jessica Kingsley.

Grief in School Communities, by Louise Rowling, 2003, Open University.

Supporting Bereaved Children: A Handbook for Primary Schools, by Erica Brown, 2009, Help the Hospices.

Then, Now and Always: Supporting Children as They Journey Through Grief: A Guide for Practitioners, by Julie A. Stokes, 2004, Winston's Wish.

Books for children and young people

A Sky of Diamonds: A Story for Children about Loss, Grief and Hope, by Camille Gibbs, 2015, Jessica Kingsley.

A Teen's Simple Guide Through Grief, by Alexis Cunningham, 2001, Jalmar Press.

All Kinds of Feelings: A Lift the Flap Book, illustrated by Emma Brownjohn, 2003, Tango Books.

Always and Forever, by Alan Durant and illustrated by Debi Gliori, 2003, Random House.

Are You Sad, Little Bear? A Book About Learning to Say Goodbye, by Rachel Rivett and Tina McNaughton, 2009, Lion Hudson.
Badger's Parting Gifts, by Susan Varley, 1992, Picture Lions.
Bridge to Terabithia, by Katherine Paterson, 1995, Puffin.
Goodbye Mog, by Judith Kerr, 2003, Harper Collins Children's Books.
Goodnight Mr Tom, by Michelle Magorian, 1993, Puffin.
Granpa – The Book of the Film, based on the story by John Burningham, 1991, Ladybird Books Ltd.
Michael Rosen's Sad Book, by Michael Rosen, 2011, Walker Books.
Miss You: A First Look at Death, by Pat Thomas, 2001, Barron's Educational Series.
Missing Mummy, by Rebecca Cobb, 2011, Macmillian Children's Books.
No Matter What, by Debi Gliori, 2003, Bloomsbury Children's Books.
The Velveteen Rabbit, by Margery Williams, 1995 edn, Puffin.
Waterbugs and Dragonflies, by Doris Stickney, 2002, Bloomsbury Publishing.
When Dinosaurs Die: A Guide to Understanding Death, by Laurie Krasny, 1998, Time Warner.

Workbooks

Muddles, Puddles and Sunshine: Your Activity Book to Help When Someone Has Died (Early Years), by Diana Crossley and Kate Sheppard, 2000, Winston's Wish.
When Someone Special Dies, by Marge Heegard, 1996, Woodand Press.
Draw On Your Emotions, by Margot Sutherland, 2003, Speechmark Publishing.
Someone I Know Has Died, by Trish Phillips, 2009, Child Bereavement Charity.
Helping Children with Loss, by Margot Sutherland, 2003, Speechmark Publishing.

References

Adams, J., 2011. *How Children and Young People Grieve.* [Online] Available at: www.childbe reavementuk.org/files/5414/0868/5878/How_Children_and_Young_People_Grieve.pdf [Accessed 1 May 2016].
CBUK (Child Bereavement UK), 2011. *Information Sheets.* [Online] Available at: www.child bereavementuk.org/publications/information-sheets/ [Accessed 24 April 2016].
Dex, S. and Joshi, H., 2004. *Millennium Cohort Study,* London: Institute of Education.
DfES, 2005. *Excellence and Enjoyment: Social and emotional aspects of learning,* London: DfES.
Doka, K., 2000. *Living with Grief: Children, adolescents and loss.* s.l.:Hospice Foundation of America.
Furstenberg, F. F. and Allison, P. D. (1989). How marital dissolution affects children: Variations by age and sex. *Developmental Psychology*, 25, 540–549.
Gabell, Y., 1996. Self esteem and loss. In: B. L. and J. Elsegood, eds. *Working with Children in Grief and Loss.* London: Bailliere Tindall, p. 118.
Grandparents Plus, n.d. *Rethinking Family Life.* [Online] Available at: https://www.grandparentsplus. org.uk/wp-content/uploads/2011/03/RethinkingFamilyLife.pdf [Accessed 17 June 2016].
Kastenbaum, R., 1972. *The Psychology of Death.* New York: Springer.
Ofsted, 2011. *Children in Service Families,* London: Ofsted.
Ofsted, 2013. *Examples of Good Practice in Early Years.* [Online] Available at: https://www.gov.uk/ government/uploads/system/uploads/attachment_data/file/392203/South_20Whitehaven_20Childr en_27s_20Centre_20-_20good_20practice_20example.pdf [Accessed 1 June 2016].
ONS (Office for National Statistics), 2013. https://www.ons.gov.uk/peoplepopulationandcommunity/ birthsdeathsandmarriages/divorce/bulletins/divorcesinenglandandwales/2013#children-of-divorced-couples (accessed 1 June 2016).
Perkins, J., 2007. *How to Help a Child Cope with Grief.* 1st edn. Slough: Foulsham.
Rathbone, B., 1996. Developmental perspectives. In: L. A. Elsegood, ed. *Working with Children in Grief and Loss.* London: Bailliere Tindall, pp. 16–31.

St Christopher's Hospice, 2010. *Candle Child Bereavement Service.* [Online] Available at: www.stchristophers.org.uk/candle [Accessed 4 September 2016].

Stokes, J., 2004. *Then, Now & Always – Supporting Children as They Journey Through Grief: A guide for practitioners.* s.l.:Winston's Wish.

Winston's Wish, 2011a. *An Example of a School Response – Katy's Story.* [Online] Available at: www.winstonswish.org.uk/wp-content/uploads/2013/10/An-example-of-a-School-response-Katys-story_branded.pdf [Accessed 20 May 2016].

Winston's Wish, 2011b. *Support for Schools.* [Online] Available at: www.winstonswish.org.uk/supporting-you/schools-information-pdf-page/ [Accessed 23 July 2016].

Chapter 10

Looked after children, fostering and adoption

Anna Jones

This chapter explores:

- What is meant by the term 'looked after child' and reasons why children may be looked after
- Barriers to learning typically faced by looked after children and the importance of practitioner awareness of such barriers
- The ways in which practitioners working with looked after children may reduce barriers to learning to further inclusion and improve educational outcomes
- The importance of empathy, relationships and understanding to enable all children to thrive.

According to figures from HM Government (March, 2015), 69,540 children were looked after in the UK, a number which has increased year on year since 2011. In this chapter, we will discuss the incidence of looked after children and locate this in the context of education and inclusive practice. Education practitioners, scholars and policy makers are among those who are especially concerned with how the educational outcomes of these children may be improved, particularly due to the fact that the attainment of looked after children is considerably behind that of those who are not looked after. Closing the gap between the attainment of looked after children and all young people remains a high priority of the Department for Education (HM Government 2014). Children who are in care often experience significant barriers to learning. This chapter will seek to provide ways in which practitioners can reduce and remove some of these barriers and offer examples of inclusive practice which would benefit all children, including those who are looked after.

What is a looked after child (LAC)?

According to the Children Act 1989, if a child is deemed to be suffering or is at risk of significant harm in the United Kingdom, a local authority has the right to obtain a care order for them. If a court makes a care order in respect of a child to a local authority, the local authority assumes parental responsibility for that child. Thus, the child becomes looked after by the local authority. It is the responsibility of social workers to find a place for the child to live which, in the majority of cases, is not their family home.

In 75 per cent of cases (HM Government 2015), looked after children are placed with carers who have been approved by the local authority and are referred to as foster carers. Children are placed in the foster carer's home and may live with other looked after children and/or the foster carer's own family. Foster care placements are usually temporary, although some children remain with a foster family for many years. When a child is first taken into care or looked after, their first foster placement may be a short one. This is so that social workers can spend time finding a suitable placement. Foster care placements should, where possible, be in the same area as where the child lived prior to entering care. Children living in foster care continue to attend the school or education setting they previously attended, if this is feasible. If not, the local authority is in charge of finding a new education setting for the child to attend. Regulations made under the School Standards and Framework Act 1998 state that looked after children are given the highest priority in admission arrangements for schools and education settings (DfE 2014).

Some children may be placed in a residential care home if a suitable foster family placement cannot be found. Equally, a child may be placed in foster care but find it very difficult living with another family. The child may display challenging behaviour and a residential care placement sought. Care homes also provide more placements, so it may be possible for siblings to be accommodated together if this is not possible in foster care. However, there are usually no more than ten children in a residential care home (Who Cares Trust 2016).

In a minority of cases, children who are subject to a care order will live with their birth families, but the council will take parental responsibility for them and, as such, has the right to make decisions regarding the child's education and welfare. Sometimes children are placed with another family member, such as a grandparent or adult sibling, whilst the local authority assesses the most suitable place for the child to live. This is known as 'kinship care'. In the long term, it may be that the family members are approved as foster carers for the child, but the local authority retain responsibility for their care. The Who Cares Trust (2016) estimate that there are as many as 200,000–300,000 children living in kinship care in the UK; however, it is difficult to get accurate figures as many of these children are not subject to care orders. Parents or other family members may decide that kinship care is best for the child, without the involvement of the courts or social workers. Therefore, the child can be considered looked after, but would not appear in official statistics and the local authority would not have parental responsibility for them.

If a child has committed a criminal offence, or is judged to pose a significant risk to themselves or others, they can be detained in a secure children's home. A secure care home restricts a young person's liberty and children placed here are considered to be looked after. On-site education is provided and children typically attend 25–30 hours of school per week. In this chapter, we will primarily discuss looked after children who are in foster care or residential care homes, due to the separate consideration which should be given to those in secure care homes.

A child will stop being looked after if they are adopted, returned home, or when they turn 18 (NSPCC 2016). A local authority will make every effort to return a child to their birth family; however, if their family is unable to provide adequate care, a child may be adopted. Many children wait a long time to find an adoptive family and older children often remain in permanent foster care if a suitable match cannot be found. When a looked after child turns 18 and leaves care, they will receive support from the local authority until they are 21; this support may include assistance with accommodation, finances and employment. It is important to note that children who are adopted and, therefore, no longer considered a LAC, will, in the vast majority of cases, have been looked after previously. Therefore, it is likely that adopted children will have probably suffered similar trauma to those who remain looked after and their needs must still be considered.

Why might a child be looked after?

There are a number of reasons why a child may become looked after. The vast majority of children who are looked after by the local authority have been removed from their families in order to keep them safe, as their families are unable to care for and protect them adequately. Children may be taken into care because they have suffered emotional or physical abuse or neglect. Other incidences include children whose parents have died, are unable to care for them, or are in another country. Some children may be 'accommodated' by the council at the parents' request due to illness or emergencies which prevent or impair the parents' ability to adequately care for their child. This means that the child is looked after by carers other than their own family, but their parents still retain responsibility for them and must be consulted regarding any decisions which involve the child. Some children may be looked after for a long period of time, whilst for others it is temporary. What is clear, however, is that all children who are looked after will have experienced trauma and, in many cases, frightening and emotional situations, which means that they can display challenging behaviour and thus be challenging to work with. Schools and all those who work with such vulnerable children have a duty to understand, care for and support them in realising their potential.

Scenario 1: Millie

Millie is 6 years old; it is her first day at her new school. She had to leave the school she was happy and familiar with to come to this one. Although very anxious, Millie is somewhat comforted by the fact that Jackie, her foster carer, is taking her to school and will at least be there to speak to her new teacher. As she approaches the school gates, she holds Jackie's hand very tightly and stares at the floor. If she is quiet, no one will want to speak to her and that's just fine. If no one speaks to her, then no one will ask her why she is starting at a new school halfway through the school year, no one will ask her why on some days she is collected by social workers and, most importantly, no one will ask her why she is not allowed to live with her Mum and Dad anymore.

Millie and her younger sister, Jade, experienced sustained sexual and physical abuse at the hands of their father. Their mother, herself a victim of domestic violence and an alcoholic, knew about the abuse but was unable to keep the girls safe. Social services became involved when staff at Millie's previous school reported that her younger sister had displayed inappropriate sexualised behaviour towards her classmates. The girls were taken into foster care and although placed with Jackie and her family in the same area, it was decided that they could no longer attend the same school because it would put them at risk of being approached by their parents.

Millie is a bright girl, cooperative and quiet, although she is very anxious. She has an extremely close relationship with her sister; however, since they have been in foster care, they have had several ferocious arguments which result in violent physical fights. On some occasions recently, Millie has been defiant towards her foster carers and this change in behaviour does seem to be linked to her situation and what she has been through.

How might being looked after act as a barrier to learning?

Despite educational attainment for looked after children in England improving over time, the attainment gap between those who are looked after and those who are not is significant. This pattern is also an international concern as 'research demonstrates that low educational attainment of children in care is an issue in many countries' (Dill, Flynn, Hollingshead and Fernandes 2012, cited in O'Higgins et al. 2015). At the end of Key Stage 2 in England, statutory assessment tests (SATs) are used as the measure for attainment. The government reports that '48 per cent of looked after children achieved the expected level in reading, writing (TA) and mathematics [SATs] combined in 2014 compared with 79 per cent of non-looked after children, an attainment gap of 31 percentage points' (HM Government 2014).

It is evident from data in Figure 10.1 below that in Key Stage 2 SATs, looked after children are attaining far less well than those who are not looked after; however, there has been gradual improvement in progress over time. All children have made progress year on year, including looked after children.

There has long been a recognised link between attainment in Key Stage 2 SATs and Key Stage 4, when GCSEs are used as the attainment measure. If a child attains below the expected level in Mathematics at Key Stage 2, for example, it is highly likely that they will achieve below a grade C in their Maths GCSE. Statistics released by the Department for Education (DfE) in 2014 continue to indicate that the vast majority of children who do not meet expected outcomes in Key Stage 2 will not meet the expected outcomes of five GCSE grades at A-C. Since less than half of looked after children achieve expected

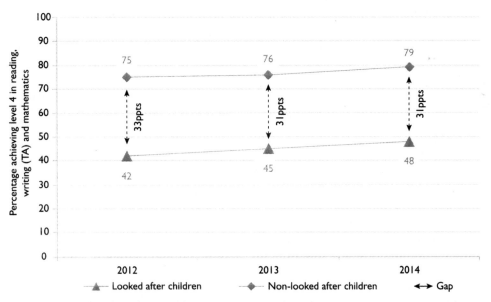

Figure 10.1 Attainment and attainment gaps between the percentages of looked after and non-looked after children achieving the expected level in reading, writing (TA) and mathematics, 2012–14 (HM Government 2014)

outcomes at Key Stage 2, it is unsurprising that only 12 per cent of looked after children achieved 5 A-C grades in 2013/14 compared to 52 per cent of non-looked after children (HM Government 2014).

A looked after child will not necessarily have similar needs or experience the same difficulties compared to their peers because *all* children, and indeed all people, are different. When working with any child, practitioners should seek to understand the needs of the individual and adjust teaching and learning accordingly through effective differentiation. However, research identifies some common factors which act as a barrier to learning for looked after children as a group and these will be discussed subsequently.

Due to the fact that looked after children will have experienced trauma and loss, it is perhaps not unsurprising that many experience poor mental health. In 2014, just half of the population of looked after children were considered to have 'normal' emotional and behavioural health (HM Government 2014). There is an established link between mental health and attainment. Vulnerable children such as these, who have at times not had their basic physiological, safety and relationship needs met, often have very low self-esteem. According to Maslow's hierarchy of needs (McLeod 2016), it will be more difficult for children who have suffered unmet needs at a basic level (food, security and love, for example) to progress and reach their cognitive and personal potential and achieve 'self-actualisation'.

According to data collated by HM Government, in 2014, 17.9 per cent of the *total* population of children had a Special Educational Need (SEN). However, 66.6 per cent (or two-thirds) of looked after children had an SEN, which is evidently much higher than the population as a whole. The most common type of SEN for looked after children are 'behavioural, emotional and social difficulties' (HM Government 2014). John Bowlby's work on attachment is very useful in furthering our understanding of the emotional difficulties a looked after child may face: '"Attachment" is a term which refers to the state and quality of an individual's attachments. These can be divided into secure and insecure attachment' (Holmes 2014, p.67). Looked after children will have experienced trauma and separation from their primary caregivers at some point, regardless of whether they are then returned to their family or adopted by a new family. Bowlby identified that if bonds with primary carers are broken, immediate distress and long-term psychological damage will occur. Bombér and Hughes (2013) highlight the fact that there is a direct correlation between emotional growth and learning. They state that the development of meaningful relationships with key adults is essential to emotional growth, with the same being true for learning. Consequently, looked after children who do not have secure and meaningful attachments with key adults will find it very difficult to learn.

An additional consequence of insecure attachment, poor mental health and low self-esteem can mean that looked after children display challenging behaviour, which can be defiant and violent in nature. As a result, the number of looked after children who are permanently excluded from school is twice as high as non-looked after children, although it is falling at a faster rate (HM Government 2014). If children are not able to access learning due to their emotional state or because of literal exclusion from it, it is inevitable that their educational outcomes will be very poor.

Jackson writes, 'Frequent movement within the care system is another of the factors which has been linked to educational underachievement. Changes of placement frequently mean changes of school and these changes often occur at inappropriate times' (Jackson 1989, cited in Goddard 2000, p.81). Local authorities have a duty to ensure that children subject to care orders are placed near to their home, do not experience disruption to their education and are placed with or near any siblings they have. However, this may not always be possible, for reasons such as availability of suitable foster care placements, requirement to move a child away for protection, or the breakdown of a foster placement. Looked after children may have periods of non-attendance during transitions between placements. This may also occur *during* a placement, if the relationship between the foster carer and child is a challenging one. Absences from school over time are likely to result in gaps in a child's learning, which makes it difficult for them to do well. For all children, starting at a new school and in a new class each year can be an anxious time. All children want to feel secure and familiar in the school and with their peers and adults. For looked after children, who have already experienced loss and separation, moving to a new school can be particularly distressing and is highly likely to have an impact on mental health and, therefore, educational outcomes.

It is necessary to emphasise that in their international systematic review of research, O'Higgins and colleagues (2015) concluded that being in care is not *in itself* a factor for poor educational outcomes for looked after children. Their review found that

> . . . there is a correlation between being in care and educational outcomes but that this relationship is mediated by a number of individual, family, environmental and risk factors . . . there is little support for the claim that being in foster or kinship care per se is detrimental to the educational outcomes of children in care.
>
> (O'Higgins et al, 2015, p.5)

As we have already mentioned, looked after children will have and continue to experience trauma and it is these pre-care experiences that are a key factor in affecting educational outcomes. Simply being in care does not mean that a child will have lower educational outcomes than those who are not. It is, however, clear that looked after children face a number of barriers to learning which will require the understanding of practitioners to ensure they are included.

Scenario 2: Millie

Millie, now 7, has settled in well to her Year 3 class; she has a small group of close friends and is doing well academically. Millie becomes very frustrated when her work, particularly writing, does not turn out exactly the way she had planned it. This means that sometimes her work is incomplete as she 'gives up' on getting it 'right'.

She has formed a good relationship with her class teacher and can be relied upon to be a good role model; she continues to be cared for by a foster family and has occasional 'contact' meetings with her Mum supervised by social services. Some mornings, Millie arrives at school teary and visibly morose; she joins her peers at her table, but puts her head in her hands and withdraws. Her class teacher has seen her like this before and quietly calls her for a chat, while the teaching assistant continues taking the register with the rest of the class.

Millie explains to her class teacher that she is upset due to a fight she had with her sister Jade that morning, during which Jade has told Millie that she hates her. The teacher reassures Millie and organises some time for her and her sister to speak to the learning mentor about the argument later that morning. Millie is able to join the class and participates fully in the lesson. After lunch, Millie returns to the classroom upset after a quarrel with a friend; there is another adult covering the class as the class teacher has non-contact time. Although the cover teacher is known to the class, they tend to misbehave when she is in charge. That afternoon, the children were taking part in a practical group activity, but the cover teacher found it difficult to manage the behaviour of some of the pupils which resulted in arguments within the groups, shouting and an unacceptable level of noise. Feeling unable to inform the teacher of her distress due to the continual noise, without asking permission Millie left the classroom and set off towards the school gates in order to leave.

How might practitioners improve educational outcomes for looked after children?

Section 22 of the Children's Act (1989) states that 'The duty of a local authority under subsection (3)(a) to safeguard and promote the welfare of a child looked after by them includes in particular a duty to promote the child's educational achievement.' In England, every local authority must appoint someone to promote the educational achievement of all the children looked after by that council. This person is known as a Virtual School Headteacher (VSH). The VSH is responsible for all looked after children in the borough and even though the children are physically attending different schools, they are on one 'virtual' school roll. Since 2009, it has been statutory for schools to have a designated teacher who is responsible for the educational achievement of any children in care in their school. The designated teacher is often the head teacher or other member of the senior leadership team, the inclusion manager, or Special Educational Needs Coordinator (SENCO), for example. It is the duty of the VSH and designated teacher to ensure that other practitioners in an education setting understand the issues which affect looked after children. They should also promote a culture of inclusion and high expectations for the outcomes of children in care. However, to return to the principles of inclusion, it is the responsibility of *all* practitioners to ensure the best outcomes for *all* children.

Figure 10.2 shows the key recommendations in the DfE guidance (2009) in improving the attainment of looked after children. The guidance was produced based on the good practice observed in a sample of fourteen primary schools. A fundamental message from this report and from what is known about good inclusive practice is that practitioners should 'do what they do for all children but more so' to raise the attainment of looked after children.

All looked after children must have a care plan and an integral part of this is a Personal Education Plan (PEP). The PEP is an evolving document detailing intended outcomes and objectives for the child and the steps that will be required to meet the child's needs. The PEP is essentially the document which sets out an individual plan to support the child in achieving their potential. It is crucial that practitioners have high expectations of what a looked after child can achieve, just as they should with all children, but that they are realistic about the support a LAC may require to get there. LAC are one of the groups of children who attract pupil premium funding; that is, local authorities will receive a pupil premium grant based on

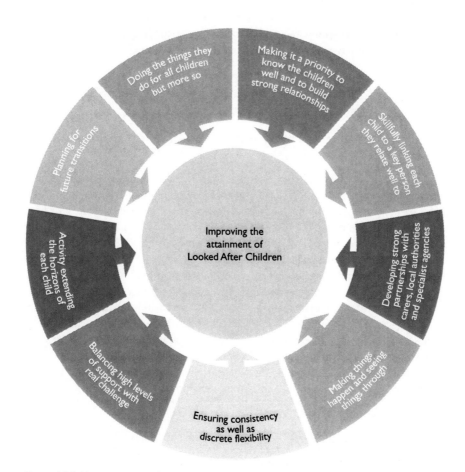

Figure 10.2 Key recommendations in the DfE guidance (2009) in improving the attainment of looked after children (HM Government 2009)

the number of children who have been looked after for at least one day. The additional funding is provided to help close the attainment gap between LAC and their peers. It is likely that the PEP will identify specific interventions for those children falling behind or indeed to challenge those who are performing well, and pupil premium funding can enable these interventions to take place. The designated teacher will take the lead on the development and implementation of the PEP and 'should use it to support the personalised learning of the child' (DfE 2014, p.14), but all relevant professionals such as social workers should have input. Most importantly, the child should be involved in the creation of the PEP. The child's voice should be taken into account when understanding and identifying the child's needs. Of course, an inclusive practitioner should take account of any child's views and ideas in relation to their learning and provision, but for looked after children this is especially important to ensure they feel empowered.

As there are many professionals across different agencies involved in the care of a looked after child, it is of utmost importance that good communication is established between them. The PEP contributes to this because

. . . when they are used effectively, PEPs improve the educational experience of the child by helping everyone gain a clear and shared understanding about the teaching and learning provision necessary to meet the child's education needs and how that will be provided.

(DfE 2014, p.13)

Becoming better informed about supporting looked after children

It is good practice for schools to hold regular meetings for staff to keep them updated about the needs of individual children. Information concerning LAC must be treated as confidential and shared on a need to know basis only; however, to help staff better understand the needs of looked after children, it may be appropriate to ask a school SENCO/inclusion manager to organise a visit from an educational psychologist or social worker who can give an overview of what it means to be a LAC, and the impact this can have on a child's educational experience and progress.

Some schools and educational settings have created a staff reference booklet that is kept in a secure area which identifies LAC and gives helpful information about possible triggers or difficulties they may face within the educational setting. Information included might be: who the designated teacher is, which key adults the child has good relationships with and strategies to use in those people's absence. It is not necessary, or appropriate, for everyone to know the details of the child's situation, but it is helpful to know if more care and sensitive understanding is needed.

Source: Knowles 2010

Central to supporting looked after children, whose mental health is often particularly fragile, is supporting them to develop positive relationships with adults and their peers. As discussed, many vulnerable children have been let down by the very adults they have relied upon and, as such, LAC often find it difficult to trust others. As Golding and Hughes (2012, cited in Bombér and Hughes 2013, p.3) state: 'all children need relationships to thrive; traumatised children need relationships to heal'. Bombér and Hughes (2013) go on to say that the provision of an attachment figure such as a key adult in an education setting *in addition* to an attachment figure at home can make a real difference to a child in terms of their emotional health. It is hoped that a looked after child will have formed an attachment to their primary carer, whether this be a foster or kinship carer or key worker in residential care, who will provide consistency, reliability and adequate care.

It is important then, that education settings are able to provide at least one key adult with whom the child can form an attachment in order for that child to experience feelings of safety and security. Geddes (2006, p.141, cited in Bombér and Hughes 2013, p.25) describes these adults as a 'surrogate secure base' for the child. A child who feels safe and cared for in an educational setting will be much more likely to be able to settle to learn. Showing empathy towards children can also have a positive effect on emotional state and therefore ability to learn. Empathy involves having awareness and showing an understanding of how another person may be feeling or thinking: 'Our pupils need to experience our empathy if they are to experience value, understanding, safety and the desire to learn when they are with us' (Bombér and Hughes 2013, p.142). If practitioners are able to approach interactions with vulnerable pupils such as those who are looked after with empathic understanding, they will be optimising the conditions to enable learning to take place. Being empathic does not mean excusing challenging behaviour, however; it is necessary for children to understand the behaviour that is acceptable and what is not. Nevertheless, if we are able to relate to children with empathy, we can provide emotional and mental safety for them leading to greater inclusion for all.

Supporting LAC whose behaviour might be challenging

During their pre-care experiences, looked after children are likely to have experienced adults who are:

- Unavailable
- Stern
- Distant
- Insensitive
- Cold
- Shut down
- Cut off from feeling
- Frightening.

Practitioners in education settings have the opportunity to be:

- Available
- Warm
- Present
- Sensitive
- Reassuring
- Opened up
- Connected to feeling
- Kind.

In education settings where there are usually many children, practitioners are responsible for ensuring behaviour is managed effectively to create a safe, calm and purposeful learning environment. This is indeed necessary; however, quite often we relate to children in some of the negative ways listed above in order to maintain 'discipline' and order, or because we fear that if we are 'too soft', challenging behaviour will be unmanageable. If we consider the benefits of showing empathy and providing additional attachment figures, relating to children positively seems more beneficial.

- Try relating to children in the positive ways listed above.
- What difference does this make to behaviour in your setting?
- Note down differences in children's responses when you approach a situation in this way.

Source: Adapted from Bombér and Hughes 2013

Supporting transition – what happens when a child leaves care?

As discussed earlier, a child stops being looked after for three reasons: adoption, turning 18 years old, or being returned to the family. In most cases, a child leaves care because they are adopted or because they reach adulthood; a smaller number of children return home. In an education setting, the most likely end-of-care scenario practitioners will experience is that of adoption. If an adoptive family has been found for the child, social services have a responsibility to support both the child and the new family with the transition, but it is equally important for the education setting to support the child. If the child's adoptive family is in a different area, not only will the child be moving to a new home, they will move to a new school also.

Scenario 3: Millie

Now in the final few weeks of Year 3 and aged 8, Millie feels settled and content in her school and she is finding arguments with her sister easier to deal with. She now has very limited contact sessions with her Mum and although regularly expressing that she wishes to live back at home with her family, she is, for the most part, happy with her foster family.

Millie is aware that the courts will soon meet to decide whether she may return, along with her sister, into the care of her parents. Millie's behaviour at school begins to deteriorate and her foster family notice that her bed-wetting is becoming more frequent. The school increases the frequency of the time that Millie spends with the learning mentor, both in class and as a therapeutic intervention out of lessons.

The learning mentor works with Millie on an art project which documents Millie's life through photographs and drawing. A few weeks before the summer holidays, the court rules that Millie and her sister will not return to their family and that a permanent adoptive placement will be sought. Millie withdraws and refuses to discuss the subject. It is eventually the learning mentor whom she chooses to talk to, initially expressing anger, fear and resistance. Experience tells the learning mentor that while Millie and Jade still have many challenges ahead of them, with the support from school and others around them, adoption will provide the girls with a stronger long-term chance of settling into a loving situation which will provide the basis of security and support needed to enable the girls to thrive.

As highlighted in the scenario above, the permanence of the decision that a looked after child will not return to their family is a difficult experience. Even if a child is fully aware and accepting of the reasons they are not able to return home, fundamentally children love their families and do not want to be separated from them. It is very likely that a looked after child's behaviour will change leading up to or following a court hearing, making empathic understanding from practitioners of utmost importance. If a child is found an adoptive family in or outside their local area, some of the activities detailed below may be used to enable a transition which allows the child to continue to learn.

Supporting LAC through transitions into new situations

LAC often experience many more changes and transitions than other children. Having to leave secure situations – schools, the place where we live – can cause us anxiety, sadness and fear about what might happen next. For LAC who experience these changes more frequently than others, knowing that they have to go through another change can impact on their sense of trust and self-worth.

To support looked after children during transition, you could work with them to make two identical memory books of their time at the education setting for each of you. This shows that you will remember them and provides a way for them to remember you too. You could leave some pages blank to encourage them to continue to add in details of their new beginning. It can help to maintain links via cards or letters and the child's peers can share in this with the support of the practitioner. The child should also be given opportunities to develop relationships in the new setting so contact would be reduced over time (Knowles 2010).

It can also be helpful for all children (both the looked after child and their peers) to experience children's literature on the theme in order to make sense of what is happening. The following texts, all suggestions from Letterbox Library (2016), offer stories on the theme of different families, fostering and adoption and may be used in a whole class context or with individual children as a starting point for discussion:

- *The Great Big Book of Families*, by Mary Hoffman, illustrated by Ros Asquith
- *Snowflakes*, by Cerrie Burnel, illustrated by Laura Ellen Anderson
- *Scarlet Ibis*, by Gill Lewis
- *The Red Thread: An Adoption Fairy Tale*, by Grace Lin
- *Motherbridge of Love*, by Anonymous, illustrated by Josée Masse.

In this chapter, we have discussed who a looked after child is and reasons why they may be looked after. We have provided an overview of the many possible barriers to learning that looked after children may face. In suggesting ways practitioners may help to reduce such barriers, ways of working which can benefit *all* children and support them in improving education outcomes have been highlighted. Finally, consideration has been given to periods of transition and adoption. It is necessary to remember, though, that children who have been looked after at any point in their lives will benefit from our time, understanding and empathy in working to ensure that they are included in our education system.

References

Bombér, L.M. and Hughes, D.A. (2013) *Settling to learn: Settling troubled pupils to learn: Why relationships matter in school*. London: Worth Publishing.

Children Act 1989, c. Available at: http://www.legislation.gov.uk/ukpga/1989/41 (accessed 12 March 2017)

DfE (Department for Education) (2014) Promoting the education of looked after children statutory guidance for local authorities. Available at: https://www.gov.uk/government/publications/promoting-the-education-of-looked-after-children (accessed 12 March 2017)

Goddard, J. (2000) The education of looked after children, *Child & Family Social Work*, 5(1), pp. 79–86. doi: 10.1046/j.1365-2206.2000.00143.x (accessed 12 March 2017)

HM Government (2009) *Improving the attainment of looked after children in primary schools guidance for schools*. Available at: https://www.gov.uk/government/uploads/system/uploads/attachment_data/file/190244/01047-2009.pdf (accessed 12 March 2017)

HM Government (2014) *Statistical First release outcomes for children looked after by local authorities in England as at 31 March 2014*. Available at: https://www.gov.uk/government/uploads/system/uploads/attachment_data/file/384781/Outcomes_SFR49_2014_Text.pdf (accessed 12 March 2017)

HM Government (2015) *Children looked after in England (including adoption and care leavers) year ending 31 March 2015*. Available at: https://www.gov.uk/government/uploads/system/uploads/attachment_data/file/464756/SFR34_2015_Text.pdf (accessed 12 March 2017)

Holmes, J. (2014) *John Bowlby and attachment theory*. 2nd edn. Hove: Routledge.

Knowles, G. (ed.) (2010) *Supporting inclusive practice*. 2nd edn. New York: Routledge.

Letterbox Library (2016) *Letterbox library*. Available at: www.letterboxlibrary.com/

McLeod, S. (2016) Maslow's hierarchy of needs. Available at: https://www.simplypsychology.org/maslow.html (accessed 27 April 2017)

NSPCC (2016) Children in care. Available at: https://www.nspcc.org.uk/preventing-abuse/child-protection-system/children-in-care/ (accessed 12 March 2017)

O'Higgins, A., Sebba, J. and Luke, N. (2015) *What is the relationship between being in care and the educational outcomes of children? An international systematic review*. Available at: http://reescentre.education.ox.ac.uk/wordpress/wp-content/uploads/2015/09/ReesCentreReview_Educational Outcomes.pdf (accessed 12 March 2017)

Who Cares Trust (2016) Available at: www.thewhocarestrust.org.uk/ (accessed 12 March 2017)

Chapter 11

Supporting and including children from low income families

Fabienne Benoist

This chapter explores:

- What we mean by low income and poverty and how poverty is defined
- The families living on low income in the UK today and the impact of low income and poverty on children's well-being, development and learning
- Supporting children from low income families
- The attainment gap between children from low income backgrounds and their peers
- The pupil premium and how schools have used the extra funding to raise attainment
- Key aspects of good practice and what schools can do to enable all children regardless of income to achieve.

What do we mean by low income and poverty?

Although low income and poverty are not quite interchangeable terms, they are nonetheless often used synonymously and it would be difficult to discuss one without defining the other. So what do we mean when we talk about poverty? Is it just about a family's or an individual's lack of money or could it also be about people's inability to achieve well-being in the society they live in? If income is the measure we use to define status on the one hand and quality of living standards on the other, it is important then to define these terms also.

Absolute poverty

During the World Summit for Social Development in Copenhagen, 6–12 March 1995, the United Nations first adopted a definition of absolute poverty. One hundred and seventeen countries agreed that absolute poverty was characterised by the severe deprivation of basic human needs, including food, safe drinking water, sanitation facilities, health, shelter, education and information (UN 1995). These absolute measures are the minimum subsistence standards – in other words, having enough income to cover minimum living standards. However, these measures tend to hide the real extent of poverty, as it does not include a broader aspect of the life quality individuals are able to achieve within their society. Extreme or absolute poverty is understood as living with under US$1 a day, the poverty line rule of thumb measure adopted by the World Bank in 1990. This amount was increased in 2009 to US$1.25 and again in 2015 to US$1.90 (Hickel 2015).

Relative poverty

Relative poverty is based on contemporary norms and social standards which change over time (Lansley & Mack 2015). The official measure of relative poverty in the UK is when a household income falls below 60 per cent of median income (Seymour 2009). Median income is accepted as accounting for the total income, including all benefits but minus direct taxes. These measures are accepted and used internationally to allow for comparisons between countries and for the study of trends over time. In 2013–14, the median income in the UK was approximately £21,900 per year (HM Revenue and Customs 2016) and 60 per cent of this is £13,140 per year. Hence, any households falling below this income would be considered in relative poverty. Poor people lack sufficient wealth to meet life's necessities or comforts and are unable to live in a manner that is considered acceptable in a society.

There are issues with this definition of relative poverty as it does not take housing costs, debt repayments, or changes in the cost of living, etc. into account and in effect it is likely to give a much lower poverty count than in reality (Lansley & Mack 2015). Income is important as it determines people's living standards but it is also an arbitrary measure. Living standards are referred to as a 'household's level of access to goods, services and recreational activities' (Parliamentary Office of Science and Technology 2015, p.1). In other words, living standards are not exclusively about wealth in monetary terms, but include notions of how comfortably people are able to live and participate in their society. Hence, it is argued that looking in depth into people's standards of living/way of life will provide a better answer to the question 'how poor is too poor?' (Lansley & Mack 2015, p.12).

The capability approach

The concept of the 'capability approach' was developed by Armatya Sen (1979), an Indian economist and philosopher who became the Nobel laureate in Economics in 1998. The capability approach was subsequently developed further by Martha Nussbaum, an American feminist philosopher and ethicist (Nussbaum & Sen 1993). The main premise of the framework is that well-being is not just a matter of resources. Freedom, rights, choices and values individuals have determine what they are able to be or do, and hence the life they are able to live.

This approach is not an explanatory theory; it does not explain poverty, inequality, or well-being. However, it is a notion that helps conceptualise these ideas and assists in describing poverty, inequality, quality of life, or social change. It is in effect a framework which evaluates the lives of individuals. The focus of this approach is on individuals' beings and doings, which Sen calls 'functionings', and the opportunities they have in achieving those beings and doings, which he refers to as 'capabilities'.

> *Examples of beings:* being well fed or not, living in a warm house or not, being educated or illiterate, having a social support network or being part of a gang, being healthy or depressed, etc.

> *Examples of doings:* caring for a child, travelling, voting, heating a house, giving money to charity.

Capabilities are understood within this framework as individuals' real freedoms and opportunities to achieve these functionings. Being poor seriously curtails people's capabilities, that is their ability and opportunity to achieve a quality of life without shame, and arguably leads to social exclusion.

The consensual method

The notion of the consensual method started with a television programme in 1983: *Breadline Britain*. Subsequent studies were carried out in 1990, 1999 and 2012 (Lansley & Mack 2015). It is based on the idea of consensus and on society's perception of contemporary needs at the time. Members of the public across the UK were gathered in small representative focus groups and made a consensual decision regarding the minimum standards of living in contemporary society today. They devised a list of items and activities deemed a necessity to achieve minimum living standards and allow for inclusion and participation in society. They also listed items and activities that were desirable, but not a deemed a necessity. These necessities have altered over the last three decades, some have been taken out and others added in order to reflect the changes in society. Gordon and colleagues (2013) listed a number of items and activities which are broadly representative of living standards. These necessities go from the most basic such as food, shelter and warmth to societal activities such as dining out, going to the cinema, or visiting relatives.

Breadline Britain

The *Breadline Britain* report (Lansley & Mack 2015) made adjustments to the list of necessities to reflect changes in living standards since 1999. The members of the public who took part in the selection compiled two lists. The first combined twenty-five items or activities which were deemed absolute necessities for all adults in contemporary Britain. The second was targeted at children and again contained twenty-five items or activities deemed necessities for all children.

Poverty is not just about lack of income. It is about the consequences of this lack of income, which translates into not being able to participate fully in society and, more often than not, means the poor are effectively socially excluded.

Think about what the bare necessities required in today's society are to allow for full participation as valued members of said society. From a sociological viewpoint, social participation means people's ability to be involved directly or indirectly in the economic, social, cultural and political processes which affect their lives. Make two lists: one for adults and one for children.

Redefining poverty

In 2012, the UK coalition government commissioned the Centre for Social Justice, an 'independent' think-tank established by Iain Duncan Smith who at the time was the Secretary of State for Work and Pensions, to have a rethink about how poverty should be defined. The think tank published the 'Rethinking Child Poverty' paper (CSJ 2012), which laid out the basis for the subsequent *Measuring Child Poverty* document (HMG 2012).

The main premise for a redefinition of poverty can be clearly construed from the following quote:

> The Centre for Social Justice (CSJ) is clear that in order to construct a measure of poverty that is both accurate and useful, it is vital that the main drivers of poverty – family breakdown, educational failure, economic dependency and worklessness, addiction and serious personal debt – are made the priority for measurement.
>
> (CSJ 2012, p.1)

Poverty was now to be measured by people's behaviour and characteristics and not their circumstances. The Department for Work and Pensions (DWP) survey sets out criteria to measure child poverty in the UK and states that these criteria 'should be widely accepted by the public as being a fair representation of those children growing up in poverty' (DWP 2013, p.2). These characteristics included: having parents addicted to drugs and alcohol, living in a local area which is not safe, growing up in a household with unmanageable debts, experiencing family breakdown, going to a failing school, or having parents lacking qualifications or skills for employment. It could be argued that the aim of this redefining was to downgrade the importance of income and living standards by focusing on parenting skills, health, drug and alcohol addiction, and family stability. The Conservatives' argument was that poverty is caused by individuals' failings and therefore being or becoming poor is a personal choice lying in people's lack of social and personal responsibility. This notion was made clear by Iain Duncan Smith: 'the nature of the life you lead and the choices that you make have a significant bearing on whether you live in poverty' (CSJ 2009, p.9, cited in Lansley n.d.). However, in early 2016, when he was faced with huge opposition from other political parties, church groups and poverty campaigners, Mr Duncan Smith abandoned the project and the current system of defining relative poverty by measure of median income threshold is being maintained for the foreseeable future (Allen 2016).

Examples of negative media coverage of those living on low incomes

Figure 11.1 Examples of negative media coverage of those living on low incomes

There are many examples such as these types of headlines and articles in the British press. On reading, note down the words used to describe a particular section of society. What is being implied here? What is the perception of people claiming benefits?

Who are the families on low income?

The activity above highlights how a negative dominant discourse about those on low income is created and maintained. Discourse denotes how people think and communicate about different subjects or people, and it becomes dominant discourse when the notions about any subjects or people are the accepted norms within a given culture or society. The language used, whether in speech or in writing, is a reflection of the ideologies of those who have the most power in society (Foucault 2002).

The dominant discourse about poor people and benefits claimants is expressed by the press in the use of words such as 'scroungers' or 'work skivers' who are depicted as draining the public purse whilst living on far too generous benefits. There is unfortunately a large part of the British media perpetuating this myth. One could further argue that this may be politically and ideologically motivated, a way for the general public to accept and ignore the consequences of the austerity measures put in place after the coalition government gained power in 2010.

The reality is in fact quite different. Over half of poor households in the UK have at least one person in employment. Those households where there are sick or disabled relatives or a carer looking after the family will also have someone in employment (Lansley & Mack 2015). The *Breadline Britain* survey (Lansley & Mack 2015) found that the most significant shift in poverty statistics in the last three decades has been the increase in the number of households in work living in deprivation.

The group Poverty and Social Exclusion in the UK (PSEUK) published a final report on child poverty and social exclusion in 2014 (Pemberton et al. 2014). Although the findings did outline a significant association between worklessness and poverty, the report also clearly highlighted that the majority of children living in poverty came from a household with at least some paid work (65 per cent). Where at least one adult was in full-time work, nearly half of the children in these households were living in poverty. Although the majority of poor children in the UK live in a household with two or more adults, the PSEUK 2014 findings further indicate that it is children in single-parent families who may be at a greater risk of living in poverty.

When it comes to ethnicity and poverty, Lansley and Mack (2015) report no change in over a decade. Black/Black British and Pakistani/Bangladeshi households were more likely to be at risk of living in poverty (56 per cent and 42 per cent respectively). These findings are very much similar to the PSE 2014 report, which also highlighted that across all poverty measures, the greatest number of poor children were White British.

The Joseph Rowntree Foundation's latest report's (Fitzpatrick et al. 2016) findings on poverty and destitution in the UK supports the 2015 *Breadline Britain* report (Lansley & Mack 2015). Necessities include the most basics of needs: the ability to afford food and shelter as well as staying warm and dry and clean. At some point during 2015, 1.25 million people, 79 per cent born in the UK, were destitute, including 325,000 children. As this is considering the more extreme end of the poverty spectrum (i.e. destitution), it is likely that when including families struggling on low income, numbers are much higher than these figures.

Scenario 1: Angel and Georgia

Angel and her twin sister Georgia live with both their parents and baby sister in B&B accommodation and have had to change school three times over the past academic year. When Angel's father was made redundant, the family lost their home and thus began the journey of a life in temporary accommodations. The family was moved from one London borough to another and it has been difficult for Mum and Dad to find temporary work, even occasionally. Recently, their father has been offered a zero hours contract; however, there is not enough income for the family to afford a rented home or enough food to feed everyone properly. Mum and Dad often do without so that the children have something to eat, and the family is clearly struggling to afford the most basic of necessities. The children's latest school is very keen on the use of information and communication technologies (ICT) for parents to get more involved and for the children to complete their homework. The precariousness of the family's living situation means that the children do not own a computer or have access to the Internet. Angel and Georgia are regularly being told off by their teacher for not completing their weekly homework. They are both too ashamed to explain why they are not able to do their work.

How can a school or education setting support Angel and Georgia?

What could your educational setting in this case do as far as good practice is concerned? Moreover, what can be done about digital poverty? How does your setting bridge the digital divide?

The Children's Commission on Poverty report (Holloway et al. 2014) highlighted that in their survey nearly a third of the children who lived in poverty had fallen behind on their homework, due to the fact that they did not have a computer or Internet access at home. These children were often met with disbelief by teachers and thought of as trying to get out of completing their work. Children reported feeling shame and embarrassment at having to disclose their lack of access to ICT. Schools' answer is usually to set up lunch time or after-school homework clubs; however, these were often seen as the *poor kids'* homework clubs. Moreover, these children were missing out on other more exciting extracurricular activities organised by the schools. The report clearly highlighted that reducing the impact of poverty was not only about providing support, but more importantly, teachers needed to develop their understanding of how poverty affects children and young people's lives and the stigma that is attached to it.

What is the impact on children's well-being, development and learning when living on low income or in poverty?

Shame

The effects of poverty are well researched by psychologists and there is clear evidence to suggest that people who live in deprived circumstances suffer significant psychological problems. The group Psychologists Against Austerity (PAA) published a briefing paper highlighting how austerity policies are having a real, measurable impact on mental health. To experience humiliation and shame, fear and distrust, instability and insecurity, isolation and loneliness, feelings of being trapped or powerless increases the likelihood of mental health problems (PAA 2015).

Shame is a self-conscious and social emotion. When people feel disempowered and lack agency, they become highly critical of their abilities to cope financially, when they are in fact showing enormous efforts in managing scarce resources. For parents, these feelings only instil a sense of failure in their ability to care for their children.

Furthermore, Chase and Walker (2013) describe shame as a co-construction: the combination of how individuals judge their own inabilities on the one hand and, on the other, the anticipated judging of others who may demonstrate verbally or symbolically their own sense of social and moral superiority. There is a long history of qualitative studies which highlight the overwhelming feelings of shame and helplessness that are experienced by poor people and that these feelings have consistently been associated with chronic depression (Yongmie 2013).

Social exclusion and isolation

Lister describes the psychological pain experienced by people living in poverty with the following words: 'disrespect, humiliation and an assault on dignity and self-esteem; shame and stigma; and also powerlessness, lack of voice, and denial of full human rights and diminished citizenship' (2013, p.112). Moreover, it is the concept of the other or 'othering' (Lister 2013) which seems to give society permission to treat the poor as not only different but also inferior, establishing and maintaining social distance – in other words, excluding and isolating a vast number of adults, families and children.

Pemberton and colleagues (2014) highlighted the stigma attached to low income households through a pervasive and dominant discourse of portraying a distorted view of life on low income as disseminated through the media. This discourse not only stereotypes individuals but to some extent institutionalises the poor. The poor are viewed with suspicion and their morals are evaluated: the single mothers, the sick or disabled, the young offenders, etc., all gathered under the same pejorative umbrella of benefits claimants. The same report also outlines the disrespect that people on low income receive throughout their daily lives, with participants in the survey offering numerous examples of verbal abuse and bullying when accessing services, or sometimes directly experienced in their children's schools.

Health and well-being

There is consistent evidence in the body of literature about the wide range of negative outcomes associated with living in poverty. These outcomes relate to children's physical health, cognitive and language development, attainment in education and academic achievement. There is also increasing data which support that poverty is a causal influence on the mental, emotional and behavioural health of children (Yoshikawa, Aber & Beardslee 2012).

The effects of poverty are cumulative and do not occur in a vacuum or in isolation. Children's academic achievement or lack of it, for example, is multifaceted and a number of factors can be accounted for educational attainment: from family history – the mother's educational background, for example – to genetics. However, there is mounting evidence of increased rates of depression in low socio-economic-status (SES) households. Furthermore, depressed parents and marital conflicts are related to higher rates of disorganised attachment in early childhood (Yoshikawa et al. 2012).

Research by Akee and colleagues (2010) is often cited in support of the causal link between poverty and children's overall well-being and educational attainment. The researchers investigated the impact of an increase in income to American Indian households (the opening of a casino on a reservation allowed for profits to be distributed equally to all American Indian families). They found that an increase in income translated to sustained decrease in behavioural problems in children, as well as raised educational attainment. There were also substantially fewer recorded minor offences and arrests by age 16 and an increase in the number of young people finishing the equivalent of secondary schooling.

Further evidence was highlighted in Wilkinson and Pickett's report *The Spirit Level* (2010). This book examined outcomes in education, mental and physical health, life expectancy and obesity across wealthy societies. The authors argue that it is not just about how affluent a society is but the inequalities in the distribution of resources which impact the most on the above-mentioned. The societies with the largest gaps in income between the 20 per cent richest and the 20 per cent poorest have the worst outcomes. The highest gaps were found in Singapore, the USA, Portugal and the UK. The lowest gaps were located in Japan, Finland, Norway, Denmark and Sweden. Wilkinson and Pickett (2010) concluded that in a more egalitarian society, there is better social cohesion, trust, involvement in community life and a lower level of violence.

Supporting children from low income families

In 2016, the Child Poverty Action Group updated and published the following figures (CPAG 2016): 3.9 million children in the UK lived in poverty – 28 per cent of all UK children – or to make this a more concrete, visual and meaningful figure it is the equivalent of nine children in every class of thirty who are living in poverty today. This figure is established on a median income base line and although it is the usual way for poverty researchers to come up with numbers, it is only a rough estimate, as was discussed earlier in this chapter. Due to recent changes in tax and benefits, the International Monetary Fund (IMF) estimates this number will rise to 4.6 million by 2020.

In a systematic review examining possible causation of households' financial resources onto children's outcomes, Cooper and Stewart published compelling evidence – gathered from thirty-four studies worldwide – denoting clear indications that 'money makes a difference to children's outcomes' (2013, p.5). Most of the evidence gathered suggested that lack of money had a direct impact on children's cognitive development and school achievement. This was followed closely by social and behavioural development. Published under the umbrella of the Joseph Rowntree Foundation, the authors posit that an increase in households' incomes would bring substantial reductions in differences in children's outcomes between the low income and others. It would not, however, completely eliminate that gap. Cooper and Stewart (2013) went further as to suggest that a £7,000 increase in income in households with children on free school meals (FSMs) would halve the attainment gap in KS2 SATs (between FSM and non-FSM children).

The link between low income, poverty and educational achievement

On behalf of the Joseph Rowntree Foundation, Connelly, Sullivan and Jerrim (2014) published a comprehensive review of educational attainment in primary and secondary schools in the UK. The authors drew the following conclusions:

- The level and/or experience of parental education was in itself a strong predictor of children's educational attainment.
- Economic, cultural and social capital had a direct impact on educational inequalities.
- The socio-economic gap in educational attainment was greater than the ethnic or gender gap.
- Socio-economic disadvantage was equally damaging for children of both genders.
- Educational inequalities start in the pre-school years and continue to grow through primary and secondary schooling.

The attainment gap

According to figures published by the DfE (2015), the UK has one of the largest performance gaps between pupils from more and less disadvantaged backgrounds amongst all OECD countries, although the attainment gap at KS2 level 4 or above has narrowed in the last couple of years from 19 per cent to 16 per cent. However, whilst there is an association between low educational attainment and being poor, low income is not the only cause of social inequalities in educational outcomes (Connelly et al. 2014). Sociologists such as Bourdieu and Passeron (1977) would argue that social class differences in attainment can be explained with reference to three forms of capital: economic, social and cultural.

Financial resources do matter, as was highlighted earlier in this chapter (Cooper & Stewart 2013), not only in the sense that money can buy private schooling or tutors, but well-off parents have the ability to afford housing in a catchment area with good public-funded schools (Ireson & Rushforth 2004). Economic capital can have a direct impact on the quality of children and young people's environment; for instance, having one's own room to study, or access to a computer and the Internet.

What Bourdieu (1986) refers to as 'social capital' can be best described as the relationships between people in families, schools and communities (Connelly et al. 2014), a network of social connections which may explain the realities of social inequalities. In an education context, people on low income could be at a social capital disadvantage; for example, working long hours may leave parents little time to connect or get involved with the school or school activities.

Prieur and Savage (2013) explain that the notion of cultural capital was developed originally as a tool to explain that children's successful educational attainment depended on the level of their parents' education and Connelly and colleagues (2014) made this their first conclusion from their report, as highlighted above. The main idea is that capitalist society reproduces itself, and its power is maintained through the transmission of culture. Over a number of years, culture is acquired consciously or not, first through socialisation within the family and then schooling (speech pronunciation or appreciation of the arts, for example) (Madigan 2002; Ball 2004). Bourdieu (1986) argues that children from what is seen as the higher social classes start with an advantage because their families are well off and free from economic worries. They are more likely to possess books or have access to music tuitions, for instance. Working-class children are taught in schools with the values of the dominant classes, which are embodied in the education system and the school curriculum. Dominant classes maintain their power because their children already possess the cultural capital demanded in schools.

A deficit model?

Deficit theory in education refers to pupils differing from the norm, whether it is through disability or special learning needs, ethnicity, or language and culture, and as such these pupils are considered deficient. The process of education will correct these perceived deficiencies. Gorski highlights the myths of the culture of poverty, or the belief that poor people share 'a consistent and observable "culture"' (2008, p.32). The author cites numerous studies which concluded that there was no such thing as a culture of poverty and differences in behaviour and value systems were just as great between poor or wealthy people. Gorski goes on to explain that the concept is a construction based on stereotypes that have become unquestioned facts. Myths such as poor people lack motivation and work ethics, poor parents are not involved in their children's education and learning, being poor also means you are more likely to be a drug or alcohol addict and poor people are 'linguistically deficient' (2008, p.33). For Dudley-Marling (2007), it is cultural and linguistic differences which are constructed as deficiencies needing to be fixed and disadvantaged pupils are made to learn the appropriate and correct cultural and linguistic practices of the middle classes. The author further argues that the deficit approach aims to mould poor children to the image of the dominant middle class.

Scenario 2: Angel and Georgia

Angel and Georgia will both be attending a local secondary school for the first time in the new academic year. Their living situation is still precarious and there has not been any money for going away on holiday over the summer break. Now both Angel and Georgia's parents are worried about the cost of their girls transitioning to secondary school. The exact and prescriptive requirements of their new school uniforms are an expense that the parents can ill afford. The emblazoned blazers and school sweaters, book bags and PE kits can only be purchased from one specialist supplier. Angel and Georgia's parents are unable to get a crisis loan and will have to cut back on other necessities, such as food or heating, in order to be able to afford the girls' uniforms.

DfE (2013) non-statutory guidance on school uniforms policy makes clear that cost and value for money should be the highest priority consideration when schools set out their uniform policy. The guidance suggests that school uniforms should be available for purchase in supermarkets or other good-value shops. The Children's Commission on Poverty's inquiry *Through Young Eyes: At what cost? Exposing the impact of poverty on school life* (Holloway et al. 2014) reported that on average families spent £800 a year on school costs. The commission found that more than two-thirds of parents struggle with school costs and the three main items parents worried about providing for their children whilst in full time education were school uniforms, other extracurricular activities such as school trips, and school meals. Children are aware their parents struggle to afford these items and this has led many to feelings of shame and embarrassment, and more than a quarter of children taking part in the inquiry stated they had been bullied as a result.

When it comes to school materials and trips, again government guidelines are clear that schools cannot charge for any materials (books, instruments, or other equipment) relating to the teaching of the national curriculum during or outside school hours; with regards to school trips, schools should not exclude pupils if parents are unwilling or unable to pay and, if this is the case, children must still be given an equal chance to participate to the visit (DfE, 2014). Schools can ask for voluntary contributions but must make clear there is no obligation to contribute.

However, the commission found that there are schools which charge for many materials, adding to the financial burden of struggling and disadvantaged families. The inquiry found that children from less well-off backgrounds were avoiding certain subjects due to the costs of materials, specialised equipment, or trips associated with these courses (one in six of all children, rising to 30 per cent of children from disadvantaged backgrounds).

The inquiry also found that many schools did not make clear to parents when asking for contributions to school activities that these were not compulsory. In the study, 37 per cent of all children stated they had missed a school trip due to the cost, rising to 67 per cent of children from disadvantaged backgrounds. Sometimes the trips are mandatory and part of the curriculum (a visit to a museum or an art exhibition, for example). This affects children from less well-off families' ability to participate fully in their education, as well as missing out on the social aspect of school visits/trips. Poor children are in effect excluded from full participation as citizens in our society.

How might a school or educational setting provide further support for Angel and Georgia?

The governing bodies of schools and educational settings are responsible for setting up uniform policy. Have a look at your school governing body's policy. How is the DfE guidance taken into account regarding cost and value for money?

Look also at your school's or setting's policy on charging for additional educational materials and school trips. Again, does the school adhere to the DfE guidelines?

How does your school or setting manage the financial barriers experienced by some children and families that may curtail children's full participation in their education?

The pupil premium

In April 2011, the coalition government introduced the 'pupil premium' in order to tackle the performance gap between pupils from disadvantaged backgrounds and their peers, and to increase social mobility (DfE 2015). The pupil premium is added funding given to publicly funded schools according to the number of its disadvantaged pupils. Pupils who have been registered as eligible for free school meals (FSMs) at any point in the previous six years or who have been in care for six months or more are counted in the allocation of the pupil premium (Ofsted 2014). The school can use the funding in the best interests of all its eligible pupils. In 2013–14, the premium was £953 per academic year for each primary pupil and £900 per secondary student.

How schools use the pupil premium funding

The Department for Education (DfE 2013) surveyed schools in England to investigate how the extra funding was being spent and found that the majority of schools (primary, secondary, pupil referral units and special schools) were aiming to support all disadvantaged pupils, with a minority of schools targeting specific groups of individual pupils who were not making good progress. Schools provided a range of support including one-to-one tutoring or small group teaching, additional staff such as teaching assistants, learning mentors, or family support workers, help with school trips, parental support, out-of-hours activities, or provision of material and resources.

In 2015, the Sutton Trust and Education Endowment Foundation (EEF) published recommendations for the next steps with the pupil premium. The EEF 2015 survey found that 76 per cent of schoolteachers thought the premium had allowed schools to target resources to raise attainment to a great or to some extent, and the use of early intervention schemes has seen a significant increase, from 16 per cent in 2012 to 31 per cent in 2015. Because the premium was only introduced in 2011, there has been little research done and thus evidence on the effectiveness the extra funding has had in bridging the gap in attainment between disadvantaged pupils and their peers is sparse. Current data shows that in primary schools the gap in attainment has been narrowed, but in secondary schools the data is inconclusive. The percentage point gap for pupils achieving five or more A*-C GCSEs including English and Maths was nearly the same between 2011/12 and 2013/14, 27.2 per cent and 27.4 per cent respectively (EEF 2015). It will be interesting to see if the gains made by the practice of early interventions in primary settings will carry over when this generation of children reaches secondary schools.

Key aspects of good practice

Improving the outcome of educational attainment for children from low income families has been on the political agenda of all mainstream parties for decades. Successive educational policies and changes in curriculum provision have not changed the status quo: children and young people from disadvantaged backgrounds are still lagging behind their peers. The OECD's report (2012) is clear and unequivocal about this issue: the reality is that children and young people from disadvantaged backgrounds are at higher risk of low performance.

The National Foundation for Educational Research (NFER) was commissioned by the Department for Education to investigate what schools across the country were doing to improve the performance of disadvantaged pupils and, when successful in this task, what set of common features could be drawn from this (DfE 2015). The study found that no single intervention led to success. The strategies that schools found most effective were focused on teaching and learning strategies including paired or small group teaching, improved feedback and one-to-one tuition. In secondary schools, the use of meta-cognitive learning (helping pupils to learn how to learn), as well as independent and peer learning strategies, were found to be related to success in raising the attainment of disadvantaged pupils. Schools that had started interventions early were also the most successful in bridging the attainment gap.

The lower performing schools were also found to have common characteristics with regards to disadvantaged pupil education attainment. Schools with higher levels of absence, higher proportions of disadvantaged children, larger year groups, higher proportions of children with special educational needs, higher proportions of White British ethnic backgrounds, and rural schools were all associated with lower performance among disadvantaged pupils. There were also some localised UK regions associated with low performance compared with schools in London or the North East, namely in the South East, South West, the East of England and the North West.

Lewis and Demie (2015) also identified similar key good practice in their schools case study. These strategies included strong leadership and an inclusive curriculum meeting the needs of working-class pupils. They also found that engaging with parents and breaking the cycle of low aspiration contributed to the schools' success in narrowing the attainment gap. Of interest also, the authors found that the most successful schools were led by head teachers with white working-class roots, who had a strong commitment to the issues of white working-class communities. Demie and McLean (2015) suggest that factors which assist in successfully closing the gap include strong leadership, high-quality teaching and learning strategies, inclusive curriculum, effective use of data, one-to-one support and the use of the best teachers in interventions. These findings support what Ofsted (2014) had identified, in that the schools showing the most improvement were committed to closing the attainment gap and had robust tracking systems of their pupils' learning needs.

Conclusion

This chapter has attempted to explore some of the issues faced by children who live on low income and its subsequent impact on their educational attainment. It is clear that the effects of poverty reach further than the school gates. There is a need for educational practitioners to appreciate the far-reaching consequences of living in poverty, as well as to understand why socio-economic disadvantage impacts on learning. There is a lot that schools can do to raise the attainment of low income family children, but to achieve social justice in education will certainly remain dependent on the allocation of state funding where it is needed (Lupton & Hempel-Jorgensen 2012) and the pupil premium funding will need to be maintained.

Social mobility may possibly increase through educational attainment; however, poverty levels are the result of structural inequalities in the economy and society and this cannot be addressed by only reforming schools (Connelly et al. 2014). The achievement gap between children on low income and their better-off peers also raises questions with regard to the cultural elements of schools and the curriculum. If schools in disadvantaged areas have been successful in raising attainment, the research shows than an inclusive curriculum was part of the solution. This would suggest that schools need to be flexible and listening in to the needs not only of their pupils, but also of the wider community they serve.

References

Akee, R. K. Q., Copeland, W. E., Keeler, G., Angold, A. & Costello, E. J. (2010) Parents' incomes and children's outcomes: A quasi-experiment using transfer payments from casino profits, *American Economic Journal: Applied Economics*, Vol. 2 pp86–115

Allen, K. (2016) Tories drop attempt to redefine child poverty after wide opposition. *Financial Times*. Available from: www.ft.com/cms/s/0/2c0617e0-dc80-11e5-a72f-1e7744c66818.html?siteedition=uk (accessed 12 March 2017)

Ball, S. J. (ed.) (2004) *The Routledge Falmer Reader in Sociology of Education*. Abingdon, Oxon: RoutledgeFalmer

Bourdieu, P. (1986) The forms of capital. In J. Richardson (ed.) *Handbook of Theory and Research for the Sociology of Education*. New York: Greenwood, pp241–258

Bourdieu, P. and Passeron, J. C. (1977) *Reproduction in Education, Society and Culture*. Beverly Hills, CA: Sage

Chase, E. & Walker, R. (2013) The co-construction of shame in the context of poverty: Beyond a threat to the social bond, *Sociology*, Vol. 47(4) pp739–754

Connelly, R., Sullivan, A. & Jerrim, J. (2014) *Primary and Secondary Education and Poverty Review*. University of London: Centre for Longitudinal Studies

Cooper, K. & Stewart, K. (2013) Does money affect children's outcome? A systematic review. Joseph Rowntree Foundation

CPAG (Child Poverty Action Group) (2016) Child poverty facts and figures. Available from: www.cpag.org.uk/child-poverty-facts-and-figures#footnote1_zzou99o (accessed 12 March 2017)

CSJ (Centre for Social Justice) (2009) Why is the government anti-marriage? Family Policy derived from strong evidence would lead to policies which supported marriage. Available from: www.centreforsocialjustice.org.uk/library/government-anti-marriage-family-policy-derived-strong-evidence-lead-policies-supported-marriage (accessed 12 March 2017)

CSJ (Centre for Social Justice) (2012) Rethinking child poverty. Available from: www.centreforsocialjustice.org.uk/library/rethinking-child-poverty (accessed 12 March 2017)

Demie, F. & McLean, C. (2015) Tackling disadvantage: what works in narrowing the achievement gap in schools. *Review of Education*, Vol. 3(2) pp138–174

DfE (2015) Supporting the Attainment of Disadvantaged Pupils: Articulating success and good practice. Available from: https://www.gov.uk/government/publications/supporting-the-attainment-of-disadvantaged-pupils (accessed 12 March 2017)

DfE (2014) *Charging for School Activities: Departmental advice for governing bodies, school leaders, school staff and local authorities*

DfE (2013) *Evaluation of Pupil Premium – Research Brief*

Dudley-Marling, C. (2007) Return of the deficit. *Journal of Educational Controversy*, Vol. 2 pp1–14

DWP (2013) *Public Views on Child Poverty: Results from the first polling undertaken as part of the Measuring Child Poverty Consultation*

EEF (Sutton Trust and Education Endowment Foundation) (2015) *The Pupil Premium: Next steps*

Fitzpatrick, S. et al. (2016) *Destitution in the UK*. London: Joseph Rowntree Foundation

Foucault, M. (2002) *Archaeology of Knowledge*. London: Routledge

Gordon, D. et al. (2013) *The Impoverishment of the UK. PSE UK first results: Living standards*. PSE UK: ESRC

Gorski, P. (2008) The myth of the culture of poverty. *Educational Leadership*, Vol. 65(7) pp32–36

Hickel, J. (2015) Could you live on $1.90 a day? That's the international poverty line. *The Guardian* 1 November. Available from: https://www.theguardian.com/global-development-professionals-network/2015/nov/01/global-poverty-is-worse-than-you-think-could-you-live-on-190-a-day (accessed 12 March 2017)

HMG (2012) *Measuring Child Poverty: A consultation on better measures of child poverty.*

HM Revenue and Customs (2016) *Distribution of Median and Mean Income and Tax by Age Range and Gender*. Available from: https://www.gov.uk/government/statistics/distribution-of-median-and-mean-income-and-tax-by-age-range-and-gender-2010-to-2011 (accessed 12 March 2017)

Holloway, E., Mahony, S., Royston, S. & Mueller, D. (2014) *The Children's Commission on Poverty Inquiry: Through Young Eyes: At what cost? Exposing the impact of poverty on School Life*. The Children's Society

Ireson, J. & Rushforth, K. (2004) *Mapping the Nature and Extent of Private Tutoring at Transition Points in Education*, BERA, UMIST Manchester

Lansley, S. (n.d.) Redefining poverty. Available from: www.poverty.ac.uk/analysis-poverty-measurement-life-chances-government-policy/redefining-poverty (accessed 12 March 2017)

Lansley, S. & Mack, J. (2015) *Breadline Britain: The rise of mass poverty*. London: OneWorld Publications

Lewis, K. & Demie, F. (2015) Raising the achievement of white working class pupils: Good practice in schools. *Review of Education*, Vol. 3(1) pp1–21

Lister, R. (2013) 'Power, not Pity': Poverty and human rights. *Ethics and Social Welfare*, Vol. 7(2) pp109–123

Lupton, R. & Hempel-Jorgensen, A. (2012) The importance of teaching: Pedagogical constraints and possibilities in working-class schools. *Journal of Education Policy*, Vol. 27(5) pp601–620

Madigan, T. J. (2002) Cultural capital. In Levinson, D. L., Cookson, P. W. Jr & Sadovnik, A. R. (eds) *Education and Sociology: An encyclopaedia*. New York: RoutledgeFalmer

Nussbaum, M. & Sen, A. (eds) (1993) *The Quality of Life*. Oxford: Clarendon Press

OECD (2012) *Equity and Quality in Education: Supporting disadvantaged students and schools.* OECD Publishing

Ofsted (2014) *The Pupil Premium: An update*

Pemberton, S. et al. (2014) *Life on a Low Income in Austere Times.* PSEUK

PAA (Psychologists Against Austerity) (2015) *The Psychological Impact of Austerity. A briefing paper*

Prieur, A. & Savage, M. (2013) Emerging forms of cultural capital. *European Societies*, Vol. 15(2) pp246–267

Sen, A. (1979) *Equality of What?* Stanford University: Tanner Lectures on Human Values. Available from: http://tannerlectures.utah.edu/_documents/a-to-z/s/sen80.pdf (accessed 12 March 2017)

Seymour, D. (2009) *Reporting Poverty in the UK: A practical guide for journalists, revised edition 2009.* Joseph Rowntree Foundation

The Parliamentary Office of Science and Technology (2015) Measuring Living Standards. *Postnote*, No.491 pp1–5

United Nations (1995) *Report of the World Summit for Social Development, A/CONF.166.9.* New York: United Nations Publications

Wilkinson, R. & Picket, K. (2010) *The Spirit Level: Why equality is better for everyone.* Penguin

Yongmie, N.J. (2013) Psycho-social dimensions of poverty: When poverty becomes shameful. *Critical Social Policy*, Vol. 33(3) pp514–531

Yoshikawa, H., Aber, J. L. & Beardslee, W. R. (2012) The effects of poverty on the mental, emotional, and behavioral health of children and youth. *American Psychologist*, Vol. 67(4) pp272–284

Index